CRUISING YACHTS

By The Same Author(s)

Cruising Boats — Sail and Power
(4 editions; 1968, 1969, 1970 and 1971)

Practical Ferro-Cement Boatbuilding
(with Herman Husen. 3 editions; 1970, 1971 and 1972)

Designs and Services
(2 editions; 1971 and 1972)

Boatbuilding and Design Forum
(Robin Roberts, editor; 12 issues 1973)

The Benford 30
(with Robin Roberts Benford. 3 editions; 1975, 1976 and 1977)

Cruising Designs
(2 editions; 1975 and 1976)

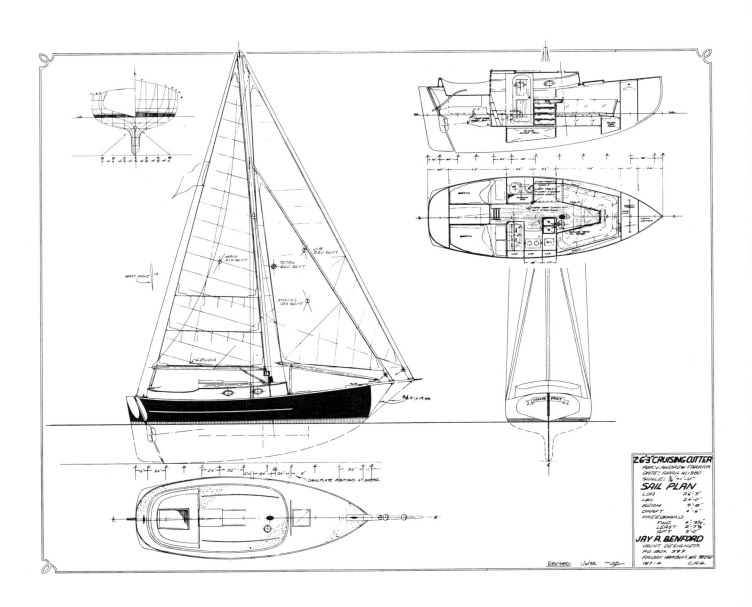

CRUISING YACHTS

by Jay R. Benford

with more than a little help from
Robin Roberts Benford, Frank Madd, and Lilly Wite

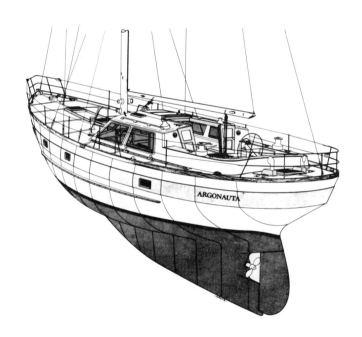

Published By

Tiller

P. O. Box 399
Friday Harbor, Washington 98250

ISBN 0-9610396-0-4
Library of Congress Catalog Card Number 82-74074

Typesetting by King Typesetting, Friday Harbor,
   Washington
Printed and bound by Whitmore Printing Company,
   Annapolis, Maryland

Published by Tiller
P. O. Box 399, Friday Harbor, Washington 98250
(206) 378-4244

Chapter 4 was originally published in Nor'Westing
   magazine.
Chapter 7 was originally published in Pacific Yachting
   magazine.
Chapters 10 and 14 were originally published in
   Yachting magazine.

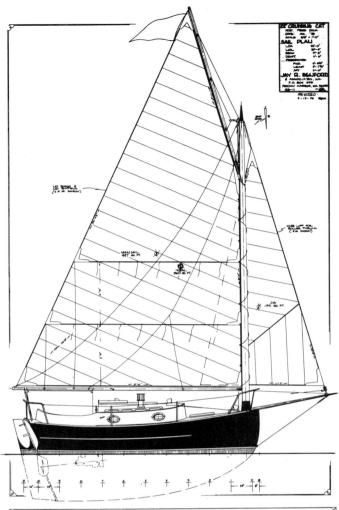

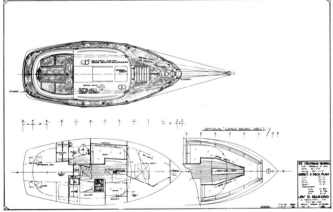

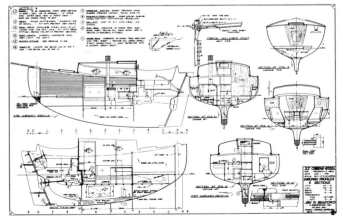

Dedication:

I've always loved to pour over published drawings
of yachts — sometimes I think my bookbuying habits
keep several publishers solvent — and have been pleased
to learn that there have been many requests of a more
extensive publication of my own designs.

Seven years ago we published a small book of my
designs, called *Cruising Designs,* and this was generally well received. However, the most serious criticism of
it — by ourselves as well as others — was that the
drawings of the boats were so small as to require a
magnifying glass. Some said this was a ploy to boost
our study plan sales. The truth of the matter was that
publishing costs dictated the size of the book.

I'm not sure how we were so lucky as to convince
the Tiller to put out this larger format book, but we are
grateful for their faith and funding. Thanks also go to
them for their editorial assistance and helpful suggestions on content and layout. Thus, it is both logical and
fitting that this book should be dedicated to them:
   To Frank and Lilly, the best of shipmates.

Table of Contents

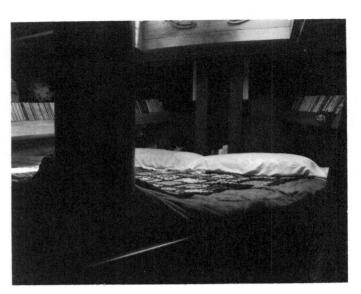

The lovely sky-light, left, is over the comfortable double berth, right, in SUNRISE's forward cabin. The bookshelving is made to be a snug fit to the paperback books.

Roy Montgomery Photos

SUNRISE's galley is handy to the cockpit for easy feeding of the crew. The stove is properly located to radiate heat into the whole cabin for chilly times. The oven fits an 11" pie pan and will nicely roast up to a 14-pound turkey. There is a large pots and pans locker under the stove. The two drawers hold the silverware and cutlery and miscellaneous galley utensils. The locker under the outboard counter has a shelf in it and holds a large quantity of jars and canned goods. A second galley pump has been fitted to provide sea water as well as fresh to the sink. The three-tier spice rack is handy to the stove. The counter cutout for the sink serves as a large cutting board.

Preface

Those of us addicted to "messing about with boats" are — fortunately — regarded with some suspicion by the populace at large. I've never been sure whether this is because they see this archaic mode of transport as a form of madness, or whether they find it sinful for some people to enjoy something so much.

I say fortunately with good reason. If they all understood it and joined in, there would be no room for those currently sharing this "madness" to continue what peaceful cruising we now have.

So; perhaps we sinners should do all we can to perpetrate this misconception. We should complain of exorbitant moorage and maintenance costs; repeat sailing descriptions such as, "compares favorable to thrill of standing fully clothed under a cold shower tearing up $100 bills," and "as exciting as watching grass grow."

Admittedly, there may be some professional social meddlers who will want to study why we continue something that we complain about so much. However, by taking them out at the proper times, they will get a taste of all the complaints and retreat to their (heated) ivory towers.

As a beginning student of yacht design, many years ago, one of the major frustrations I experienced was trying to find published drawings for more than just the profile and arrangement views.

Now, having been in the business of yacht design for more than twenty years, my position is reversed: I keep getting requests from other students for more detail drawings. (I still enjoy studying as many drawings from other designers as I can find.) Having been given a pretty free hand on the content of this book by the Tiller, I took the opportunity to include a great variety of construction and outfitting sheets in addition to the lines and profiles and arrangements.

Some years back, Phil Bolger wrote an article talking about the business of doing a custom design. In it, he said he often marked his plans "Follow exactly except for mistakes," which is always good advice. Even though most of the plans in this book are for boats that have been built, there is still the possibility for errors on the drawings. We make our best efforts to cross check all drawings for agreement with others in the set, and try to update them when we get feedback from the builders. However, I recently had a case where a builder called up and asked me if we really wanted the engine exhaust outlet to be two feet underwater. This design was then over ten years old, and there were over sixty builders of it all over the world. So over 60

notices were sent out rectifying the oversight. Yet, my caller was the first one who'd found the error noted by one of our draftsmen way back when the original drawings were done. . . .

I try to make a point of telling clients to call if there is some question about interpretation of what's on the plans. It's very difficult for the person making the drawings to know what the person reading the drawings has for knowledge and background. Thus we may assume something when making the plans that is not understood or assumed when the builder is reading it. It's far better for the builder to call and question something then, than to have to rebuild it later, or to have both of us disappointed with the results.

Like most designers, our plans are tailored to the initial client and how much detail they require. The 34' Fantail Cruiser, *MEMORY,* was done for a local boatshop who'd built from our designs before, and both of us felt comfortable with a lightly detailed set of plans. The 41' D.E. Cutter, *QUIET BIRD,* was designed for production in a yard in Taiwan where we felt that communication would be difficult and delayed due to the distance. Thus, it was a more extensively detailed set of plans. Both of these sets of plans are reproduced in this book so that the range of possible detailing can be seen. Most of the rest of the plans are excerpted from the complete sets which we offer as stock plans.

A word about the plans in this book is in order. The plans presented here are more extensive than normally offered by designers as "study plans." In some cases, the complete drawings are reproduced here. However, the great reduction needed to make them fit on the pages of this book makes it that much more difficult to use them for actually building the boat.

The plans thus are presented herein for study and enjoyment by the readers and students of yacht design. Anyone interested in building the boats should write to us at: P. O. Box 399, Friday Harbor, WA 98250 U.S.A. We can then send you the price list for the stock (building) plans and building rights for the boats.

Jay R. Benford
P. O. Box 399
Friday Harbor, WA 98250

SUNRISE patiently waiting for her crew to return so she can be off on another cruise.

Chapter

1

Happy

LONG DISTANCE RECORD SETTER
14' Offshore Cruiser
For: Howard Wayne Smith
Design Number 168
1978

John Guzzwell made history when he sailed back into Victoria in 1959 aboard TREKKA. He set a record, for the smallest boat on a solo circumnavigation, that stood for many years. In recent years, several sailors have set out to break his record, and at least one has succeeded.

When Howard Wayne Smith came to us in December of 1977, he was a crewman on a Canadian West Coast tugboat. He had been reading and planning for some time. His dream was to make a distinctly smaller boat to break the record set by his hero, John Guzzwell.

To a smaller group in the boating world, John Guzzwell is equally famous for his skill in fine yacht construction. Earlier in 1977, he had set up shop on Orcas Island, the next ferry stop over from our San Juan Island office. There he had the first of the 37' pilot-house cutters of our design, CORCOVADO, being built, we were able to talk with him about some of the questions we had about his voyaging and about TREKKA.

Howard Wayne Smith's specification to us was to try to get the maximum amount of boat we could in under 14 feet of length. After considering many alternatives, we came up with the plumb ended cruiser shown in the accompanying drawings. Howard wanted everything kept as simple as possible, for each pound of weight would be important.

The designed auxiliary power was a small outboard engine. The locker in the stern was designed to be watertight, sealed off from the rest of the boat. This locker holds the engine as well as the fuel tanks.

The companionway hatch is hinged, making it easier to seal against water coming inside. The boat can be well ventilated in warmer climates through the 6 opening ports, 2 dorade vents, the foredeck hatch, and the companionway hatch.

The raised deck amidships provides an area in which there is sitting headroom below. The pipe berths shown on the drawings extend aft under the cockpit seats, keeping the crew in the area of least motion when at sea. The forward part of the boat is devoted to storage and has space for the very simple galley that is used for cooking aboard.

The mast is stepped through to the keel, making for a very strong mounting. The jib and genoa can be poled out opposite each other for downwind runs. A wind vane, mounted on the boomkin, is hooked to the trim tab on the rudder. Mooring and rigging cleats, not shown on the deck plan, were through bolted to the deck. The pair of small winches are more than adequate for sheeting the genoa.

The small area of hollow in the keel amidships gives a place for bilgewater to collect and makes it easier to pump it out. This is one of the things that were incorporated in the design as a result of comments from John Guzzwell.

"Hull speed" is just about 5 knots. Howard Wayne Smith wanted to be able to average 3 knots for most of his passagemaking. The motion on a short and fat boat like this is much better off the wind than bucking to weather. With the NACA foil sectioned keel, she has the lateral plane and lift to sail to weather, but Howard prefers to do most of his sailing off the wind.

The basic hull construction was done by Finn Nielsen at Maple Bay on Vancouver Island. Howard did a lot of the outfitting himself. Most of the construction materials in her are native to the Northwest, including a lot of fir and cedar. The construction is cold-molded cedar planking over fir longitudinal stringers.

Particulars of HAPPY — design No. 168

Item	English	Metric
Length over all	13'-10"	4.22m
Length designed waterline	13'-8"	4.17m
Beam	6'-3"	1.91m
Draft, coastal cruising trim*	3'-7"	1.09m
Displacement, coastal cruising trim*	2240lbs.	1016kg.
Ballast	750lbs.	340kg.
Displacement-length ratio	392	
Sail area	180 sq. ft.	16.72 sq. m
Sail area-displacement ratio	16.82	
Prismatic coefficient	0.55	
Wetted surface	84.4 sq. ft.	7.84 sq. m
Sail area-wetted surface ratio	2.13	
Pounds per inch immersion	285	
Entrance half angle	28 degrees	

*CAUTION: The displacement quoted here is for the boat in cruising trim. That is, with the fuel and water tanks filled, the crew on board, as well as the crews' gear and stores in the lockers. This should not be confused with the "shipping weight" often quoted as "displacement" by some manufacturers. This should be taken into account when comparing figures and ratios between this and other designs.

Howard's story of working his way from the idea for a solo circumnavigation in such a small craft, through the design, construction, transportation and sailing phases is highly entertaining. He writes in a personable style, and a number of magazine and newspaper articles by and about him have been published around the world. His plans include a book or two, and we'd recommend the reader keep an ear out for news of these, if stories of adventure, determination and skill are of appeal. Excerpts from some of his early writings follow:

"Once Jay and his young associate, Peter Dunsford, heard more of the story and saw my preliminary

HAPPY anchored off Tahiti.
Photo courtesy Howard Wayne Smith

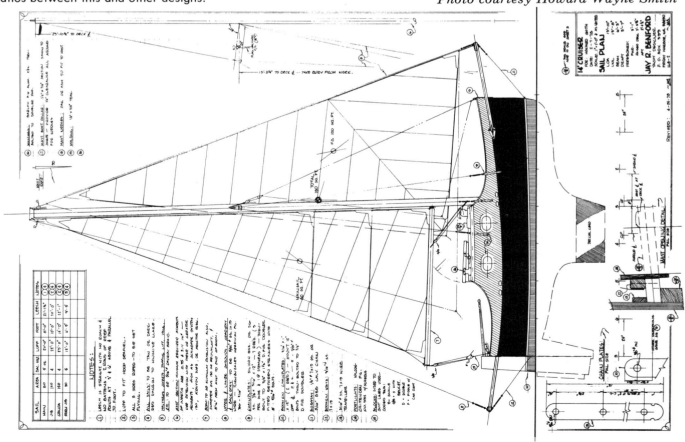

plans, their eyes lit up and they were 'tossing ideas back and forth a mile a minute. They were enjoying themselves. I sat there fascinated. Realizing that this might have been the last time I could go custom with a boat, I wanted to go all the way: all wood, with lots of varnish and bronze, tan bark sails, etc. I had been thinking in terms of single carvel or strip planking for the hull, but Jay immediately informed me that for my size vessel, these were too heavy a medium, and we'd have to go with a cold molding method. . . . Well, we talked for a few hours that day, and I was very pleased when Jay agreed to start work on the design even though he said it would take about three months by trying to squeeze it in with other work.'' . . .

"By March, 1978, the design was completed, and as you can see, *HAPPY* turned out really nice. Jay did a fine job. I think he really enjoyed himself on this one, as she's a little out of the ordinary, and that's his bag really.'' . . .

"With the 8 hp diesel engine I installed and plenty of plywood (there are bins and drawers in every available space), *HAPPY* really gained some weight, and is now about 2500 to 2600 pounds.'' . . .

"I found that, for her size, *HAPPY* is pretty stable, and I could walk around on her deck without heeling too much.'' . . .

After a slow trip across the Gulf Stream for a shakedown cruise to the Bahamas, and a holiday there,

Howard seemed pleased to make another report. "The trip back across the Stream was a very quick one, just under 12 hours. We were surfing about half of the way back, and averaged a little over five knots!'' . . .

After sailing 10,000 miles from Miami, Florida, through the Panama and across the Pacific, touching at the Galapagos, Marquesas, Fiji, Tahiti and on towards Australia, he touched a little too hard on a reef off Noumea, New Caledonia. There, towards the end of November, 1982, the beautiful *HAPPY* was lost, an hour before Howard was due on watch in the early hours before dawn. Howard was able to scramble into his dinghy and surfed his way over a number of treacherous reefs (spending the night on the overturned hulk of a steel wreck), landing in Noumea the next day. Friends he'd met in the Marquesas took him back to *HAPPY* to salvage all possible gear, but she was otherwise a complete loss.

However, Howard Wayne Smith is a determined adventurer. With the aid of an aluminum builder in Noumea, he will be putting together yet another miniature offshore yacht. Economics and record-breaking tables ever in mind, the *HAPPY II* is now on our drawing boards at 9½ feet. Howard feels that his most-used space on the 13'10'' *HAPPY* is really the equivalent of the space he'll have available in the smaller vessel. He'll have to mainly forego stores-carrying ability and speed.

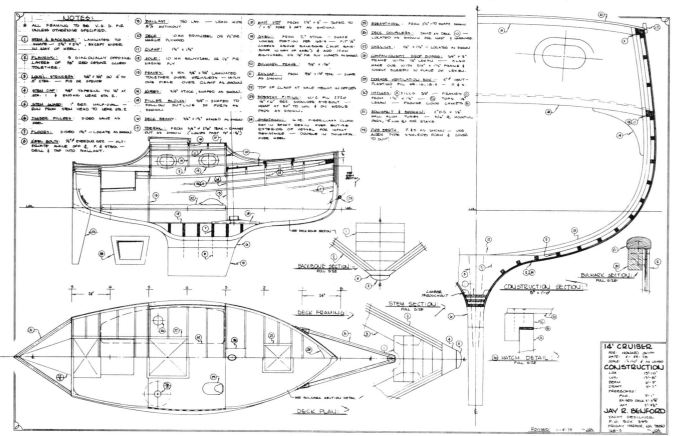

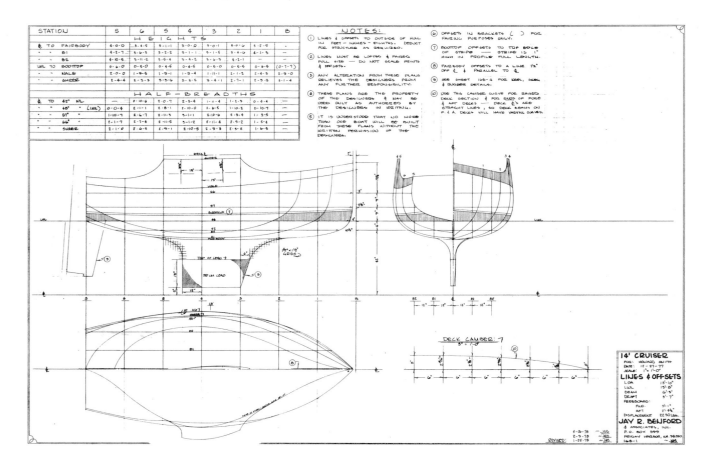

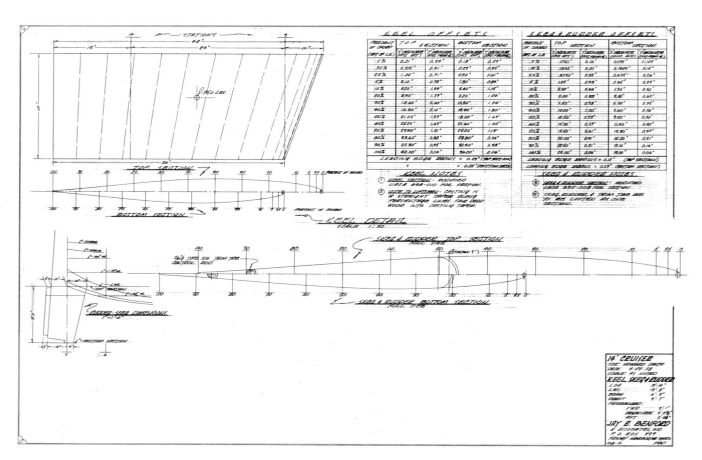

Chapter
2
The Philosophy Of Choosing A Vessel

by Robin Roberts Benford

An Unreachable Dream?

A vessel reflects a state of mind.

That there is a huge variation in states of mind is evident in the variety of craft which find themselves bobbing about the waters. Contrary to times of yore, it is coming to look as though most boats are made in Detroit. Growing weary of this, we have set out to change the trend a bit, and would like to take the time to discuss some of the reasons for choosing one particular kind of vessel over another. Hopefully, this little dissertation will prove to be a helpful guideline for the prospective boatowner.

Too often, a sailor sighs as he sees one of the few remaining beautiful vessels passing him by on a summer cruise: she seems so enticing, yet so tauntingly remote. For some reason, it never occurs to him that if he really likes that lovely siren, then he ought to possess her! She and her sisters need not be only an unreachable dream.

How?

The first decision to be made is that of the vessel's intended use. Is she to be for work or for pleasure? And if for pleasure, is she to be for power or sail, for cruising or racing? Each of these different requirements will place different demands on the vessel. If there is to be an overlap in services of the craft, there will necessarily be a compromise. How much compromise depends on the owner's relative priorities. But whatever the vessel's use, it is our belief that there is no excuse to buy an ugly boat.

The Purpose of a Vessel

Work or play? What her use is to be will determine what sort of performance is to be expected of the vessel. If she is to be purely for work, then she must be a no-nonsense vessel laid out with utility as her main function. She must provide a steady working platform, must stow her cargo and/or carry her gear in as efficient and abundant a manner as possible, must move efficiently to, from and in her working grounds so that her crew can continue to profit by her, must provide comfort and security in rough going, and overall, must be able both to take her crew out to sea and bring them safely back again.

"But wait!", we hear the reader say — "She should do all these things if she's to be for pleasure, too!" Quite so. We wouldn't want her any *other* way. It's interesting to contemplate that the more wholesome pleasure boats have evolved from working craft, and we'll digress a little later to discuss this evolution.

On Racing and Its Opposite

Some mention should be made also of the use of a vessel for racing. The IOR and other racing rule systems stemmed from the innocent desire to establish a system for comparing performance of differently sized and shaped vessels. By establishing handicaps, it became possible for these different types to compete against each other more or less fairly. The handicap is subtracted from the vessel's time after she goes round the course, leaving her with a correct or comparative time, which determines her rank in the outcome of the race. Naturally, what evolved was a competition among designers to see how they could design a vessel to have the lowest rating (highest handicap) possible, yet still to create a high performing craft. Handicaps are allotted on the basis of such things as overall length, waterline length, beam, draft, sail area, and so on.

The handicap system has evolved considerably, for new ways to circumvent the rules are constantly being discovered by the designers. In much the same fashion as the system of the income tax (a system which also has increasing penalties for performance), more and more loopholes have been unearthed until the rules have become as cumbersome in technicalities as the boats have become ungainly in appearance, to the detriment of overall sailing qualities. These boats excel to windward, on which point races are most often won, while cruising off the wind, ease of keeping a course, and interior comfort are held as distant second considerations. The point has now been reached in today's cruising boats, which are designed without a glance at the rating rule, that they may very well sail faster than their racing or racing-cruising sisters.

From a nostalgic perusal or the yachting journals of the turn of the century, it seems apparent that there used to be a time when one could sit overlooking a friendly harbor and have one's eyes delighted with the sight of a wonderful variety of graceful sheers and delicately balanced rigs. Today, vessels appear to be more conducive to eyestrain, and watching them a sorry pasttime. Straight and/or triangular lines have become associated with the sleek, racy look, and those who may not be planning to do any racing have found themselves caught up in the game of playing status with their neighbors, without a very good look at the practical results of playing the game. Status players generally end up with a vessel which may be well suited to another's way of life — but isn't really what they want for cruising comfort and beauty. If they were honest with themselves, they might discover that it makes more sense to satisfy their own cruising needs and aesthetic notions instead of those of their neighbors.

This is not intended to be a slur on racing per se, but rather an attempt to enable the reader to rethink his actual desires while attempting to make the choice of a vessel, and to examine the effects of a strict and somewhat arbitrary racing rule on today's typical racing/cruising boats. The outcome of races themselves provide much food for thought for designers, and can thus have a most beneficial effect on the creation of new designs for both other racing and cruising boats. But the use of boats designed with the IOR rule solely in mind should be kept strictly to those who wish to race seriously, for outside of racing, such boats are constructed around so many compromises that they should not be expected to be ultimate or even satisfactory cruising boats. The good cruising boat can apply some of the beneficial lessons gleaned from her racing cousin's trophies, yet can totally turn her nose at the IOR rule itself in an effort to optimize the cruising needs of her individualized crew.

In an effort to overcome the stigma of being cast as a racing boat, some cruising boatbuilders and designers seem to have swung the pendulum to the opposite extreme. Ads can be seen declaring "The Nostalgia 34 is almost an exact replica of 'SEASHANTY', which Henry Globegirdler sailed on his many famous ocean voyages of 1892 to 1899." The implication, of course, is that if Henry Globegirdler did it, and did it in "SEASHANTY", then of course anybody else can do it if only he has a "SEASHANTY", too: the Nostalgia 34.

Several fallacies are inherent in the analogy, but the idea most often overlooked is that a replica of an 1892-99 vintage design can be handsomely improved. "SEASHANTY" may certainly have served her proud captain well at the time, but people of her era were also quite happy living without electricity, flush toilets, and other conveniences which most of us today take for granted. The point, of course, is that improvements in design need not detract from the worthiness of the original concept. To the contrary, they should add to the comfort, sailability, and efficiency of the vessel. Too often, Nostalgia 34s turn out to be unresponsive tubs in comparison to their modern day sisters who took advantage of the "SEASHANTY's" sturdy tradition, but went further. They combined that tradition with design improvements learned from experience, advancement allowed by use of modern materials, and results learned also from the racing fleet.

Very well now, let us suppose that one wishes not to join the ranks of the racing elite, but merely to have a fine performing, comfortable, easy-to-handle, safe, and beautiful cruising vessel. What further points must be considered before arriving at a craft which culminates in satisfying these criteria?

Considerations of Location

Where will the vessel be used? If she is to cruise coastwise, she may well do best with a larger rig for the often lighter coastal winds. Offshore, a smaller rig may prove more prudent. Where the intracacies of island hopping and bayou exploring are enticing, a shallower draft vessel may be desired. Contrarily, for ocean sailing, a deeper draft can perhaps mean a stiffer vessel in stronger winds and larger seas, and will also mean a vessel with more stores carrying capability.

In discussing location, we would not be remiss to mention also what part of the globe. In warmer climates, consideration should be given to hull material for ease of maintenance, ventilation, and resistance to marine borers which seem more abundant in warm water. In extremely cold areas, where icing may be hazardous to navigation, the hull should be strong enough to provide safe passage through the ice, and/or remain unharmed when at dock should the harbor ice up. Hull, deck and sail color should also be considered if she is to be sailed in relentlessly sunny areas. A darker hull and deck color may mean suffocatingly hot interior accommodations and hot feet on deck. White sails often produce severe glare problems which leave long distance sailors returning home bloodshot, swearing in favor of tan and colored sails.

For those folks who have developed webs between their toes from the wet overcast of their cruising grounds, perhaps a pilothouse with inside steering may be a realistic consideration. Pilothouses are also popular with tropical sailors who need good shelter and cool shade from the sun's constant heat. If the cruising locale is one with fickle winds, more accent might be placed on motorsailing and/or just plain powering considerations, so that maximum benefit can be reaped from getting around and seeing all the interesting places there are to explore despite the weather. If one is a powerboat buff, but dislikes tossing about on windier passages, it might become practical to have a steadying sail to keep the vessel over on just one angle of heel. This would also carry the fringe benefit of emergency power in the unhappy event that the engine ceased functioning.

Sorts of Cruising

After mulling over the vessel's needs as dictated by her cruising location, another consideration should be what sort of use she'll be put to. Is she to be purely for day sailing — such as for short jaunts to attractive fishing grounds, or for beach exploring around home? Will she be lived on? Or worked with? As these cases progress, the criteria for choosing her become a little more complex. Progressively, more stowage capacity is needed, more "at home" comforts are necessary (in the way of head, stove, berths, headroom, and so forth) and more elbow room is generally required in order that her crew does not turn cannibalistic after being confined in small compartments with each other for an overly long period of time. The shorter the time period of her individual uses, the more adept each individual usually is at putting up with what can psychologically be acknowledged as a temporary situation. If she is to be used for an extended period at a time, such as for a long passage, or for living and/or working aboard, then much time should be spent on deciding how one's own living philosophy will create the ultimate in personal comfort in her interior. What will work well for one person may have nothing at all to do with what an Interior Decorator may dictate as the "ultimate" in layout. Only by seeing the interiors of many vessels, thus gathering helpful ideas, and by crewing and/or chartering aboard a good number of vessels, thereby really trying them on and seeing how they fit individual quirks and cus-

toms, can a person best decide what is the most useful interior and rig for himself. However, a fine starting point is to define the goals for the use of the boat. the next step is to decide which use is the most important single one. Then the sailor can plan around that choice.

For instance, it seems that the fashionable Interior Decorators of today's modern vessels have decided, after first being dictated to by IOR or "SEASHANTY", that the next most important criterion is sleeping. (Either the crew is exhausted by all that racing, or they are a swinging crowd whose secondary life revolves around the bed.) At any rate, the most common question asked of yacht brokers is, "How many does she sleep?" Thus, the chart table is shrunk or thrown out as an unneccessary frill to navigation, stowage lockers are discarded as wasted space, galley counters are foreshortened in a panic to get the food part over and done with, the engine room is non-existent (who ever needs to look at an engine, anyway?), the dining table collapses at inopportune moments, but by god, she CAN SLEEP 17!!!!

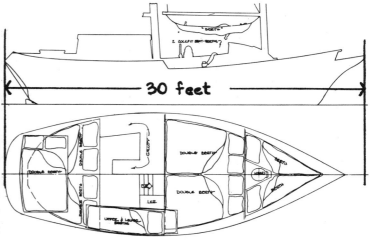

Figure 1: "How many does she sleep?" . . . "How many can you stand to have her sleep?"

Which brings us the opportunity of discussing another consideration. How sociable does the vessel need to be? If she must crew a large family, then some family members must either be put ashore in hotels or tents when overnighting, or they must plan to be accommodated in the boat, "somehow". Will all the family want to cruise all the time, or will some of them make do with roughing it in the cockpit under the boom tent and/or stars during their occasional excursions away from shore? If the crew consists only of one, or one with a soulmate, then the size of the craft can be limited, or the number of uses to which the interior is put can be increased. If the vessel must of necessity be a good overnight social event, then the skipper will want to make sure that her exterior appointments are likewise able to provide appropriate amenities by way of cockpit seating, deck lounging space, and room for working the rigging around the various bodies. All this, without the skipper's either having to trip over them and fall overboard himself, or feeling as though he'd like to toss a few of them overboard because there's no other convenient place for them to be.

On Rigs

Another personal consideration is what sort of rig will best suit the owner's needs. Does the vessel need to be singlehanded, or can she be laid out intricately for the purpose of keeping a crew of seventeen gainfully employed? If the former, which is perhaps most often the case, then it is important to see that the size of each sail is within the capabilities of one person to both set and furl under the most trying conditions. If it is not an all inboard rig, but necessitates the use of bowsprit and/or boomkin in order to increase the sail area horizontally but not vertically, is the rig set up so that her skipper needn't balance at the end of a slippery stick in order to take down the sail? (The bowsprit needs to be a steady platform built within a secure bow pulpit, and/or the headsails need to be on roller furling.) If the rig is all inboard, it may be helpful to look at its height. Does the vessel have to go under a number of bridges in her cruising grounds, and how does the mast meet these passes? If her rig is excessively tall, is this affecting what her angle of heel will be (i.e., will she be sailing on her ear and keeping the crew somewhat lopsided all the time?)

Then, of course, there is the consideration of type of rig — ketch, schooner, sloop, cutter, yawl, catboat, catketch, motorsailer — gaff or marconi, spinnakers or squaresails?

If a rig is designed to optimize the performance of the shape of her hull, as any good rig should be, then this leaves no room for discussion about whether a sloop or a ketch is a faster rig. It is often the hull which makes the boat a fast of a slow one, and as long as the layout of the rig maximizes the shape beneath her, then the question of choice boils down to personal preference. Will the vessel go well to windward? — She'll go to windward as well as her underwater shape will allow her, assuming her rig has been designed to take advantage of this. If she's a tubby scow, no variation in rig will make her better to windward.

Of course, there must be a fair sense of reason within the choice for rig, as well. One wouldn't want to put a catboat rig on a 50-footer, for example. (Imagine the single 1500+ square foot sail!) One of the main reasons for choosing a split rig is to reduce the size of the individual sails so that each sail is more easily handled. Some people are prone to look at a split rig and then look at a single-sticker, and say of the former: "Wow, look at all those lines to handle." This sort of comment is oblivious to the fact that it will be much easier to handle smaller sails on the split rig than larger ones on the cutter or sloop. It really isn't any more difficult to learn what the various lines do on two single masts than what those same lines do on one mast.

There is also the great controversy between marconi and gaff rig proponents. One of the most frequently heard comments in favor of the marconi is that it will send the vessel better to windward. This is erroneous, for as mentioned before, if both marconi and gaff rigged vessels had been designed to optimize their hull shapes, and if both hull shapes will go to windward equally well, then the gaff and marconi rigs will perform equally well to windward. Perhaps this discussion evolved from those who'd sailed some of the huskier old vessels such as the "SEASHANTY", that were old enough to have gaff rigs, but also sufficiently old that their hull shapes were not designed with optimizing windward performance in mind. To be fair in the comparison, one should sail the different rigs on the same hull shape, assuming the designer of the rigs knew what he was about.

Another discussion of gaff versus marconi centers around the weight of the gaff when hauling up the sail. On the reasonably small cruisers, the gaff should always be light enough in weight for one person to set. By the time the vessel is up to about 60 feet in size, multiple purchase tackle and/or multiple persons must come into play in hoisting sail. However, a vessel of this size usually involves more complex rigging and/or a more sizeable crew, no matter whether gaff or marconi. The proponents for the gaff will tell listeners that in this rig, the sail area is spread out more horizontally, making the center of effort lower and therefore heeling the vessel less than a taller marconi rig. As a consequence, for long bouts of sailing, the gaff rig makes her crew more comfortable, for they can walk about in a more flatfooted fashion. Also, the gaff rigged sail is often readily lowered without having to luff up. This can be a valuable safety feature.

Of late, most of the Detroit model boats have come out with immense rainbow hued spinnakers. Doubtless, spinnakers can be a good deal of fun. (Can't they? . . . "Everybody" has them. . . .) They are the most used, light air, downwind sail. But why is it that we hear so many tales of So-and-So's spinnaker blowing out — or hanging up — or dropping in the water — or being sworn at by a crewmember unable to furl her in that moment of need? Aren't spinnakers fun?? Well, we would propose another answer, which may seem quite radical (for it is quite old), but it is well tried, and with a modern approach to its use, it can be infinitely less trying and more convenient than spinnakers.

This is the squaresail.

But wait! Do not snort, "Squaresail — how archaic!", and throw this dissertation in the garbage. A squaresail is a sail made for going downwind, and with good design, it can also broad reach, reach, and close reach, and thus it satisfies the common use of the spinnaker, as well. However, the main difference is that the squaresail is set inboard of the headstays, and will not wrap around them when the wind drops, while the spinnaker dangles off outboard, way forward. It takes little imagination to picture which is the safer sail, and also which is the more easily managed. Why then, has the squaresail been abandoned in favor of the spinnaker? We can only assume that mythology deserves the blame. "Squaresails mean yards, and yards mean people dangling dangerously off them, don't they?"

Squaresails mean yards — yes. People dangling — no. Squaresails rigged in the manner of the old West Coast Trading Schooners can be handled entirely from the deck. They are set by pulling on the outhauls and sheets, which in turn pull the sail(s) out along the length of the yard. They are furled by pulling on the buntlines, which slide the sail back along the yard (in much the same fashion as sliding a curtain along a curtain rod.) Once they are furled, no sail ties are needed, for when the buntlines are pulled, they gather and hold the sail in place along the length of, and parallel to, the mast. A modern advancement on this technique is to sew the squaresail with a wire down the centerline, and to then rig her with roller furling — thus eliminating numerous extra lines and yet further simplifying the squaresail's speedy use.

The squaresail thus rigged doesn't need to be taken down and stuffed into a sailbag, as does the spinnaker, for it is quite happy and out of the way furled up in place. Because squaresails can be handled so easily, they receive better treatment and care than spinnakers. Being set inboard, they keep their crew in greater safety, and they make it much easier on the crew to handle changes in wind direction, for a slight trim in the braces and sheets is all that is needed. When wending his way through crowded marinas or through high-walled locks, the skipper need only adjust the lifts so that the yards are cock-billed at an angle toward the deck to reduce their horizontal clearance.

Another evolution on the square rig is the Great Pyramid Rig, as used on our ketch *Sunrise*. In this, all 1,000 square feet of sails are set flying from on deck. It's not only grand fun but highly effective as the downwind to close reach rig on our 34-footer. (For more details, see the description of this rig on page 97.)

As in any discussion of rigs, and boats, one will always hear the tune of those whose personal experiences have dictated their favoritisms. The untried is often condemned. But there are so many factors involved in the success or failure of a particular rig, that it's a pity to discard any type of rig until all these factors have been fairly assessed.

As to Cost

The next consideration is one which usually brings us all down to earth (and back to land.) Cost: — both initially and long term. Her first cost can be on a graduating scale, depending upon how she is built and outfitted. Going from the most expensive route to the least expensive route, she may be: entirely custom built, semi-custom built, all production built, used, semi-production and semi-home built, or all home built. "Expensive" is a relative term in this instance, for it is predicated upon one's assessed value of his own time. If his time can be spent more profitable earning the money to pay someone else to do all or part of the building for him, then that may well be the most economical way for him to build the boat. It is also likely that a professional builder can best do the kind of work that will optimize the future resale value of the vessel.

The boat's second cost — her long term cost — includes her moorage, fuel, repair, maintenance, insurance, and property taxes. In different areas, these costs will vary as much as 500% or more from one another, but the serious boatbuyer will want to research these in advance for his area, so that he is not rudely shocked once he has all-too-gleefully dashed off the showroom floor with his beloved craft.

Dissertation on Design

While the reader is fingering the last lonely pennies in his pocket, we thought he might wish to consider some other realistic considerations, such as what he is getting for his money in the way of a safe and seaworthy vessel. To start, quite properly, at the beginning, he should ask whether or not the vessel in question was designed by a competent yacht designer, whose job it is to conceive the ideas which will make the boat owner and builder's time and money a worthwhile investment. It is ridiculous to contemplate spending thousands of dollars on an object which may end up killing one at worst, or infuriating one at best, just because no-one thought to spend a small percentage of those thousands of dollars to make sure the investment would perform to its maximum from the outset. And if the designer is worth his salt, he can well help save the boatbuilding crew hours of head-scratching in putting all her components together, and thus hold down her purchaser's cost.

Assuming that she has been designed by a good yacht designer, the customer has ammunition which he can use to his advantage in seeing whether or not this new vessel will be likely to serve him well. The ammunition is to ask what sort of vessels this designer has already produced, or been involved with. How are they performing? Are they the sort of craft which one could come to love? Is the designer still involved with the current vessel? Can the designer be consulted about it? Or has the boatbuilder taken over the design and is he now out of touch with the designer; if so, why? If the designer is no longer alive, what do designers of similar tastes have to say about the craft? Can the design, if it is an old one, be improved, based on the intervening years of experience with it? If the designer is new to the field, what is his background and with what other designs has he been involved? The answers to these questions will help give the prospective boatowner a good feel for the aura which surrounds the new vessel, and it will also give him a basis upon which he can proceed further, if he chooses.

In olden times, the lines of a vessel were determined by the lessons of sea and weather. The underbody was usually long in profile to help hold the vessels on course with minimum effort by the man at the helm. Gradually, the lines evolved as experience taught her masters what would make the hulls move better. It was found that a shallower entry forward made the vessel more responsive to turning, and thus also gave her more windward ability. Designers came to the accompanying realization that the center of lateral lane (or underwater profile) must be kept aft so that the vessel would hold her course well. The keel could be slender and well located without being bulky and burdensome.

As time passed, it was discovered that a fine, smooth finish of both the entry and the exit of the vessel let the water pass by with less resistance and turbulence and again produced a vessel which was faster and easier to manage.

It was also found that a hull whose ends were well balanced made for a safe boat which would neither poop nor dig her bow under in rough seas. A rudder had to be large and strong enough to give good steerage way, yet slender enough to allow the water smooth passage. Today, these and other aspects of each type of boat are continually refined to produce the kindest cruising boat possible.

As this gentle evolution was taking place, the IOR rule was also advancing, and fast modifying the underwater profiles. The IOR result is a vessel which has limited wetted surface, for speed, and exaggeratedly shallow entry forward with the center of lateral plane proportionately forward, for the ultimate in windward

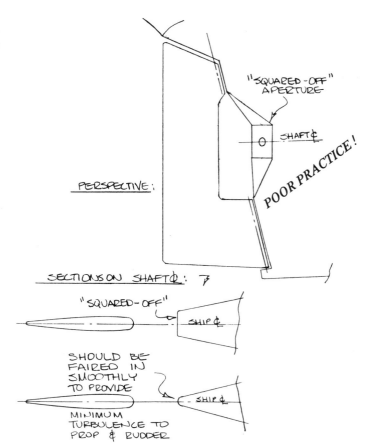

Figure 2: *It is important that both the entry and the exit of a vessel let the water pass smoothly by. The above drawings illustrate an all-too-common squared off aperture, with the bottom drawing showing the preferred treatment.*

performance. Contrary to most cruising men, the racing man spends a major portion of his time beating to windward. The IOR vessel doesn't hold her course well due to her cutaway forefoot and forward center of lateral plane, and her master must hold fast to her helm lest she go astray, but he has his compensation when his vessel brings home the trophies according to the IOR regulations.

The amount of beam in a vessel will be of great help in providing interior space. Of course there are extremes, and some of the IOR boats have taken advantage of this, not for the purpose of bedding, but of beating the Rule. A vessel having excessive beam will provide that much more exposed surface area to be blown about by the winds, and be that much harder to maneuver in tight circumstances. Likewise, excessive freeboard can multiply this problem. We know of some poor innocent souls who bought a "modern" production boat with tremendous freeboard, under the assumption that if plenty of these boats were sold, they must be good. They did not discover 'til later that plenty of these boats were out — to equally innocent sailors — and the realization hit them terribly hard when they

Cruiser   Racer

Figure 3: It's easy to see from these drawings how the racing machine has her lateral plane well cut away aft. The carefully designed cruising profile will hold her course better, yet be lively and responsive to sail as well.

tried to bring their boat in with a bit of wind running off the dock. The minimum underbody and keel was unable to get a good enough bite to counteract the windage of the freeboard, and they spent the better part of a frustrating quarter hour in a maddening attempt to move her into the dock.

About Construction

Having spent considerable time discussing the various aspects of design with which a boatowner should be acquainted, we would be remiss in overlooking the matter of construction. Most people are well acquainted with general construction in houses. But building a boat is not like constructing a house. Everything which goes into the boat must be put there with the thought that the seas are going to do their best to work each piece loose, and tear the boat apart. In house construction, rough work and mistakes can be covered over with trim and paneling. But a house does not have to test the whims of a stormy sea. Covering over mistakes in a boat may hide them from the eye for a while, but nothing will ever be hidden from nature.

One effective way to provide a sound basis for protection from the tearing seas is to build a monocoque shell — i.e., one which is an integral unit, such as fiberglass, cold molded wood, or ferro-cement, steel or aluminum. Here the skipper won't have to worry about individual pieces working against one another as in a planked boat. This is not to say that one ought to disregard other materials, for they provide very fine, seaworthy and handsome craft. However, let us for simplicity sake consider fiberglass as the material. It is probably the most common boatbuilding material used today and it is also in the greatest demand by virtue of its strength and ease of maintenance, as well as its relative ease of construction once a mold has been made.

In the highly competitive fiberglass production market, every pound of glass in the boat means more dollars out of the boatbuilder's pocket. (And at today's rising resin prices, it may shortly mean many dollars!) Thus, it is not uncommon for the high volume manufacturers to attempt to get away with the thinnest layup of fiberglass possible.

There are generally two ways to lay up a fiberglass boat: one, with a chopper gun, which shoots out chopped fibers and resin together and is therefore understand-ably much faster than the second method, which is to lay up succeeding layers of woven roving by hand, carefully saturating the whole with resin. The second method is a much more methodical application, and ensures uniform quality throughout the vessel. There are varying number of layers of woven roving applied, depending on the desired strength of the hull, and how much built-in stress resistance the designer decides the vessel should be capable of carrying. Commonly, different areas of the hull receive different numbers of layers of fiberglass, depending on where the greater areas of stress are likely to be. Such areas include the deck to hull joint, the points where the bulkheads meet the shell, and the bilge and keel areas. To understand why these are higher stress points, it might help to picture what happens to them as the vessel heels, or as she meets an oncoming wave, or as she lifts and dips from wave to wave. Considering that the same vessel must encounter these situations over and over again, the fiberglass will want to be sufficiently strong that it will have a good fatigue factor. Now 'we think back to the fact that every pound of glass means more dollars. Where does one want his dollars to go, and where does he want to save them? It may prove worthwhile — and entertaining — for the prospective boatowner to ask the various dealers and builders about their layups and to compare safety factors and dollars in this vein.

Of course, there is a reasonable limit as to how far a layup can be built up. Too much glass will make the vessel overweight (and therefore unable to respond to the ultimate of her design), and not flexible enough to give with the demands of the seas. In looking at glasswork, it is important to realize that thickness alone does not necessarily mean strength, for the conscientious fiberglass layup man will attempt to squeegee out all excess resin as he works up each successive layer. The resin in itself has little comparative strength, and it is thus ideal to compact the glass into as consistently thin a shell as possible. Thus, it is the number of layers of glass that is a better indication of strength than just overall thickness.

The ultimate ideal in glass:resin ratios is 50:50, a ratio which is seldom achieved. The "Here-Today-Gone-Tomorrow Boatworks" has not uncommonly manufactured "glass" hulls having 30:70 glass:resin ratios, much of this due to the fault of layups hastily pasted together with a chopper gun (where the man at the nozzle controls the glass content and where each boat thus has a quite different and widely varying ratio not only to other sister boats but within her own structure, as well.) If truth in advertising really had its way, such manufacturers ought to be condemned to calling their boats resin boats, and not fiberglass boats at all.

Another aspect of construction which one should

consider is the matter of fastenings and joints. They will give a good outward indication of what the philosophy of the builder has been on the innerworks of his hull. We have at times been horrified upon entering some of the stock "modern" production fleet, when we have grasped the handrail in an effort to climb aboard, only to discover the thing waving around in our hands as though it would like to walk away with us! Some of the fastening problems are not quite so obvious, however. If it is not possible to see whether it has been both glued with a quality marine glue and/or bedding compound, in addition to being screwed or through-bolted with a high quality marine-use fastener, then one should by all means ask. Where joints occur, are they cut in such a way that insidious leaks cannot occur, and are they then fastened and sealed in no uncertain terms? Such areas as the railcap, deck edge finish, rubstrip, and so forth, are places to inspect.

Where bulkheads butt to the shell, is the line visible on the exterior, or has the builder taken pains to cushion the edge of the bulkhead against the shell? As the bulkheads take a tremendous loading in their role as not only dividers but as stiffeners in the hull, they are often too prone to leaning for help on that small area of the shell along which they lie. This can create a hard (brittle) spot in the shell, and a potential place for weakness in the ultimate moment of a storm. In a fiberglass shell, the bulkheads can be cushioned by running a bevelled strip of AIREX foam along the outboard edge, and then gently glassing in two or three layers of fiberglass mat or cloth, staggering the laps outwards where they meet the shell, thereby also spreading the load outwards instead of along one single line of points.

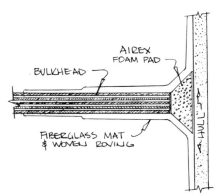

Figure 4: An AIREX foam pad and staggered layers of glass help to spread the point loading, cushioning the bulkheads against the interior of the hull.

What Value, Beauty?

Psychologically, one of the most important considerations in selecting a boat is, "Is she beautiful?" If she is, and that beauty is classical in nature, then she will never go out of style with the passing fads, and will still be thought beautiful years from now. This will keep her master attentive to her needs, giving her lasting value and serving to protect her as an investment. If she generates pride in her crew, they will get more pleasure out of every aspect of her — and that's what it's all about — a yacht is a pleasure boat and should be fun!

A Short Example from History

Having discussed some general design considerations, and the points for which the prospective owner will want to keep a weather eye out, it may prove useful to consider a specific example of how a good cruising boat design can evolve.

Up until this century, most small boats existed for the sake of earning their keep. As modern technology developed, it brought with it two accompanying benefits which altered the status of the small boat: more leisure time, and new materials and machines which facilitated construction. The cost of vessels was thus brought within the grasp of those who wished to spend their leisure time "messing about with boats". It only made sense for these folks to turn to vessels which had proven themselves capable of taking their owners out to sea and back.

One of these vessels is the Friendship Sloop. A charming boat, she was born in the late 1800's, and hailed out of Friendship, Maine. She was created by the lobstermen, who were feeling the pressure of competing fishermen beating them to the Boston fish market in their Portuguese sloops. As the New England coast is not reknowned for its docility, these hardy fishermen were already working in craft which had to withstand the strain of wild winds and unkind seas, and on top of this, they were now being faced with having to come up with a speedy sailing boat — else all their trials would be for naught when they finally arrived at the fish market.

One day, some of the fishermen came across a Portuguese sloop on the beach. They quickly made a close study of her underwater lines, and set about building a new vessel which encompassed all the fine qualities of both their own and the Portuguese model. What evolved was the Friendship Sloop. The Friendship was a stout little ship, docile and well mannered. She steered easily running off the wind in a sea, and kept her crew dry and on an even keel. Gradually, she began to be used for other sorts of fishing, such as mackerel, for which the laying of nets was an exacting task, especially in inclement weather. At the conclusion of laying the nets, one man hiked out to the end of the bowsprit, and with a long pole, held the net in place as the sloop eased out: of course, demanding a steady boat. As this proved relatively safe, the sport of harpooning swordfish from the end of a bowsprit found the Friendship a good soulmate. In addition to these fine assets, she sailed briskly, leaving most all the competition behind her. It is estimated that there were well over a thousand Friendship Sloops by the early part of this century, so successfully had they evolved. In the early 1900's, the gasoline engine began to replace sails as power in the commercial world.

It is reported that there were only a dozen or so more Friendship Sloops built from the time the gasoline engine took over, until the early 1960's. In 1961, a Friendship Sloop Society sprang up, "dedicated to reviving the venerable Friendship to make the boating public fully aware of her potential as a family sailing yacht. Everyone who had ever seen one admired them, but now suddenly everyone wanted one." (For those interested in a more detailed history of the evolution of this fine vessel, and in seeing some lovely photos of both early and modern versions of her, we'd heartily recommend The Friendship Sloop Society's book, *Enduring Friendships.)* At any rate, what could make better sense for those interested in a beautiful, safe, seaworthy, fast vessel than to turn to a type of craft which was known to have already encompassed all these qualities? To take these features and combine them with the advantages of technological advances in design and materials would produce the ultimate in family cruising.

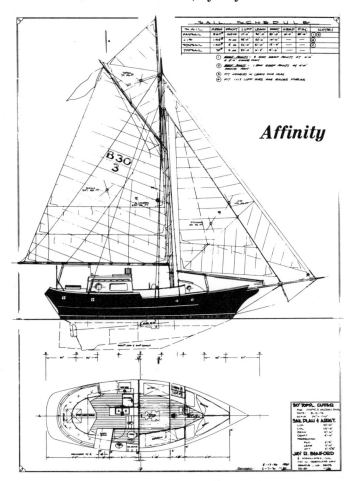

Affinity

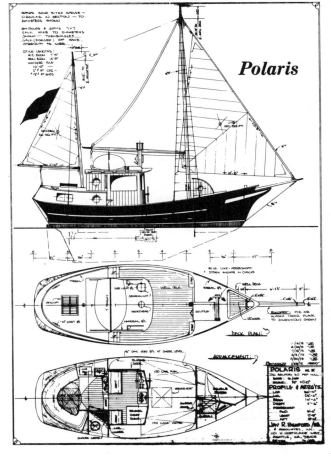

Polaris

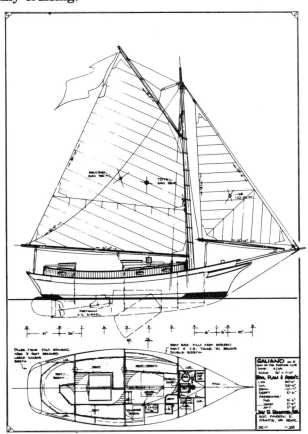

Chapter
3

The Benford 30:

A Philosophy And A Yacht
By Robin Roberts Benford

Her Heritage

The Benford 30 is a vessel for those who wish to step out of the mainstream of IOR dominated racing and racing/cruising boats. She is a yacht with individuality as a truly fine cruising vessel. The Benford 30 belongs to those who would object to being classed as a group of anything (unless it were a group of individuals.)

Her purpose is practicality: cruising performance and cruising comfort are her abilities. She can be worked, for those who wish her to earn her keep, for it is from work that her heritage stems. She'll be fast, and she'll turn to windward smartly, but not to the detriment of tracking well.

The Benford 30 evolved from the Friendship Sloop. In the charming book, *Enduring Friendships,* The Friendship is typified as follows:

"All have the graceful clipper bow, from which the line of the rails swing aft to a low point at the cockpit and turns up gracefully to a rounded stern. . . . You will notice that her bow is very fine; indeed it is actually concave in section. This hollow runs aft under the boat and increases as it goes. As you approach the stern, you will find that in cross section the side of the boat turns in sharply just below the water line, runs almost flat, with little deadrise, until nearly the middle of the boat, and then turns down to quite a deep keel."

Her Evolution

How have we modified her? Well, in the olden days, she needed low freeboard so that the lobsterman who worked her could more easily haul their pots aboard. These fishermen weren't after creature comforts so much as space in which to store pots and gear, and run the boat. As we desire to use the vessel for comfortable cruising, we have raised the freeboard slightly to provide more in the way of interior accommodations. The after deck is raised for further headroom aft, and her bold tumblehome is carried around the stern to create a very pretty elliptical deck line on the quarterdeck, and a more svelt impression overall. We have cut away her forefoot to quicken maneuvering. The volume distribution of her hull has been slightly modified to minimize drag and increase speed. In her early days, the Friendship carried her ballast of loose rocks inside, for this was most economical and practical. Not requiring this interesting feature, we have modified her keel sections for solid lead or iron and concrete ballast, and the keel is shaped for maximum performance.

The Benford 30 has a modern full keel configuration and large rudder which helps her keep her course by herself, aided by her well balanced rigs. Under power, offsetting her propeller shaft line allows the boat to be more efficient, as she will go straight ahead instead of crabbing off to one side in reaction to the torque from the rotation direction of the propeller. Her carefully shaped hull with cutaway forefoot gives her surprisingly good windward performance under sail. The Benford 30's beam is saucy — in the Friendship tradition — generous enough to give room, but not so fat as to detract from performance. This enhances the interior accommodations, yet is balanced with the freeboard and healthy keel so that leeway never becomes a problem.

The Benford 30 herself is actually several steps along the evolutionary development road from the original 30-footer we designed in 1968, and then called the Fortune Line. One variation of this, the *Polaris*, had a great cabin in the stern, and raised quarter deck aft, but the remaining several versions had the lower sheer from bow to stern. From the Fortune Line, we evolved the *Belle Amie* series in 1971. These were designed for ferro-cement construction, a much heavier building material than the original wood and fiberglass ones. To gain the extra displacement needed, we redesigned the underbody to give wineglass sections and about an extra ton of displacement. A little over a year later, the original Great Cabin version of the Benford 30 was created. By 1975, a mold for building the latest hull was constructed. The drawings in this chapter show the evolution of our hull designs, the first of which in herself was quite evolved from the original Friendship herself.

PARTICULARS:

Item	English	Metric
Length over all	30'-0"	9.14m
Length designed waterline	23'-6"	7.16m
Beam	10'-6"	3.20m
Draft	4"-6"	1.37m
Freeboard:		
Forward	4'-9"	1.45m
Least	3'-0"	0.91m
Aft	4'-5¾"	1.37m
Displacement, cruising trim*	10,975 lbs.	4,978 kg.
Ballast	3,300 lbs.	1,497 kg.
Displacement-length ratio	377	
Sail area: (Varies with Rig)		
(Cutter with Main & Jib)	435 sq. ft.	40.41 sq. m
(Sloop with Main & Jib)	450 sq. ft.	41.81 sq. m
(Cutter with both Headsails)	560 sq. ft.	52.03 sq. m
(Sloop with Genoa)	600 sq. ft.	55.74 sq. m
(Tops'l Cutter w/all 4 Sails)	700 sq. ft.	65.03 sq. m
Sail area-displacement ratio:		
(Cutter with Main & Jib)	14.09	
(Sloop with Main & Jib)	14.58	
(Cutter with both Headsails)	18.14	
(Sloop with Genoa)	19.44	
(Tops'l Cutter w/all 4 Sails)	22.68	
Center of Bouyancy	54.8% aft	
Wetted surface	254 sq. ft.	23.60sq. m
Hull Surface Area	510 sq. ft.	47.38 sq. m
Prismatic coefficient	0.55	
Pounds per inch immersion	807	
GM	3.98'	1.21m
Moment to Trim 1"	917 ft.-lbs.	

*CAUTION: The displacement quoted here is for the boat in cruising trim. That is, with fuel and water in the tanks, the crew on board, as well as the crew's gear and stores in the lockers. This should not be confused with the "shipping weight" often quoted as "displacement" by some manufacturers. This should be taken into account when comparing figures and ratios between this and other designs.

Jay R. Benford, Photo

RUNAWAY GIRL (Benford 30 #2) at her coming-out party. She was dressed in her finest: — dark green, glossy gel coat, so fair that her admirers were able to see themselves reflected true to shape in her mirror-like surface.

Roy Montgomery Photos

AFFINITY, Benford 30 #3, at her launching.

Two Benford 30's under construction, overlooking the Benford 22. The drape in the background closes off the area of the shop where new hulls are molded.

Her Amenities

The Benford 30 has a large capacity for carrying stores, varying with the arrangement desired. The motor launch can be used readily for fishing excursions. Any of the sloop or cutter rigs make practical day-sailers, while the split and square rigs prove a joy to those sailors desiring more options in combinations of sail to set for a variety of wind and weather situations.

For those whose accent is on the bed side of sociability, there is even an arrangement to sleep seventeen! However, it should be noted that plans for this version are available only on prepayment of four hundred ounces of .999 fine gold.

For those who value their privacy, we have models about which her owners can say, "Gee — I'd love to take you on a cruise with us, but our boat only sleeps two (or four.)" For those whose joy centers around abundance in private repose, there are models with two heads. Those who like to have secure sea berths aft for offshore work, and who also like ample working room around the engine, might enjoy studying the arrangement in the Staysail Schooner version. And for those who like combinations of the above ideas, these can generally be accommodated.

The Benford 30 is capable of going almost anywhere. Certain versions will prove better suited to certain cruising areas than others. For instance, the motorsailer models, with a pilothouse and inside steering, will appeal to those who find the water in their cruising grounds descends from above (in the form of rain) as well as beneath their vessels. The Great Cabin versions will be welcome in any climate. Although some interiors may be intended more for local coastal hops, while others are carefully laid out to maximize the needs of the long distance cruiser, with her heritage of being able to claw off lee shores in heavy weather, the Benford 30 will make a worthy offshore vessel.

Rig? What is desired? We can design them all: sloop, cutter, yawl, schooner, ketch, motorsailer ketch, or brigantine, with squaresail, gaff, and/or marconi. Each is designed to make the most of this seakindly,

fine performing hull. Individual sail areas are kept within the means of the single-handler. Rigging is arranged so that all sails can be set and furled from inboard on deck, and in many cases, right from the cockpit. Any of the rigs shown in the accompanying profiles are possible with the cabin shown with it, and several versions are already detailed in the plans. Of course, a straight powerboat is also quite possible.

Roy Montgomery Photo

BAKEA daysailing beneath the Space Needle on Seattle's Lake Union, before her cruise to Mexico.

Her Statistics

In addition to the design data presented, we thought the reader might like a little more detail about the Benford 30's statistics. Her lines help portray her sweet shape.

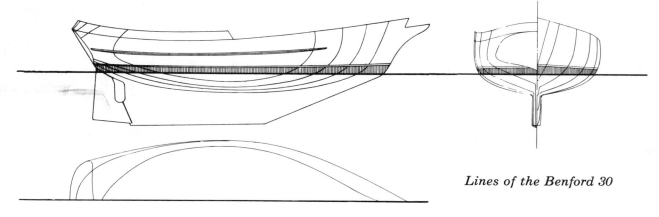

Lines of the Benford 30

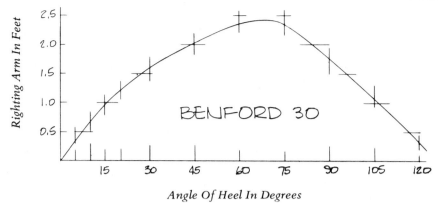

Benford 30's Righting Arm

Diagram showing the Righting Arm

From the stability curve for the Benford 30, the righting moment can be calculated by multiplying the righting arm by the displacement. This provides the force to oppose the heeling moment generated by the wind on the sails. Interpretation of these curves by the designer indicates this is a pleasantly stiff vessel, inclined to sail more on her bottom than on her ear.

A word of caution is in order about the top end of the righting arm curve. The method of calculation used to produce these figures does not take into account the volume of the deck camber, the houses, spars, and so forth that will serve to increase the righting arm at extreme angles of heel. Thus, although the curve is headed down, this is a normal situation, and if all the hatches were shut, she would readily right herself from putting the whole rig in the water.

The sail carrying power graph shows relative angles of heel for four different sail combinations under increases in wind velocity. This is calculated from the formula shown in Wind Pressure drawing, and perhaps more easily understood by a study of the illustration accompanying the formula.

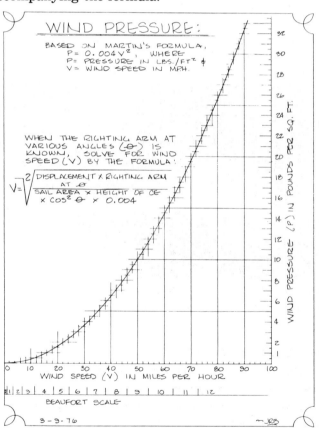

Wind Pressure Based On Martin's Formula

Sail Carrying Power and Angle of Heel for the Benford 30 with varying amounts of sail set in different wind velocities.

The Angle of Heel vs. Wind Velocity Curve shows the boat heeling more than is the case in real life, for the formula assumes that the sails are sheeted flat, and that the wind is blowing from directly abeam, a combination rarely seen when sailing. Thus, the angle of heel would be less than shown for the various wind velocities. Condition One, with 600 square feet of sail area, would be just about the same for the schooner rig, and Condition Three would be close to the schooner with just her main and jib set.

Her Longterm Cost

Looking at her long term cost, the economical Benford 30 will not find her skipper often at the fuel dock, for she'll burn less than a gallon of diesel fuel an hour, under power — and of course, the wind is free! On the maintenance side, fiberglass is well known for its relatively carefree aspects, but loving owners will take pride in giving her a pretty wax polish when it seems prudent. (Plans for her are also available strip planked or cold-molded in wood, ferro-cement and multi-chine steel.) For ease of hauling and docking, we have designed the bottom of the keel with a flat, straight section. The engine is on a close to level plane (not steeply angled), so it works more efficiently, and thus more economically. Access to the engine varies with each model, but we try to make her easy to tend — again minimizing repair effort and time. The rigging specified is of simple, traditional style, employing modern materials, so that all parts are of long-lasting quality, but are also open for inspection with no hidden inner parts.

Roy Montgomery Photo

Benford 30 Airex cored hull with the doubler for the guard rail and main bulkheads in place.

Her Construction

The Benford 30 has extra reinforcing at higher stress areas, and generally husky scantlings. The layup is one which is commonly seen on larger vessels from production builders who are more conscious of the pound/dollar measurement. Being care conscious, we prefer to measure the layup on terms of strength rather than dollars. She'll withstand a good deal of impact from unforeseen objects such as deadheads. This is just one example why we feel this makes the Benford 30 a better long term investment to her owners.

We specify all through hull fastenings for the Benford 30 to be securely backed and thoroughly bedded in a good marine bedding compound. Joints are carefully made away from high stress areas, and are cut and

joined in such a fashion as to keep the weather outside where it belongs. Bulkheads are gently cushioned along a strip of closed-cell AIREX foam, so as to spread their loading instead of concentrating it on one line.

The deck to hull connection on fiberglass boats has become notorious as a potential source of leaks. We specify building our boats with a flange on the hull which turns inboard for the deck to land on and seal to. This is not the easiest way to laminate a hull, but it gives the best chance for a complete seal and elimination of leaks. As a side benefit, it also serves to increase the strength of the hull and hold it in the correct shape during construction.

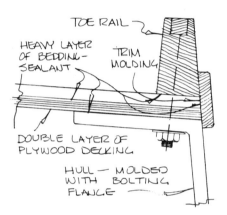

Illustration of the secure hull-to-deck joint

Ballast, consisting of iron or lead pigs set in concrete, and glassed over, is set inside the keel molding, so there are no keel bolts to worry about. Also, the ballast amount and position can be varied to suit the various versions without making a new keel casting, or having to modify the notch in the mold to suit the new ballast location.

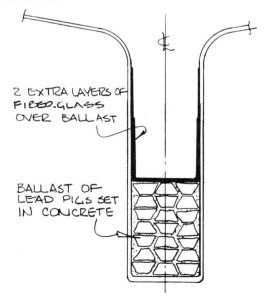

Benford 30's Ballasting Arrangement

Her Engine Requirements

The recommended engine size would be a 15 to 25 horsepower diesel. The power curve shows the estimated speed that might be expected in the smooth water with the power indicated. Practical considerations, such as the power required to charge the batteries, and the power absorbed in the reduction gear, suggest the installation of an engine with 10% to 20% more power than shown on the curve. This also gives a reserve for powering into head seas or towing another boat. Most any of the little diesels in this power range will fit in the Benford 30's engine room.

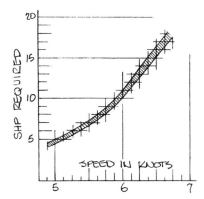

Benford 30's Speed/Horsepower Curve

Sailing the Benford 30

We have proudly provided many figures and statistics on the Benford 30. A reader may well look at the figures, and remark, "Well, fine, that's all very impressive, but computers, calculators and mathematicians have been known to be wrong once their figures get out on the open sea." It may be reassuring to remember that the Benford 30 design is based on a proven hull shape, the changes in which have been made to evolve her into a vessel which encompasses all of the advantages of the previously proven hull, and more: advantages which reports of experiences sailing the vessels indicate would further improve their good qualities. Our experiences with sailing several Benford 30s, serve to reinforce this. The Benford 30 will make 80 degrees tack-to-tack (40 degrees off the true wind). She is indeed comfortably stiff, responsive, and a delight to sail!

As a matter of background, one of the Benford 30's early sisters is a cutter, built then as one of the Fortune Lines, as shown in the little silhouette above. Her original owners sailed her for about five years and are impressed with her performance. They remarked that she is responsive, yet holds her course easily, and that she is stiff in a seaway. They had her out one time in the Straits of Georgia near Vancouver, British Columbia, when the wind was blowing between 35 and 40

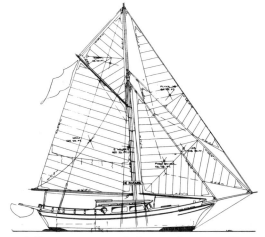

knots, and the seas were eight to nine feet. Even under those conditions, they decided they didn't want to bother reefing. They left the full 600 square feet of sail up, and never once did she heel enough to bury her rail. The only complaint came from the mate in the galley, who mentioned that she had trouble keeping all the dishes on the stove while cooking under such conditions. (!) Though she was stiff, they said her motion was comfortable. The Benford 30 is also comfortable, and is even stiffer.

Several Benford 30s are now happily cruising. The first to be launched was *Bakea*, and she was soon to face a harsh introduction to her natural element, for her owners were anxious to take her from her Seattle building yard to their home in Portland, Oregon, and didn't wish to await the fickle weather which abounds in mid-fall. After a pleasant cruise north to Victoria, B.C., *Bakea* headed determindly out the Straits of Juan de Fuca for open waters. The Pacific brewed up a good storm, and for dessert treated *Bakea* to one of her well-known gales. The crew remarked that they were most glad they had inside steering, and that they gained a good deal of confidence in their little ship, which gave them the feeling that she could withstand much more than they could. As their previous sailing experience had been limited to production-line boats which they'd been too scared to take offshore, their oft-repeated expressions to us of their feeling of security in sailing *Bakea* under such trying conditions meant quite a bit to us.

The following spring, *Bakea* began a longer voyage, again heading south off the Pacific Coast. Upon reaching San Diego, Eliane LeBeck wrote us of their journey, saying:

"Our conclusion is the BAKEA has performed beautifully . . . the engine runs perfectly, so does everything else on the boat."

From San Diego, *Bakea* headed for Mexico, and spent some time anchored in La Paz, where she underwent Hurricane Lisa, and then cruised on to Mazatlan, before returning north again to San Diego.

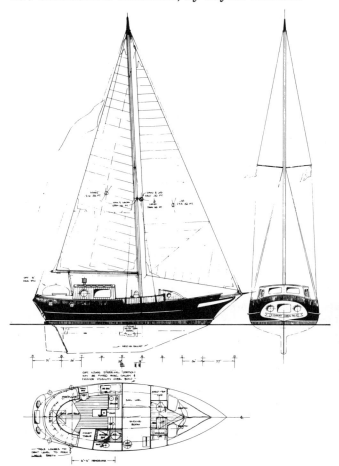

The original great cabin version of the Benford 30

Roy Montgomery Photo

NOVELTY, Benford 30 #4, standing up to a breeze, footing nicely to windward while her crew is tucked comfortably inside the high coaming around her center cockpit.

The second Benford 30 out of the shop is *Runaway Girl*, whose skipper is a retired merchant seaman currently making her his home. The summer of '76 found the two of them making a long cruise in the opposite direction from *Bakea:* to the north end of Vancouver Island, and then back to Seattle. At persent, *Runaway Girl* is based in Friday Harbor, and we have the pleasure of seeing her red sails often beckoning to us as we sit at our office window overlooking the harbor, while she heads out amongst the neighboring San Juan Islands. She's made several trips northwards along our island-strewn Pacific northwest coast.

Another professional seaman makes Benford 30 #4, *Novelty,* his home. Sisterships in a variety of materials, profiles, rigs and interiors have been built in France, England, Switzerland, Norway, Australia, Canada, Yugoslavia and Brazil, as well as many east and south coast states in the United States.

The third Benford 30 to find herself under construction was *Affinity,* and she's the first to have a gaff rig.

Aboard the Benford 30

Although all Benford 30s share the same hull, if a client is interested in customizing the rig and interior to suit his sailing philosophy, this can readily be accomplished. Some of the possibilities are discussed herein.

The interior arrangement of the Benford 30's great cabin is really unique. She was designed for the romantic soul who yearns after those large vessels with windows in the transom, and a roomy saloon from which to look out those windows. The settee aft will seat six comfortably. Two more portlights each side (port and starboard) in the stern let in more light, while overhead, the hatch also sports a skylight if desired. The galley places the cook in her (his?) own area out of the traffic, with everything in reach, and with excellent lighting and visibility while working, for the little pilothouse has a healthy sized window and portlight each side.

Enclosed head aft has room for a shower installation and sink, and doubles as a nearby wet locker for those coming out from a storm. If it's desired to stay out of the storm completely, inside steering can be accommodated in the passageway, as eye level is such that there's vision over the bow, from either cabin sole, or, for shorter souls (5′8″ or less) they, too can see over the scuttle by standing on the companionway steps. A hinge-down seat can also be fitted off the head bulkhead over the passageway for greater comfort while steering. The chart table is within handy reach from this position as well, as shown in the accompanying photograph.

BAKEA's chart table is to port, handy to her inside steering station.

AFFINITY has remote control autopilot, and her crew can thus opt for inside steering at any vantage point. The chart table is conveniently within a step or two of the companionway.

passageway under the starboard cockpit seat with four (+) feet of headroom, which would come into the forward end of the aft head compartment. Also, the foc'sle and engine room arrangement of the great cabin version could be swapped with that of the staysail schooner. Additionally, if one prefers the below decks arrangement from midships forward in the Staysail Schooner version, this could be accommodated in place of the one shown for the Great Cabin 30 version. There's a surprising three feet (+) of headroom over the double berth under the cockpit seat, and twenty-one inches under the footwell in the Staysail Schooner version. This double berth area is made lighter with the addition of deck prisms or small portlights into the cockpit well.

Eliane and Michael LeBeck, at left above, enjoy entertaining in their spacious great cabin aboard BAKEA. The settee converts to a double berth, shown below, and also provides comfortable space for two sea berths longitudinally.

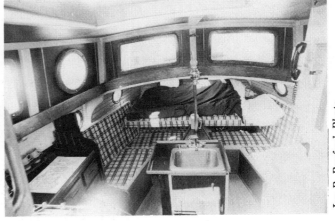

Above decks, the midships cockpit will seat six (+) in comfort, and vision is excellent from this vantage point. In the foc'sle, an optional second head helps eliminate potential middle of the night trips out through the cockpit to the aft head. Or, if a second head is deemed unnecessary, it can be replaced by moving the starboard hanging locker to port, allowing a

Although *Bakea's* aft cabin does not have the warm curves in her settee that *Affinity* has, the straighter shape has the advantage of allowing sea berths port and starboard, or a convertible double berth can be made aft by swinging up the settee's back, where in rough weather it would be more comfortable to sleep than in the foc'sle.

Affinity has a wonderfully warm curving settee in her aft cabin, as shown in the accompanying photograph.

Roy Montgomery Photo

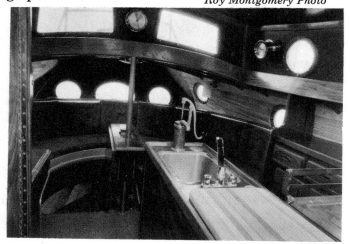

AFFINITY's great cabin's settee is luxuriously inviting.

BAKEA's compact galley (below) has a range with oven, refrigerator, drawers and lockers, and sink in an island with fresh and sea water taps.

Roy Montgomery Photos

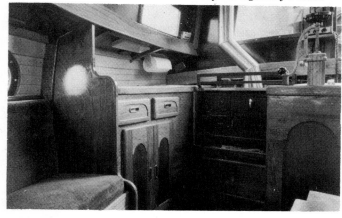

AFFINITY's galley (above) shows some fine details, with a centerline sink in a counter adjacent to the companionway, making the entire galley U-shaped.

Further interesting ideas have been incorporated in *Bakea.* Her owners requested a double headsail cut-ter rig, and a more permanent inside steering station, yet wished to keep the basic concept of the great cabin aft. Thus, the steering console has been placed a little port of midships, and the head and galley areas of the original Great Cabin version have been interchanged. With the galley on the starboard side, the skipper has maximum vision on the starboard side — which is his danger zone. Vision immediately to port can be maximized by leaving the head door open while underway. The sink has been placed on centerline in almost all the great cabin versions so that on either tack, the sink will not backfill, as it would if placed on one side or the other of the vessel. In this particular arrangement, the sink is raised in a little island of its own at the head of the drop leaf table, making it handy for clearing the table preparatory to cleaning dishes, and also making it a convenient arm's reach to the galley counter. The lower photo shows this aspect of the arrangement.

Forward in *Bakea,* there is plenty of stowage space, and good engine access to port. Also, a portion of the centerline bulkhead is removable for engine access. A head and single berth in the foc'sle are forward of the large starboard double berth. A huge (100 gallon) water tank is beneath the double berth where it is relatively easy to get at for inspection. A shelf and locker are built in on the port side just aft of the head.

The *Polaris* motorsailer/trawler yacht version of the Benford 30 is a particular favorite of ours for those who perfer a more extensive pilothouse and who enjoy the shippy feeling of being in a yacht with comfortably high bulwarks. *Polaris's* sailing rig can include one to three sails, depending upon the extent to which the captain enjoys sailing, and whether he would prefer to keep the rig limited to a steadying sail such as the fishermen use in rough seas.

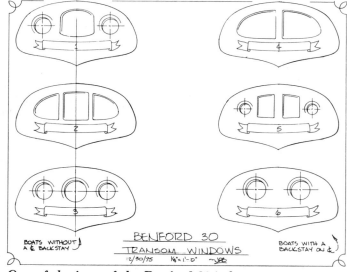

One of the joys of the Benford 30 is having great cabin transom windows. Pick your favorite from those shown above, or sketch up a new version. . . .

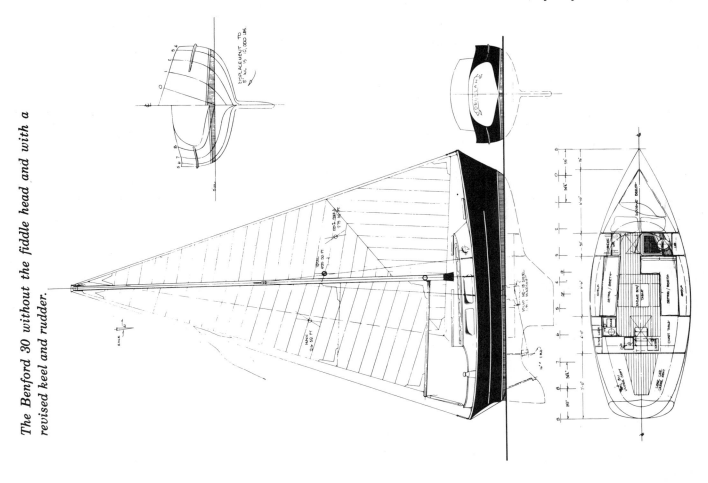

The Benford 30 without the fiddle head and with a revised keel and rudder.

Fortune Line Ketch

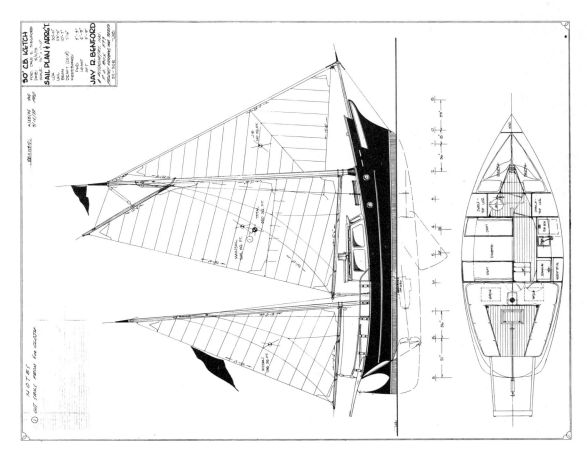

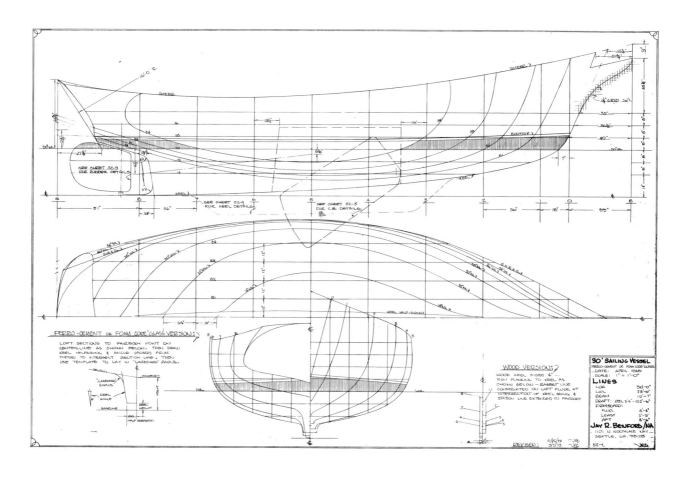

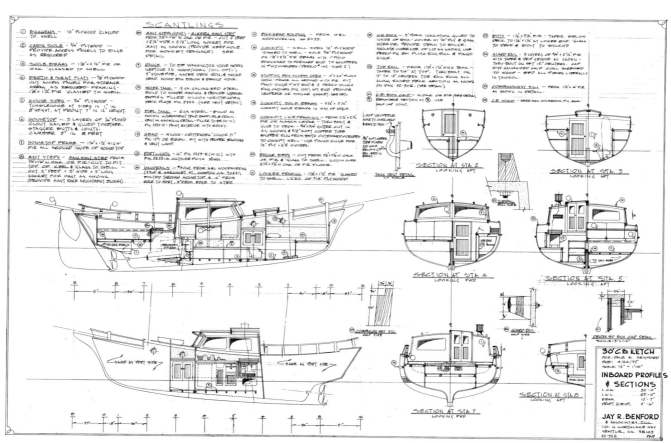

Belle Amie

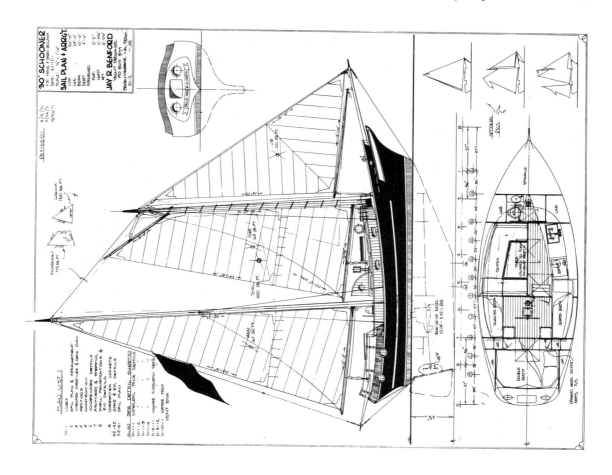

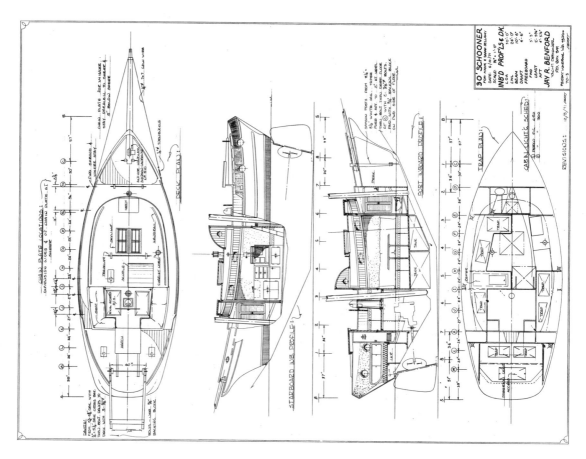

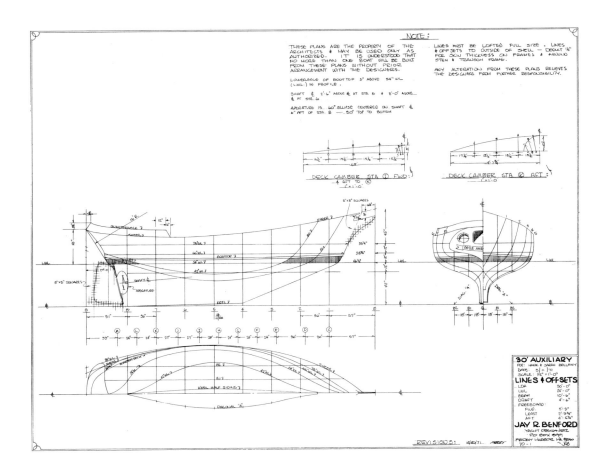

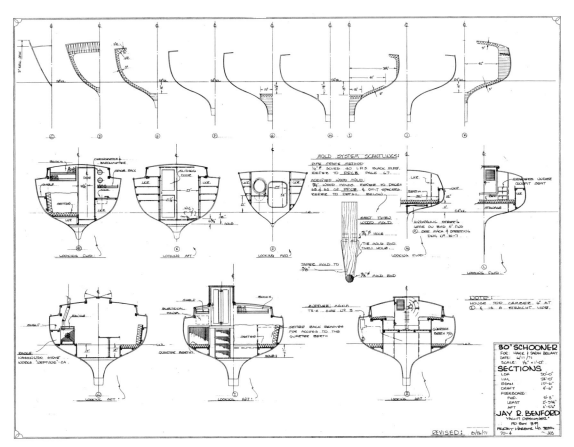

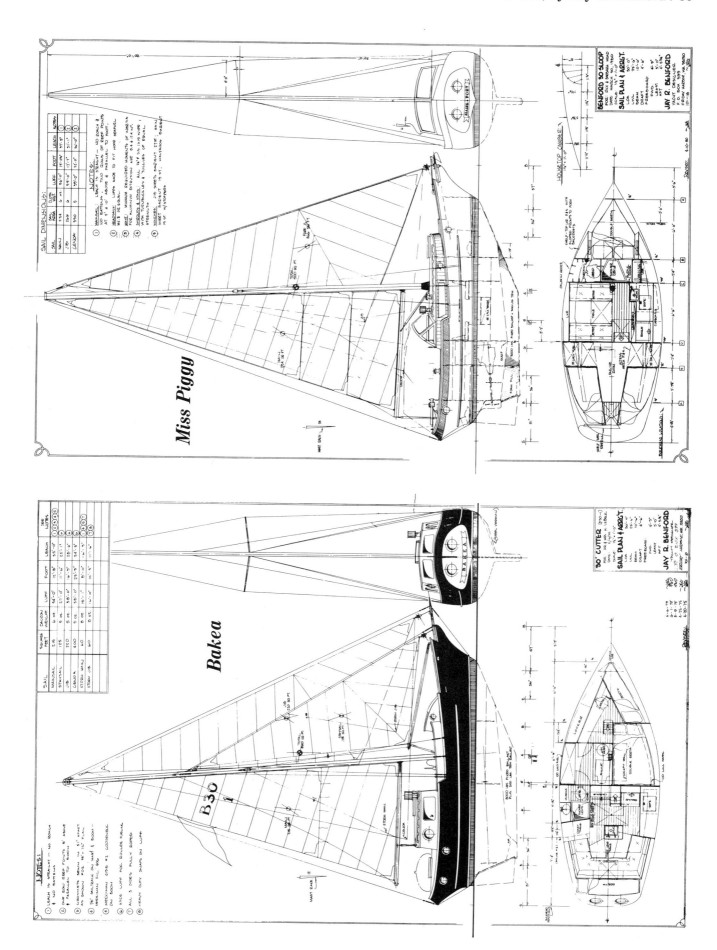

Miss Piggy

Bakea

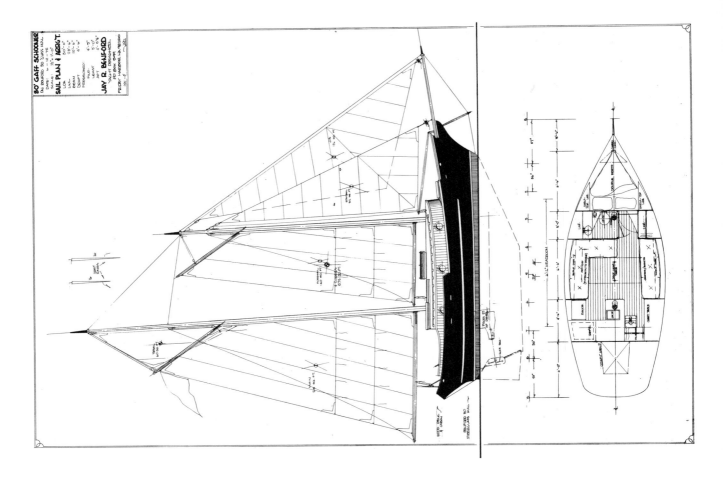

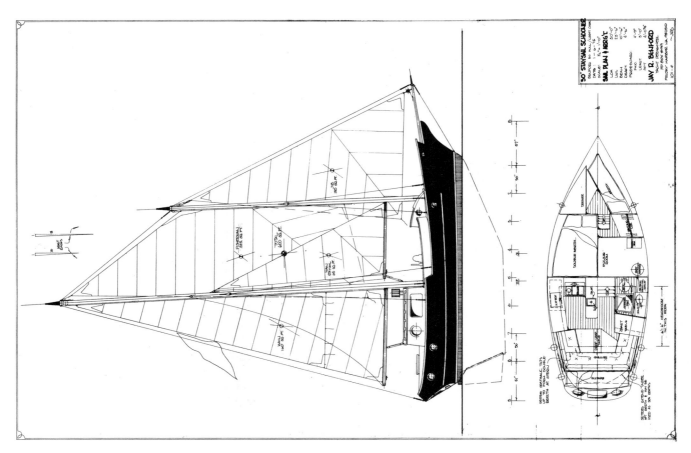

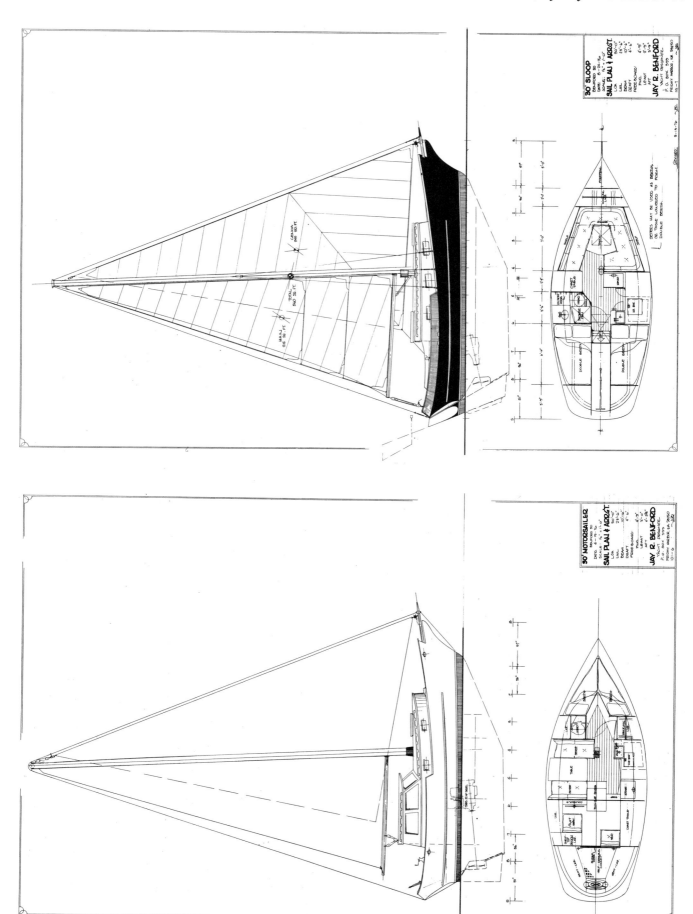

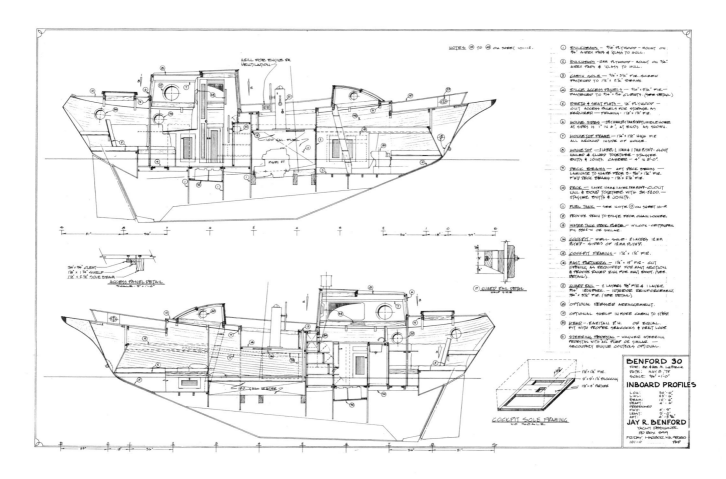

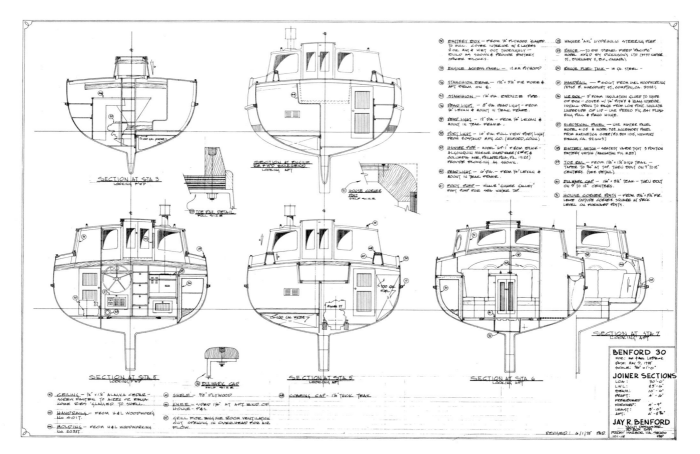

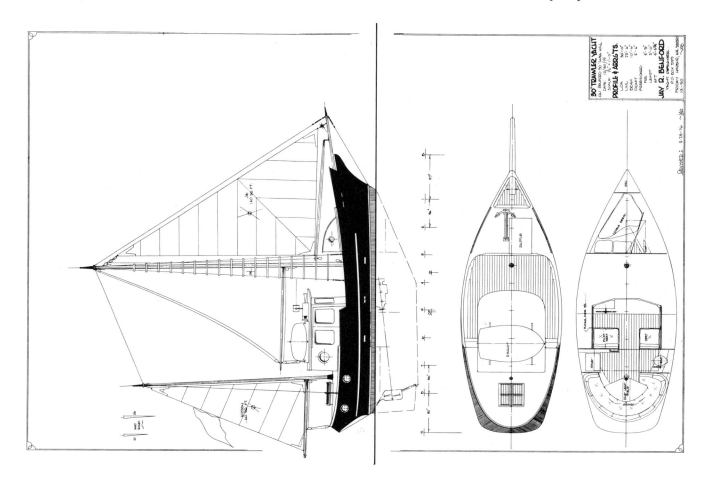

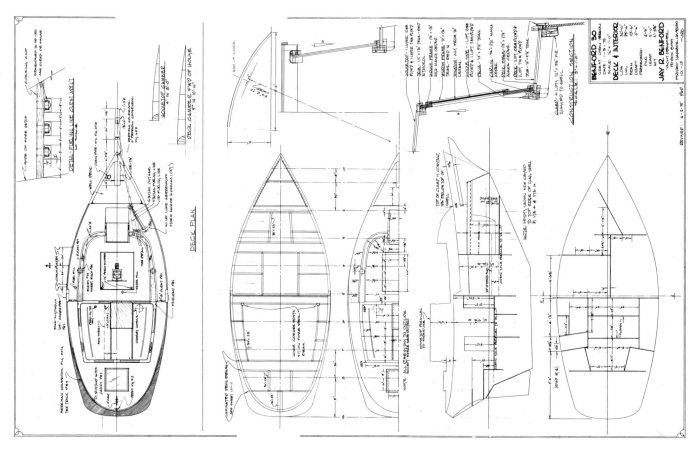

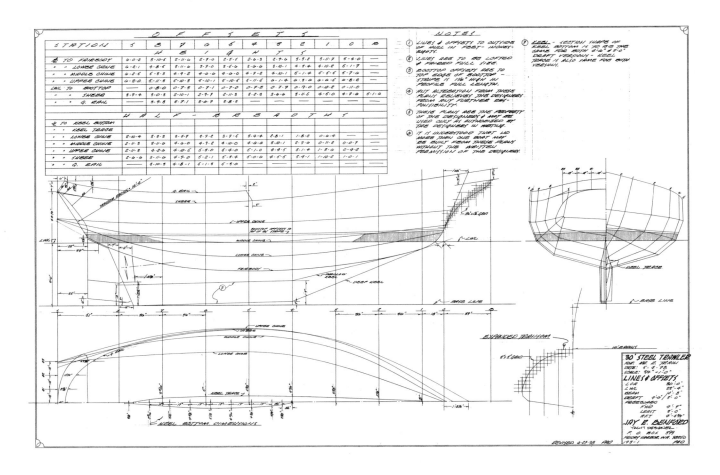

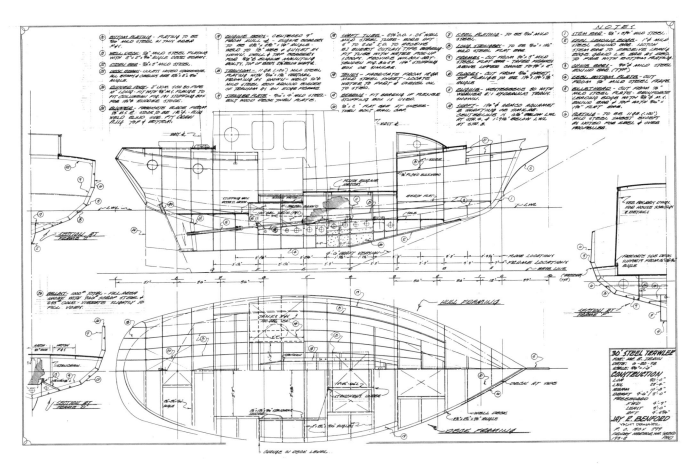

At left and below are three powerboat versions that can be built on these lines. Two have the shallower hull and the third has the deeper keel. Either keel will work on any of these boats. All of these boats will provide very economical operation at reasonable speeds.

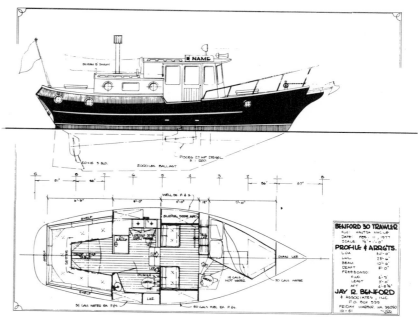

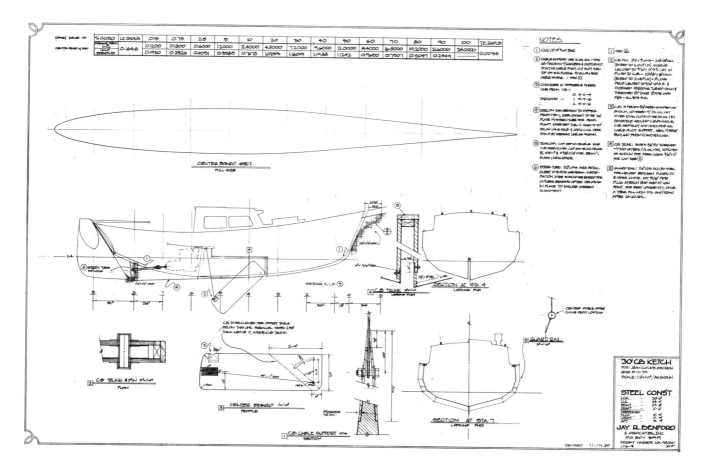

Chapter 4
The height of fuelishness

(This manuscript arrived, unannounced, in the mail one day. It caught our attention, being on a timely subject. Wanting to know more about it, we attempted to locate Ms. Wite, but were unsuccessful. We were able to reach Jay Benford. He confirmed the interview did take place, and said he thought Miss Wite was off on the 'Hatter.' Ed.)

by Lilly Wite

One winter day recently, I boarded the Washington State ferry, *Evergreen State*, at Anacortes for the two-hour ride through the San Juan Islands to Friday Harbor. The sky was sparkling blue, the air was cold, and I shivered under my blue, U-Vic float coat. I was on my way to meet and interview the reportedly reclusive and curmudgeonly yacht designer, Jay R. Benford. I had made the appointment only the day before.

Benford's salty and unique ketch, the *Sunrise*, sat in her slip alongside the Friday Harbor ferry landing. The Benford boat, I reflected, was something apart from most others I had seen, yet she was pretty and well-proportioned. I had a brisk walk off the ferry and through the hillside parking lot, where I turned left and flexed my calf muscles up another steep hill. A total of three and one-half blocks, following the directions given me, brought me to the old frame house that serves as the Benford office and design studio. It was painted off-white, and had a porch measuring about 7 feet by 10 feet. A large Herreshoff anchor leaned against the window post, and an old-fashioned set of spreaders seemed to grow out of the far corner opposite the door.

I knocked. Almost at once the door was flung open, and I faced a giant of a man, blond hair, red beard, broad shoulders and strong-looking arms and hands. He wore a blue chambray work shirt and heavy, whipcord trousers. Possibly in his early forties, he was rugged, handsome and competent-looking. "You're Miss Wite," he said. His blue eyes twinkled and his mouth broke into a broad, open grin. "I'm Frank Madd, a friend of Jay Benford's. I saw the ferry land. We've been expecting you."

I smiled, somewhat embarrassed at such a fast and warm welcome. He motioned me inside, took my coat, and asked me to wait while he checked to see if Benford was available. Then he dashed up a flight of stairs that led to the second floor, and was gone. I wondered if his parting look was questioning my attire. I had worn what has become almost a uniform for me—faded jeans and a *Woodenboat* T-shirt. I enjoy being just me, although it seems to occasionally draw some attention.

Hull models, boat photos and drawings decorated the walls of the entry area. All the craft looked businesslike and sea-kindly, yet each had its own character and beauty. Sounds of rapid-fire typing came from an adjoining room, interspersed by the occasional shuffle of a file drawer closing. A sign beside the stairs read:

> We are professionals, like doctors and lawyers, who sell our time and knowledge. Though we love to talk boats, we must give priority to our current design clients who have already paid for our services. Consultation is available by appointment at $60 per hour.

If Benford intended that notice to apply to this interview, he never mentioned it later.

Frank Madd came down the stairs and told me Jay Benford was free. He waited politely as I passed close by him, then followed me up to a large drafting room. One end of the room was partially closed in to form a library and office, and its windows looked over the lovely harbor. Within, a man was working on some calculations, seemingly oblivious to my entry, but the next instant he rose, introduced himself as Jay Benford, and motioned me to a chair. Frank pulled another chair over close to me and sat down.

Benford was medium height, with a dark beard and dark rimmed glasses. In contrast to Frank, he seemed a quiet mover, contemplative, with a certain amused outlook from behind the neatly trimmed beard. For the number of designs he'd done, I was surprised when he told me he was only 36 years old. Frank Madd, he said, had been the technical and design editor of the old *Tiller* magazine, until it was bought by a manufacturing and insurance conglomerate some time ago.

This very striking red-bearded man, I learned, was the only son of Clarence Madd, who originated the Madd Boat Works in Penobscot Bay, Maine. Their Hatter line of power cruisers remain collector's items today, and Frank owns and cruises the last one ever to come out of their yard.

Although I was becoming increasingly fascinated by this introduction, I felt compelled to begin on the stated purpose of my visit. I explained to Benford that I had come to learn about his concept of the ideal power cruiser for the Pacific Northwest.

Benford thought a moment, then said, "The proper power cruiser for this area ought to be a year-round boat. Did you notice there were almost no small boats on the water when you came over, yet the day is perfect for cruising? Too many people buy their boats in heated showrooms or at boat shows, where they are protected from the elements. They forget that the boat will be used in all sorts of weather. In this area, that usually means in dampness and cold."

"Thus, an ideal Northwest cruiser must have heat and good air circulation. Then it's pleasant to be aboard.

"The steering position must also be sheltered. It must not only be protected from the elements, it must provide a good view for the helmsman, with particular emphasis on ability to spot drift in the water. With heat, the whole area becomes comfortable, and others will join the helmsman, making the cruise more enjoyable for all. People feel inclined to repeat the experience, and thus do more cruising.''

"I like the way you emphasize comfort and pleasure while cruising. That's always been my philosophy," I said, noticing Frank was smiling in agreement.

"Well, they are called *pleasure* boats," said Benford. "The whole exercise is soon abandoned if it's no longer pleasant. Witness the great numbers of boats that never seem to leave their slips. Here is first-rate evidence that something is amiss, either with the boat or with the owner's selection of a boat to satisfy his needs."

Benford paused here, looked out the window, then selected a well-used pipe from a rack on his desk. He picked up a humidifier nearby, and from his overloaded shirt pockets produced a lighter and pipe nail. He gently tamped the tobacco in succeeding layers into the bowl, fired the lighter, and puffed thoughtfully several times. The flame alternately hovered, then disappeared into the bowl with each puff.

I asked what kinds of boats were being designed today to satisfy this kind of cruising. His answer startled me.

"Plus ca change, plus c'est la meme chose."

"He means," Frank said, "the more things change, the more they stay the same. In other words, if we were better history students, we'd realize that most of the so-called 'innovations' and 'break-throughs' are just so much organic fertilizer."

I smiled at Frank's response. He obviously got fired up quickly, and I liked that in a man.

"Look at it this way," Frank continued. "Before about 1950, there were a lot of easily driven powerboats around. They had to be easily driven. Fuel costs, as a percentage of most people's incomes, were high. But as wages went up faster than prices, we were lulled into thinking we didn't need to be concerned with the cost of fuel. We ended up with floating condominiums with pointy ends driven by very thirsty engines. This trend was abetted by marinas and boatyards that charged solely on length, leading yachtsmen to ask designers for shorter and wider boats.

"Look at the boats my father built seventy-five years ago. The problems those boats solved should still be of concern to today's power cruisers. My father's boats were much narrower, and much more lightly loaded without all the

gadgets and so-called conveniences people find so necessary today. Because they were narrow and light, they could be driven by modest sized engines with commendable economy.

"The Hatter line is a perfect example. My *Hatter* cruises effortlessly at ten knots. I have good visibility from the wheelhouse, and the diesel stove keeps the interior warm, even during this cold winter. In fact, starting this evening, I plan to go cruising for a few more days. I'll eat from the sea, drink homemade wine, and the fuel for the whole trip won't cost $10.00. What a great life!"

He looked at me steadily, and I hoped I wasn't reading too much into his gaze. I had to agree the cruise did sound like a lot of fun, and Frank looked competent enough to handle anything that came along.

Addressing myself again to Benford, who, I noticed, wore a gold wedding ring, I asked, "Where do you find boats like Frank's today?"

"Virtually all those boats are on the used boat market, if they're available at all," he replied. "Often they will have been loaded down with more gear and bigger engines over the years, but some are still relatively unspoiled.

"There are also a number of powerboats aimed at the 12 to 16 knot range recently being marketed. One of these, with a smaller engine, would be more fuel-efficient."

"This brings me to what may be the most important factor in determining the extent to which boats are used," Benford continued. "That is fuel economy. Or, more correctly, the lack of fuel economy, which is usually the overriding reason why many cruises are never made. It simply costs too much to run the boat. Most powerboats aren't economical to operate, at least at the speeds people think they need for cruising."

"What is a proper cruising speed?"

"About ten knots, with the amount of drift in the water around here. This is fast enough to make reasonable passages in a matter of hours."

"What about the so-called Taiwan trawler yachts? How do they compare?" I asked.

"Most of them are heavy, and not shaped to be driven at ten knots," Benford answered. "If they were built to lighter scantlings, with modified shapes, they could cruise efficiently at ten knots. Taking them as they are, I would suggest getting one with a smaller engine, and driving it at a lower speed-length ratio

for improved fuel economy."

I wanted to check my understanding of the term, 'speed-length ratio,' so I asked Mr. Benford to explain it for me.

"The speed-length ratio is the ratio of the boat's speed, divided by the square root of the waterline length. The hull speed of a displacement boat refers to the condition where the boat has a wave crest at the bow and a wave crest at the stern, with a trough in the middle. Usually, this occurs at a speed-length ratio of 1.33. For instance, a 36-foot waterline boat would generate this wave at 8 knots. Eight is 1.33 times 6, and 6 is the square root of 36."

I must have day-dreamed a bit, for thoughts of homemade wine and square roots were beginning to become thoroughly inter-meshed. Suddenly I was aware the Benford was talking again.

"....should not be thought of as an absolute limit," he was saying, "for there are too many cases of displacement boats exceeding 1.33. *Strumpet*, a displacement cruiser we did for Ernest K. Gann, ran right up to 1.52. She had a 32-foot waterline and made 8.57 knots in the trials. Since I'm advocating boats that cruise at 10 knots, either we must find ways of pushing smaller boats faster than 1.33, or design longer boats that make 10 knots within the 1.33 speed-length ratio parameters."

"How do you design smaller boats to move faster than 1.33?" I asked, getting my mind back on the interview.

Benford reached for one of several dozen notebooks that lined a section of his library, and turned to this graph:

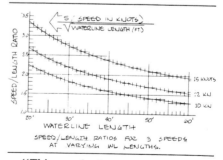

SPEED/LENGTH RATIOS FOR 3 SPEEDS AT VARYING WL LENGTHS.

"This graph shows the speed-length ratio at which a boat operates to achieve 10, 12, or 15 knots. A boat with a 25-foot waterline at 10 knots has a speed-length ratio of 2.0, while a boat with a 60-foot waterline at 10 knots has a speed-length ratio of only 1.3. The lower the speed-length ratio, within reason, the less power is required, as this other graph shows (Fig. 2):

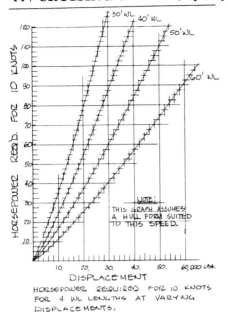

HORSEPOWER REQUIRED FOR 10 KNOTS
FOR 4 WL LENGTHS AT VARYING
DISPLACEMENTS.

"Let's say we've decided we need a 30,000 pound boat to carry us and our gear. Looking at these curves, if that boat were 30 feet on the waterline, we'd need about 127 horsepower for 10 knots. If we lengthen her to 40 feet, we'd be down to about 88 horsepower. At 50 feet, we'd need about 60 horsepower, while at 60 feet, we'd only need about 41 horsepower."

At this point, we were interrupted by a little black cat. She walked into the office, talking in almost human tones, hopped onto Benford's lap, then directly up to his shoulder. There she draped herself around his neck like a contented fur muff, purring and needling her claws in and out of his shirt. Mr. Benford gave her an encouraging little pat.

Benford resumed. "All this brings us to the specific hull shapes needed for increasing speed-length ratios. The most important thing is the shape of the stern. At higher speed-length ratios, we want to leave the aft crest of the hull speed wave further astern. Let me make a sketch of several sterns, to show how they affect performance."

As I turned from the window, he arose, cat still draped over his shoulders, and Frank looked in my direction. The four of us gathered around the drawing board. I was aware of Frank standing close to me.

"Stern A is much like the one we used on *Strumpet*, and is seen on many sailing boats. Stern B is like that of the *Kiyi*, which we lived aboard for a year, and is our favorite stern shape. Stern C is a transom stern, with the bottom just at or above the water at rest. All three of these

sterns work well at speed-length ratios up to about 1.3 to 1.5. The curvature of the bottom as it rises towards the stern is too great for them to let the stern wave move aft far enough to raise their speed.

"For speeds in the 1.3 to 2.0 and up range, a stern like D would probably be best. Its transom is immersed even at rest, and the rise of the bottom toward the stern is very gentle. Stern E is most suitable for higher speeds, and is most often used on planing boats. There is no perceptible rise to the bottom on this type."

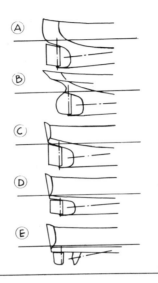

This business of comparing speed-length ratios and stern shapes to performance was starting to make sense to me. "So one of the things you're saying is that it's more efficient to make a long and narrow boat," I said. "But how can you look at an existing boat and tell how efficient it is?"

Before Benford could speak, Frank broke in. "If you don't have the actual fuel consumption data, just look at the height of the stern wave at cruising speed. If the wave's very tall, it would be the height of fuelishness to think she'd be very economical. Sorry, Jay, I couldn't let that one by."

Benford groaned, trying to suppress a smile at Frank's pun. I liked it.

"Frank's quite right, Miss Wite. Those waves can only be generated by expending energy. The bigger the waves, the more energy wasted. When we lived on the *Kiyi*, I loved watching her slip effortlessly through the water. There was almost no wake at cruising speed. The *Kiyi* is 50 feet long with a 10-foot beam, and an excellent example of an easily driven hull shape. Lately, Frank and I have been designing an economical cruiser, with the *Kiyi's* pretty stern.

She's to be about 65 feet long, perhaps 60 feet on the water, with about nine and a half feet of beam and 3 feet of draft. Her displacement in average cruising trim should work out to approximately 15,000 pounds, giving her a displacement/length ratio of 31. We think she'd be able to go from Seattle to Southeastern Alaska and back on about 125 gallons of diesel oil, cruising at about 10 knots. That's $65 worth of fuel at current costs, or just over five cents per mile.

"By comparison, the typical planing boat of about half that length but with the same displacement would make the same round trip at about 20 knots and use about 1,250 gallons of gasoline. Its cost would be about $835, or 67 cents per mile. The savings potential is obvious."

I couldn't help but think how important this concept of fuel efficiency was. The *Hatter* was becoming more attractive by the minute, and it was nice to know there were ecological and scientific rationales for the choice, as well as economic. I asked what disadvantages there might be to the long and narrow boat.

"Well, the boat would only have the accommodations of a conventional 35-footer. She would also face higher charges when paying fees based solely on length. But the fuel savings on an actively cruised boat would more than offset this, plus you could put two of these 65-footers in a slip that is usually used for only one today. You'd have to resist the temptation to load the boat with every toy offered at the boatshows, for weight is one of the detriments to fuel economy. Of course, the longer boat is less sensitive to loading, and would have more pleasant motion, so the crew would probably enjoy cruising more, which is the whole point, anyway.

By this time, the mid-winter sun was growing low, and Friday Harbor's trees were casting long, tranquil shadows over the water. A secretary carried in a handful of letters and laid them on Benford's desk for signature. I realized that Benford had quite succinctly explained his basic philosophy of the ideal Northwest power cruiser and our interview had come to an end. I thanked him, and looking away curiously from that little black cat, I turned to go.

Frank rose, his broad shoulders covering the doorway, and said, "Lilly, let me get your coat, and I'll take you to the *Hatter*. I think you'll like what you see."

"I already do," I said, and followed him down the stairs. ☐

How Much Horsepower Do You Need?

The graph below is one of the tools we use in preliminary design work. From it, we can quickly read what sized engine to specify for a displacement boat, either power or sail. It is also useful in consulting on repowering old boats.

To use the graph, read the bottom axis to find the displacement of the boat. Then go up and find the horsepower required for it. For example, the 38' Tug Yacht at right is about 23,000 pounds displacement in normal cruising trim. Therefore, she would require an engine of 35 horsepower to achieve normal hull speed — that is, a speed-length ratio of 1.33.

In actual practice, this sometimes proves to be a bit conservative. *PROMETHEUS*, the first of the 39' D.E. Cutters, was this same displacement and made 1.4 with 35 horsepower.

This graph assumes a reasonably conventionally shaped and smooth hull form, driven to a speed length ratio of 1.33. (See the preceding interview for a discussion of this ratio.) For more information on calculating power requirements for other speeds, I would suggest Robert P. Beebe's book, *Voyaging Under Power*. It contains a longer discussion of the subject, complete with useful graphs and examples.

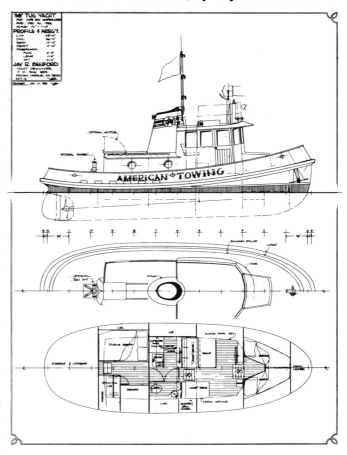

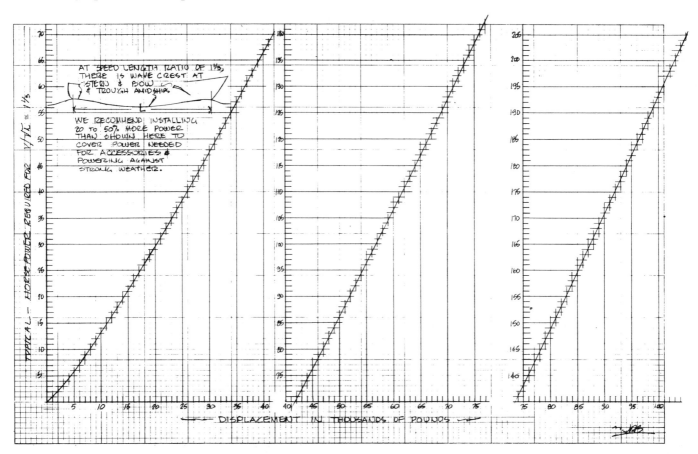

Chapter
5

Memory

34' Fantail Cruiser
For: Ash Boatbuilding
Design Number 206
1982

In 1969 I purchased a 1926, 50' fantail stern cruiser, the *KIYI*. Robin and I lived aboard for a very pleasant year (1970), and made the mistake of selling her. We thought that our expanding business required us to move into larger quarters. We should have just rented office space and kept on living aboard.

The pleasant memories of that vessel were the inspiration for this design. She is currently being built by Ash Boatbuilding in Duncan, B.C. They are doing the first couple of boats cold-molded and plan to offer the boat in fiberglass as well. The cold-molded scantlings are conservative, providing for robust structure.

Complete stock plans for *MEMORY* are included in this chapter. As you can see, this is a very abbreviated set, created thusly at the experienced builder/client's request, and quite in contrast to the complete

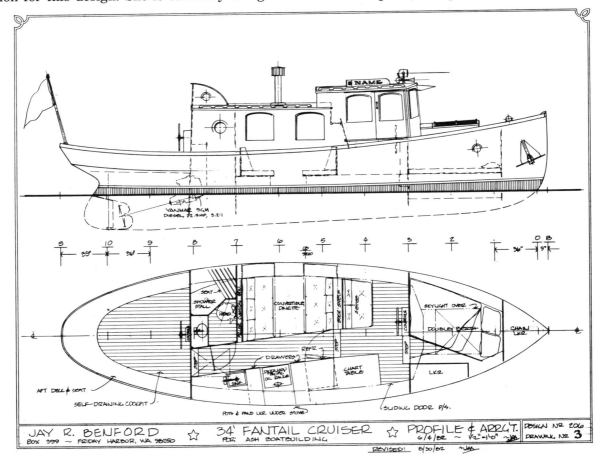

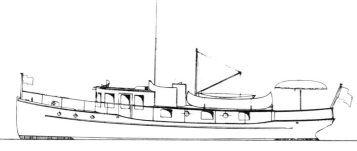

The KIYI. For small craft, we carried a 14' canoe and 14' Whitehall type skiff.

KIYI photo courtesy Pacific Yachting magazine.

stock plans for the *QUIET BIRD*, shown starting on page 148. In style, *MEMORY* is a smaller version of the *KIYI*, with much the same appearance in a boat two-thirds as long. The *KIYI* had the same beam as *MEMORY*, and was quite easily driven. Everywhere we went, the *KIYI* was admired by others who agreed with us that she was very lovely. Boats built from this

design are likely to have the same response.

Before the days of the horsepower race and before cruising became so crowded that everyone felt they had to rush to the next marina to get a slip for the night, there existed a much more economical style of cruiser. They were easily driven at modest speeds by small engines. My thoughts on this are expressed in more detail in The Height Of Fuelishness (Chapter 4, page 42.)

My comments on 10 knots being desirable, as quoted in the interview in the prior chapter, notwithstanding I'd suggest an even slower speed as being desirable and worth considering. This is particularly true with smaller vessels, such as the 34-footer shown in this chapter. A slower speed allows the shorter vessel to operate at a lower speed-length ratio which is even more conducive to good economy of operation.

This 34' fantail cruiser is intended for speeds in the 6 to 8 knot range, with 6 to 7 being quite economical. We've specified a 22½ horsepower diesel, even though she needs only about 12 to 15 horsepower to reach her top speed. This will allow a margin for adverse weather conditions as well as towing another vessel, if aid is needed. Also, she can be slightly over wheeled so the engine doesn't have to operate at full rpm's.

The pilothouse has a two person seat, raised for good visibility. The chart table is close to the helm, and is a one-fold chart size. The sliding door port and star-

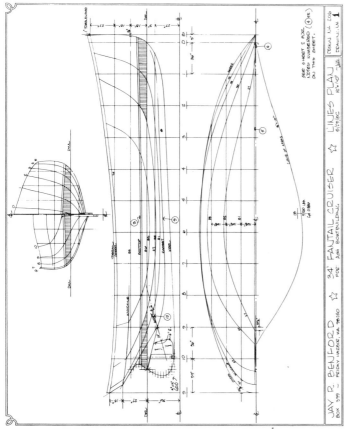

board makes it easy for the helmsman to look out and check docking situations and gives good ventilation.

Her forward stateroom has a comfortable double berth, with a large skylight overhead. This provides a good source of ventilation and makes the cabin well lit, as well as adding to the headroom and sense of spaciousness there. There is good stowage under the berth and in the locker to starboard.

The aft cabin has a convertible dinette, for guests to stay aboard. The galley opposite follows the slanted passageway to the aft door. The passage is offset to clear the engine, which is on centerline under the head sink. Keeping the engine aft, we've shortened the drive line, and kept the engine away from the pilothouse, so the pilothouse will be quieter. The enclosed head has a separate shower stall with a seat in it, so the whole head compartment won't be soaked every time someone takes a shower.

The aft deck is at comfortable sitting height from the cockpit sole. There is an outside control station for use when fishing. The fixed scuttle over the aft entry door gives headroom for going below and provides rain shelter for opening the door for ventilation in inclement weather.

As this is one of my favorite designs, I hope to do many others like it in different sizes. The *BOUNDARY BAY 44* (Chapter 22, page 168), could be the basis for a larger version. I've been working off and on, for the last several years, on a 65' variation for

ourselves, both to liveaboard and to contain our office.

This vessel was designed with the memories of a vessel we'd owned and loved 12 years ago still fresh in our minds. With this thought and because she was such a fine echo of the practical vessels of years ago, we called her *MEMORY*. Built and outfitted in the spirit of her design, she will create many more fine memories for her owners and crew.

Particulars

Item	English	Metric
Length over all	34'-0"	10.36m
Length designed waterline	31'-0"	9.45m
Beam	10'-6"	3.20m
Draft	2'-6"	0.76m
Freeboard:		
Forward	5'-3"	1.60m
Least	2'-9"	0.84
Aft	4'-0"	1.22m
Displacement, cruising trim*	9,200 lbs.	4,173 kg.
Displacement-length ratio	138	
Prismatic coefficient	0.586	
Entrance half angle	20 degrees	

*CAUTION: The displacement quoted here is for the boat in cruising trim. That is, with the fuel and water tanks filled, the crew on board, as well as the crews' gear and stores in the lockers. This should not be confused with the "shipping weight" often quoted as "displacement" by some manufacturers. This should be taken into account when comparing figures and ratios between this and other designs.

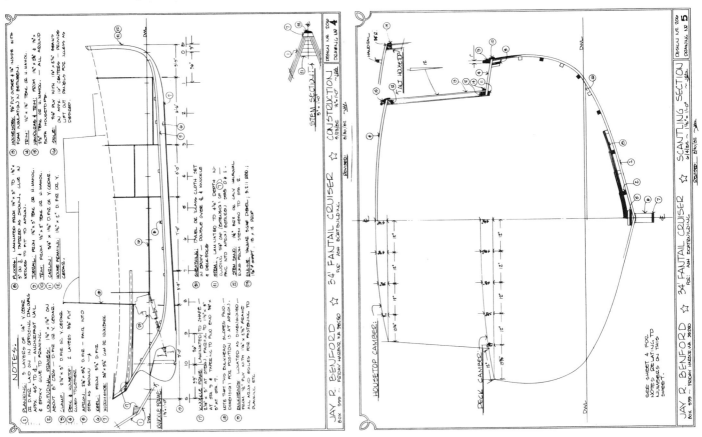

Chapter
6

The Most Economical Offshore Cruisers

The original versions of these sailing dories were designed fifteen years ago. I laid them out in trying to find the simplest sort of capable cruising boat that I could afford. Publishing them before I had a chance to build one, we've ended up with designs for several different sizes and with almost 200 of them under construction and sailing all over the world. They are being built both in home and professional shops.

Each of these sailing dories is designed with a simplified construction plan, using sheets of plywood from the bottom up. The interior bulkheads are the only transverse frames in the vessel, with the addition of the floors in way of the keel. The keel (lead or concrete

and scrap metal, depending on the version) is a sub-assembly bolted on prior to launching. The longitudinal framing consists of the chine, clamp and raised deck and/or house framing; there are no ribs to contend with. There are no deck beams, except for a temporary framework not finely fitted for the multiple layers of plywood above. The straight lines (see the lines of the 32 and 36-footers included herein) mean extremely easy lofting: a professional shop can loft one of the larger boats in a few hours! The straight lines also mean that there are no curves to contend with in outfitting; thus it is much easier to attach interior joinerwork than in a typical, (more curvacious) hull.

Jay R. Benford, Photos

These photos are of one of the economical cruisers. She is the 36' sailing dory DONNA, built by amateur builder Fred Schreiner in Alberta in only 13 months. She's since been to Mexico from Vancouver and to Hawaii and back, proving herself a first rate sea boat.

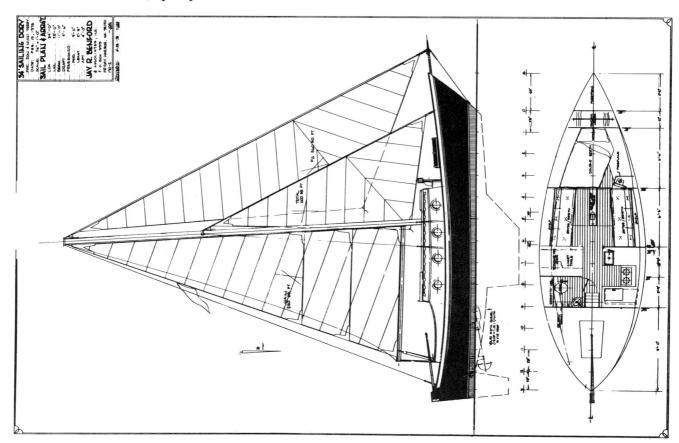

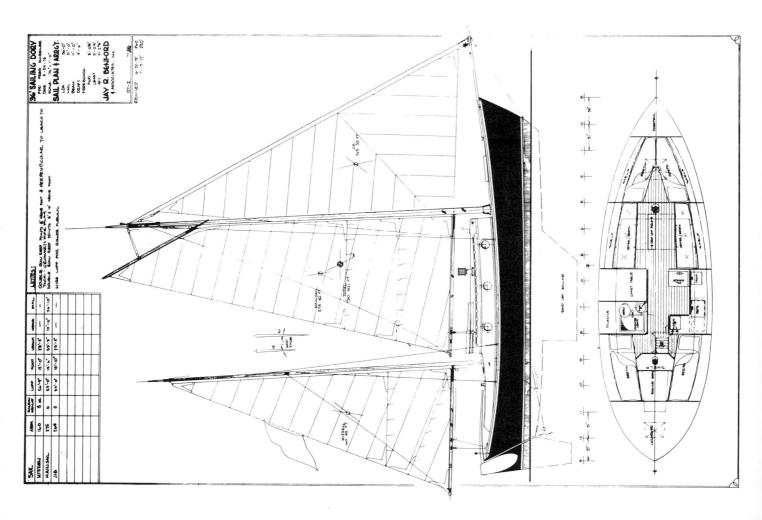

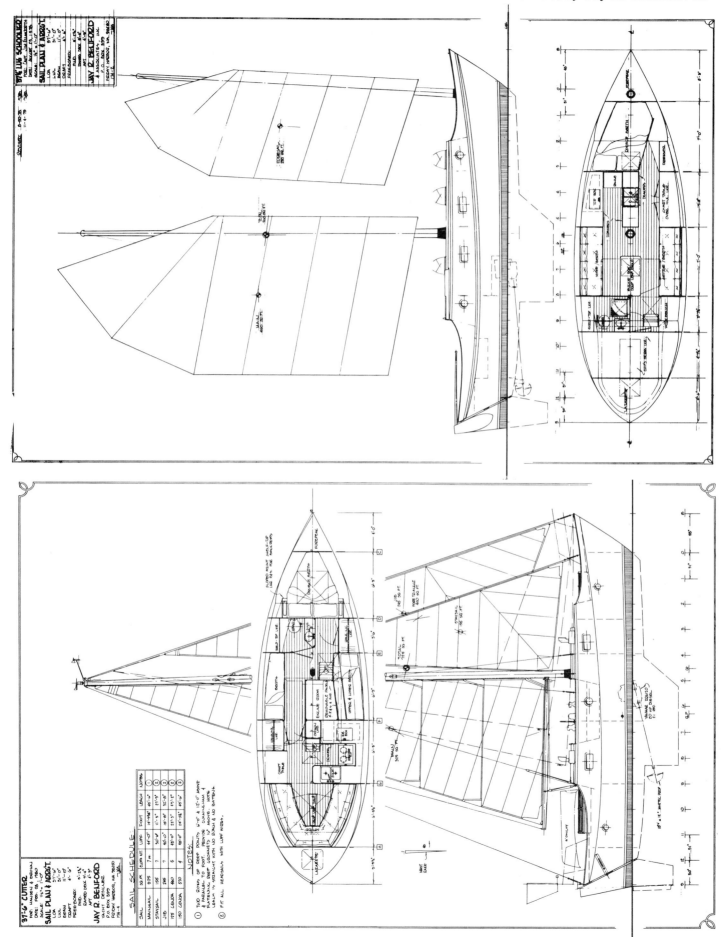

The first of the 36-footers was built in under 13 months by a shoemaker in Canada. He had never built a boat before, and didn't even have any boatbuilders with whom he could consult within his vicinity, 1200 miles from the coast. One of the first 19-footer Gunkholers was built by professional boatbuilder Paul Miller, of Port Hardy, British Columbia, in a little over 8 weeks. Thus these vessels make an ideal project for the amateur builder or for the professional yard who can set up for plywood production on a practical basis.

Though these vessels are flat-bottomed, in dory fashion, when heeled over, they present a "V" to the water, and thus move along at a good clip. We've had the pleasure of experiencing just how well this works when Fred Schreiner took us out for a sail in his 36' Sailing Dory, *DONNA,* on San Juan Channel. Fred later sailed *DONNA* from Vancouver, Canada, to Mexico, as well as to Hawaii and back to Victoria, B.C. He remarked that she tacked very easily and would hold her course well. To quote him:

"It really surfs down those big, Northwest swells with a good wind. Close hauled it steers itself. At other points I use a steering vane. It actually is a trimtab on the larger rudder with a vane and adjustments on top. It really works good. Often I do not touch the tiller for days on end, that is, if the wind stays that way."

They are thus lively and fast, with lots of sail power to carry their light, but well-ballasted hulls forth in a good variety of wind conditions. The chine on each is well immersed at the bow, to minimize or do away with pounding at anchor. Each keel and rudder are NACA foil sections. The generously large rudders maximize ease of control and minimize chances of stalling the rudder and broaching (which is common to the small racing spade rudder types.) Each of the sailing dories has a diesel engine for auxiliary power. The small (10 to 20 hp) amount of power called out is quite adequate to push these vessels to hull speed, and they have the additional advantage of being simple, safe and low in fuel consumption. Oil or wood stoves are called out for all the dories, as they make for dry heating and pleasant cooking, although other fuels could be used for cooking in the tropics.

Alternate Construction Materials

We're asked occasionally whether the dories could be built in other materials. Our answer is a qualified yes. We have done alternative construction plans for the 36' and 37½' dories for building in aluminum. It would be possible to do the smaller ones in aluminum, with similarly revised construction plans.

Ferro-cement is too heavy a method for these boats, and not suited to the flat panel type of construction in lighter weights.

Steel would be possible, but would increase the displacement because it is a heavier material. This would negate some of the advantages of these designs, so I would not recommend it as a good choice, even though it would be possible.

Airex cored fiberglass or C-Flex fiberglass could be done, but this is not the best type of design for one-off fiberglass building. The 'glass method that would work best is to make a large, smooth surfaced table. This would then be waxed, sprayed with gel coat and then the 'glass laid up on it. The large flat panels thus created would be put in place over the mold frames for the dory, and trimmed to fit. The corners would then be 'glassed together and suitably reinforced.

Plywood and epoxy is still the best choice for construction of the dories. It uses simple, inexpensive materials, and the final structure provides its own insulation. It is also easy to add items of outfit to the boat, by simply screwing on pieces inside, or bolting on deck hardware. It is my own first choice for building these boats.

A wooden boat is at least as strong as one of other materials; in addition, she's warmer, prettier, and often better finished. Because she is all of these lovely things, her owners feel greater pride in her and pay her the attention she deserves in the way of handling and maintaining her.

And what of maintenance? The very thought of "rot" makes us all creep and crawl and scurry away from contemplation. In actual fact, the major causes of rot are poor construction techniques and truly gross neglect. To quote Paul Miller, who's had years of experience repairing, renovating and rebuilding older wooden vessels, "Properly built boats rarely rot." They should be designed and built with good ventilation (so the wood can breathe) and the grain should never be exposed to weather. Aside from these few key points, maintenance of a wood boat is limited to painting. Paul points out that "today's linear polyurethane paints, applied in conjunction with the proper quality epoxy sealers can produce a finish that will outshine and outlast the gelcoat finish on fiberglass hulls." Epoxy sealers are also a boon to the endurance of bottom paints.

As to actual construction, marine grade plywood is specified in our plans. Hull, deck and cabin are assembled with bronze screws and epoxy glue, then completely sheathed with fiberglass cloth set also in epoxy resin. The reader should note that the sheathing cloth is not set in polyester resin, for polyester does not adhere as well as epoxy, nor does it last as long; we have seen too many plywood-glass sheathed boats with their outer layer of glass peeling off. The plywood-epoxy cloth method of wooden boatbuilding (much like cold molding, only with thicker or preglued "veneers") results in a strong, totally watertight, monocoque shell.

When the time comes to outfit the interior, the builder finds that plywood is infinitely easier to fasten to than other materials. Additionally, the inside of the hull needs no further insulation, and as it's pretty to the eye, it needn't be covered up for any aesthetic reason. As mentioned earlier, and as Paul enjoys pointing out, "the hard chine dory hull form makes for many straight line fits, with very few difficult curves." All of these points add up to timesavings without sacrificing beauty, which in turn translates to a lovely boat at low cost.

Rigs

There are several different rigs on the dories. Each has its virtues. You should select the one that best matches how you will use yours.

The lug rig permits handling all sail evolutions from the cockpit. It is quickly and easily reefed. It does have a bit more weight aloft and it is not as easy to add light air sails on it as on the cutter.

The ketches were designed for ease of balancing the helm and keeping the course with a minimum of effort. They are gaff rigged on the mains to keep the spars down. This keeps the center of effort low, so the heeling moments are lessened, permitting sailing at lower angles of heel.

The cutter and sloop rigs have the tallest masts. The longer luffs will give better windward ability. The height will permit flying larger light air sails, optimizing performance. These rigs are the most conventional, with a wide selection of hardware and parts available for them. They will probably enjoy the best resale value, being the most widely used and understood rig.

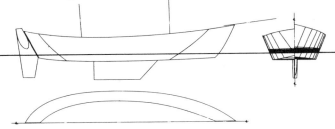

The lines of the 36' dory, above, show a boat capable of offshore cruising. The 37½' dory shares the same underbody and keel, with slightly longer bow overhang and a raised deck instead of a trunk cabin.

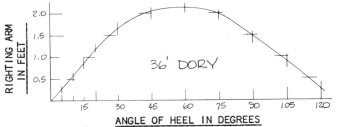

The stability curve for the 36' dory indicates a boat with excellent stability and sail carrying power. She is stiffer than most cruiser-racers of her size, and has a good range of stability. The raised deck of the 37½ will make for an extended range even greater than the 36-footer enjoys.

The Dory Hull Form and Stability

Some alarming tales are heard from time to time about the dory type of hull being "tender" — that is, heeling easily initially and then stiffening up as the deck edge approaches the water. This has been the case with the rowing dories for so long that it has become an article of faith among many that **any** dory will be tender. There are still a number of rowing dories being built where this is still the case, as this also makes for an easily rowed boat.

However, our modernized versions have relatively wider bottoms and are a bit fuller aft to give more initial stability and make for better sailing performance. This updated hull form, combined with a 40 percent ballast ratio carried low on the keel, makes for a pleasantly stiff boat. The additional design data, simplified lines plan, and the stability curve of the 36-footer on these boats should serve to silence the skeptics. Further testimony on this comes from Fred Schreiner, while sailing his 36-foot sailing dory DONNA, enroute to Mexico:

"Sailing in the ocean with the powerful winds and large swell is different than in the protected waters here. The boat is easy to steer, turn and keep under control. It reacts quickly and I can steer it in any tight spot in port. The best of all is when I have to back out in reverse gear. It goes where I want it to go. Sometimes I sailed up to the mooring buoys or piers with very little wind and hit the buoy or pier dead on, because the boat steers so precisely. The sails come down like lightning. But it takes a good crew. The boat surfs with a fair wind down those big rollers. Another good important item is the double ends. When I was offshore in the storm, I think it must have been Beaufort Scale 8, not one breaker entered the boat's cockpit. The sea was following. When it got too tough and rough we let the boat drift. The motion was violent, and the noise terrible, but the boat took on waves just like nothing. I write this because I sailed on production boats in moderate seas and they jump around. I wonder what they will do in force 8 winds. When I sailed and motored around Cape Anguello in a rough wind and confused sea another ketch got dismasted and drifted around for 3 days till the Coast Guard pulled them into port. At times the waves were 16' high. Then the boat fell off the wave top down in the trough with an awful shudder and bang. The bowsprit poked into the next wave already. But the boat withstood it all. No damage to it at all. I am well pleased with your design."

We're quite proud of the performance and sail carrying power we've designed into these boats, as we know this gives pleasure and a feeling of security to those aboard. Try it. . . .

37½' Sailing Dory

The Lug Schooner version of the 37½' dory, has an aft cockpit. The lug rig means simplified sail handling, but is not as easy to add sail area to it in light airs. The alternate interior, below, moves the galley aft and has a quarter berth instead of a workbench.

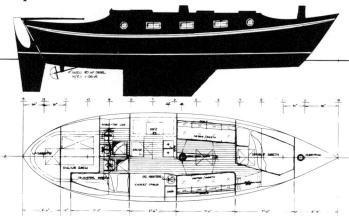

The 37½' Cutter has a midships cockpit, recessed into the raised deck. This leaves room enough to carry an 8 to 9' hard dinghy on the aft deck, over the giant skylight which is over the dining lounge.

36' Sailing Dory

The 36' dory has quarter berths in addition to the rest of her layout that she shares with the 34-footer. She could have a double berth in the forward cabin, like the 34 or 37½-footers. This interior and trunk cabin can be used on the 37½ cutter, if an alternate version is wanted. The cutter rig will probably give a bit better performance to windward.

34' Sailing Dory

The 34' dory has virtually the same accommodations that the Benfords enjoy on *SUNRISE*. This has proven to be an excellent layout for a couple to liveaboard. The galley, head, and chart table are all quickly accessible from the cockpit, making it easier to keep the rest of the boat dry, without the dripping traffic from on deck having to pass through. Her cutter rig is straightforward and will give excellent performance.

Photo by Manuela Scholz

30' Sailing Dory, PENELOPE II, on the Baltic.

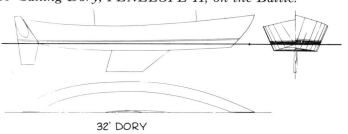

32' DORY

SAILING DORIES — Particulars

	30'	32'	34'	36'	37½'
L.O.A.	30'-0''	32'-0''	34-0''	36'-0''	37'-6''
L.W.L.	26'-0''	27'-0''	·28'-0''	31'-0''	31'-0''
Beam	10'-0''	9'-0''	11'-0''	11'-0''	11'-0''
Draft	4'-0''	4'-0''	4'-6''	4'-6''	4'-6''
Displacement	6,700 lbs	6,900 lbs	10,400 lbs	13,425 lbs	13,425 lbs
Displ/L. Ratio	170	156	211	201	201
Ballast (Ratio)	2,680 lbs. (40%)	2,760 lbs. (40%)	4,160 lbs (40%)	5,350 lbs (40%)	5,350 lbs (40%)
	(keel + 280# trim)	(keel + 360# trim)	(keel + 160# trim)	(keel + 350# trim)	(keel + 350# trim)
Prismatic Coefficient	.58	.60	.56	.63	.63
Freeboard					
Forward	4'-6''	4'-2''	5'-0''	5'0-¾''	5'-2½''
Least	2'8-¾''	2'6-¼''	2'-9''	3'0-¼''	5'4'' (raised deck)
Aft	3'3-½''	3'6-½''	4'-0''	4'2-¾''	4'-9''
Sail Area	500 sq. ft.	500 sq. ft.	600 sq. ft.	700 sq. ft.	700 sq. ft. (lug sch)
					725 sq. ft. (cutter)
Sail Area/Displ. Ratio	22.5	22.1	20.15	19.83	19.83 (lug schooner)
					20.54 (cutter)
Power	10hp diesel	10 hp diesel	13 hp diesel	20 hp diesel	20 hp diesel
Water	25 gallons	25 gallons	100 gallons	110 gallons	110 gallons
Fuel	25 gallons	25 gallons	40 gallons	55 gallons	55 gallons
Headroom	6'-1''	6'-1''	6'-1½'' to 6'-3½''	6'-4'' to 6'-6''	6'-2'' to 6'-4''

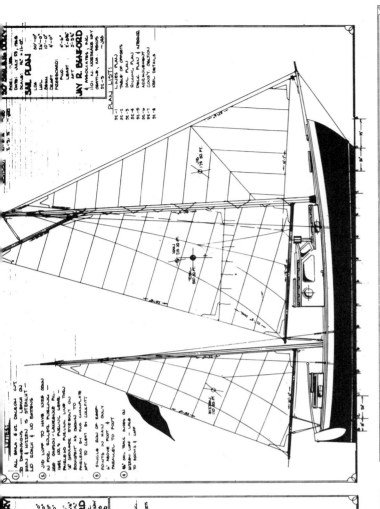

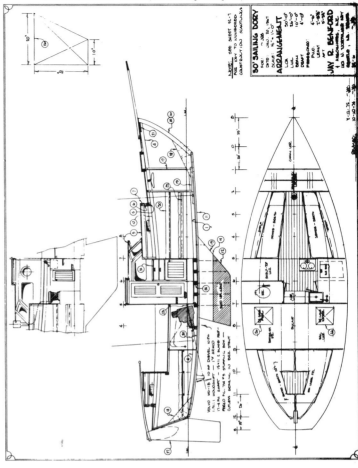

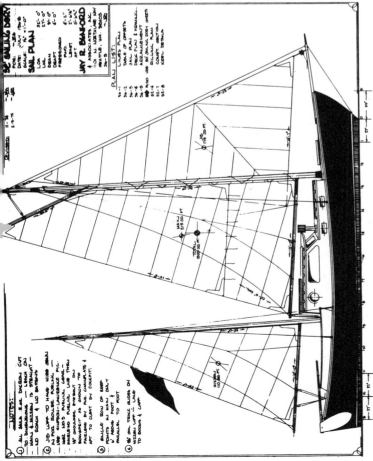

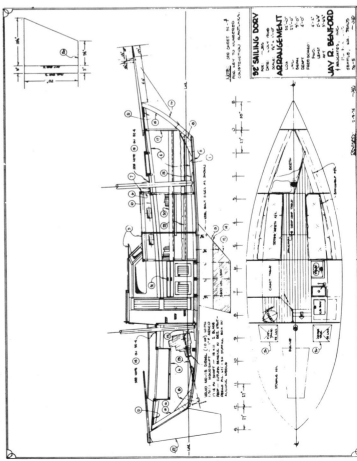

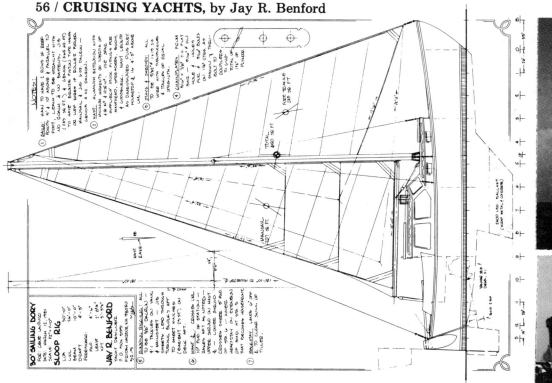

Photo by Manuela Scholz

Photo by Claus Oldag

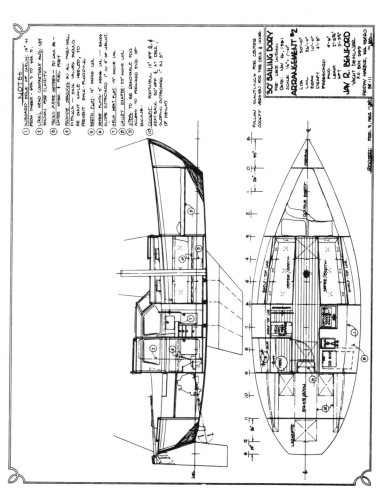

30' and 32' Sailing Dories

The 30 and 32' dories share rigs and keels. The 4'-0'' draft versions have lead ballast. The jibs on the ketches are on roller furlers, so no bowsprit work will be needed.

The booms should have topping lifts fitted, and lazy jacks for ease in dousing sail. This kind of gear makes for much easier sailhandling and is favored by singlehanders.

One builder of the 32 named his boat Shoestring. We felt it was most appropriate for a boat that could be built on a proverbial shoestring, and have thus borrowed the name for the design.

The pilothouse version of the 30 features inside steering as well as cockpit steering. This will make for a more useful year round cruiser, and she will be a very economical motorsailer. The 32 could have a similar installation where her chart table is located, or the 30 could have a larger chart table where her steering station is placed.

The lines of the 32 show how she easily will be planked with sheet plywood. There is very little twist to the plywood required in her simple, but elegant shape.

The rudders on all the dories are oversized, so that they will be effective at low angles. Large rudder angles lead to increased drag, slowing the boats down, and can lead to a broach if the rudder loses its lift and stalls, causing the boat to loose steerageway. It will be easy to fit a trim tab on any of these rudders for self-steering gear.

Chapter
7

Aesthetics of Yacht Design

By Robin Roberts Benford

If a person wants simply a good boat — or even a high performing boat — purely practically — why bother with beauty, too? It would seem that for a designer to create a truly beautiful boat, he has to be talented in all the technical chores too. Little differences, discerned but not understood by the layman, can make or break the overall effect of the boat. Yet an artist who can create a lovely, two-dimensional drawing may not necessarily be able to translate his conception as the yacht designer must into the three-dimensional, material boat upon the water.

One might argue that beauty is simply in the eye of the beholder, and that anything we might say can't change that. This is true only to a certain extent; for instance we think of the sod married to an ugly wench who nags him day in and day out. Yet he is entirely enraptured with her, and thinks of her as the star of his life. Everyone else can see the "lady's" faults — which is the point: most people do have a sense of beauty, although there is no accounting for some people's tastes.

If this majority of people were to analyze what constitutes the beauty of an object, they would probably agree with the artistic axiom that "form follows function." Some of the most commonly found shapes in nature are reverse curves, and they seem to be the most interesting — the swaying stem of a flower being blown in the wind, the opening petals of a tulip, the well-developed muscles of a track star, are but a few. These are lines that flow, and allow the eye to extend them beyond the limits defined by the actual borders of the object itself. Each item of beauty in nature has a sense of wonderful balance, one that is subtle, neither

over nor underdone, so that the result is a feeling of effortlessness and grace. When something appears effortless, it is comfortable, and perfect in every way, but one can be sure that the immense amount of energy and effort expended in achieving such a state was in direct proportion to how good it is. The best athletes appear to run, ski, or skate effortlessly — and the best boats of the most successful yacht designers appear to move with equal and effortless grace. They can be quietly resting at anchor in a harbor, yet seduce the shoreside viewer into hours of dreaming of wonderful and far-off voyages.

It has become fashionable, with the quest for favorable International Offshore Rule (IOR) ratings, that boats take on many straight and abrupt lines. Although some are successful from an artistic standpoint, all too few of these lines inspire the feeling of effortless flowing. The unsuccessful ones seem to have harsh, clashing lines. Some will comment that this is utilitarian, that the straight line is the shortest distance between points and therefore makes for the fastest looking boat. And that speed is beauty. Speed may be done beautifully, the lines may flow quickly and even gently surprise the viewer as, for example, when a house emerges from a seemingly undefinable point in the deck. But speed can also connote simply haste, and the lines become boxy and uninteresting, as though their designer did not put any thought into the container which he was attempting to draw around the package of speed.

A boat need not necessarily impart the impression of speed to be beautiful. This is not to say that she must look like a slowpoke, but simply that she can be like a lovely woman who may be quietly, outwardly beautiful, with no hint one way or another of her many capabilities which she hides beneath the surface. She doesn't need to swagger; she simply has an air about her. Her charms will be revealed as needed. This is most typical of the classic beauty, one which will never fade with passing fancies, and one which will be treasured because of this capacity.

The beautiful boat is surely the best long term investment. From the start, her builder will take great joy in creating her, and he will therefore do his best work. The maintenance yards will be more inclined to favor her with better qualified men. And if she has a fault, her owner will be more inclined to forgive her than if she were homely. She might even find moorage where a so-so boat couldn't. I once went to ask for moorage at a marina whose owner immediately told me there were no available spaces, and then I persisted by showing him a photograph of our boat. He smiled, fussed around a bit, and worked out a spot where we could tie her up. So you see, the beautiful boat will certainly hold a businessman's investment, and give him untold pleasures beyond the capabilities of the pocketbook.

The student of yacht design must train his mind to recognize the components of beauty. There is much value in studying classic beauty in art, in nature, and in yacht design. The student must be aware of the potential for beauty in the utilitarian concepts, but avoid the dangers of tunnel vision in this aspect of yacht design, so as not to sacrifice beauty to utility, or vice-versa. Some of the components which make for a yacht's beauty are the aforementioned reverse curves. Concave lines above the waterline enhance a yacht's appearance, but are unfortunately penalized by the IOR. If racing could be done without the strict and arbitrary nature of the IOR to bind it, it would seem that we'd have faster and prettier boats. The PHRF approach to racing is a step in the right direction, and has certainly gone far towards allowing more innovation instead of penalizing it.

Some of the fastest — and the prettiest — boats started out being designed purely for cruising. They are pretty because that was a natural requirement of both client and architect. They are fast because there's no reason for them not to be. Among the finest examples of the combination of speed and beauty is L. Francis Herreshoff's *Ticonderoga*. She is elegant, graceful . . . and fast. She's set records for elapsed time passages for the Transatlantic Race, the Transpacific Race, the Los Angeles to Tahiti Race, the Jamaica Race, the Halifax Race, and the Havanna Race, to mention a few. On a distance of 2,353 nautical miles (Los Angeles to Honolulu) she averaged 10.2 knots. Not bad for a

72-ft. full keel boat, whose top theoretical hull speed should only have been 10.75 knots! At the end of her record-breaking Transpacific Race, she surfed down Molokai Channel, her electronic speed indicator pegged at its limit of 20 knots, which *Ti* exceeded, in mountainous seas, and winds of 30 to 40 knots. Yet, *Ticonderoga's* primary purpose was to be a comfortable, responsive cruising sailboat. With no rating rules to hold her back, she could achieve whatever potential her designer was able to create for her. (For those interested in further numbers, her displacement/length ratio is 186, while her sail area/displacement ratio is 20.4). Friends of ours who have sailed her reported great exhilaration during a sail on which *Ticonderoga* took them all the way from the Panama Canal to Ft. Lauderdale, Florida, in only five days, with about half of this to windward. *Ticonderoga* is certainly a fine example of a very beautiful boat which is also a technical success.

Curves, especially along the sheerline, should be carried beyond the physical ends of the boat, in the design and lofting of it. This ensures that the sheerline allows the eye to continue to follow the line to an attractive imaginary conclusion. For a similar reason, masts on ketches, yawls and schooners should rake a few degrees off parallel, or else they'll appear to the eye to be converging at an imaginary point aloft. Yet with just a little bit of rake off parallel, they'll still look parallel to the eye. If a curve has an obvious conclusion — such as a spoon bow or canoe stern that has been designed to be a perfect section out of a circle, then it becomes uninteresting and often heavy looking. If on the other hand, the shape at either end has a little reverse to it, such that it will allow the eye to move gracefully in its imagination without following a vice-like trance, then it rests the eye and makes it want to keep looking at the shape. The shapes here cannot be too "busy."

All parts of the yacht should blend with each other. For example, if the bow and stern of the hull shape are drawn out finely, the imaginary extensions of the ends of the house should also appear to gradually converge with the ends of the hull. One way of doing this would be to have the centerline of the housetop follow the waterline, rather than parallel the sheerline. If, by contrast, the hull shape is huskier, and fuller at the ends in a more traditional manner, then the house should complement it, as by having the centerline of the housetop follow the sheerline.

Just as science must grow, expand and evolve, so must art. Many engineers have the ability to accurately copy a design and alter it enough to incorporate their new engineering ideas for rigging, racing, or other piecemeal ideas. However, there is a vast distance beween the clever draftsman who can trace or copy, and the one who can compose, and perhaps this explains why there are very few true artists among yacht designers. The most successful scientists and artists often stand well apart from current trends and fashions, and because of this are most often alone in their work.

In these times of rapidly advancing technology, the scientific aspects of yacht design have become a joy. Instead of the drudgery of working out varying formulae in longhand — which can take days and weeks — the yacht designer can turn to the modern calculator or computers upon approaching the theoretical potential of a new design. The software exists to "sail" a boat on a computer, to try it in many different wind and sea conditions, to change one variable, and to try it again. How much more efficient, effective, accurate — and fun — this all makes it for the yacht designer with an innovative mind. Of course, test tanks for a long time have also enabled such theoretical maneuvering to take place on a physical, but therefore more limiting basis. Once the model is tried, the only way to change it is to build another model. Contrarily, in the computer, a press of a button or two changes the shape of the hull instantly.

Of course, the effectiveness of any of these aids depends upon the skills of the users, and it is therefore essential that the yacht designer have a good grasp of past and currently successful boats, along with a good, basic groundwork in engineering. The complexities of both hydrodynamics and aerodynamics, and their effects on performance of a boat, make the study of these areas very important to the success of the yacht designer.

Within the yacht, there are numerous interrelated subsystems, which are quite a scientific study in themselves. A few examples of subsystems in yacht design would be the environmental envelope, the aerodynamic propulsion system, the mast support system, the electrical system and the food preparation system. Their affects on each other can be narrowly calculated. The human operator, ultimate user of the yacht, however, is not entirely predictable. The designer who overlooks this can end up producing a rather dehumanized boat.

Science is also offering the yacht designer much challenge in the area of materials and methods for the construction of his yachts. There is somewhat of a paradox here for the poor boatbuilder and designer who, in 1410, was quite content to do a competent job building boats in wood. In fact, he remained quite happy with wood construction and lived a psychologically healthy life for five centuries. He had many rules of thumb, and much tradition on which to base and evolve his work.

By the end of this period, the technologists entered the scene, and began to eat away at his mental security by offering him new materials which were proposed to make his job "easier". As the years rapidly progressed, he learned to "advance" from wood to such things as iron, steel, aluminum, fiberglass, ferro-cement, Kevlar, carbon fiber and Dacron — some of which had no texture, no color, and, most awkwardly, no rules of thumb. Although there was great excitement in the challenge of such materials' lighter weight and greater strength, there was also great risk-taking and decision-making, as these materials began to be used in the shop.

However, the potentials for the ultimate in yachts greatly increase as their materials options increase. With such lighter and stronger materials, as well as more efficient construction methods, new yachts can potentially attain more speed at lower fuel costs with greater cargo carrying capacity and cheaper construction and maintenance costs: quite a wonderful package to strike out against inflation! We continue to be intrigued with the Dynaship, with methane engines (for recyclable waste fuel potentials) and wind or wave driven generators for ship's services, to mention a few.

A good yacht design can be brilliant in either producing a pretty yacht or an innovatively and modernly engineered yacht. The best yacht design is one that encompasses both art and science in equal proportions of brilliance. The process of achieving this double state of excellence is a never-ending evolution, and the potential makes it exciting to be a yacht designer.

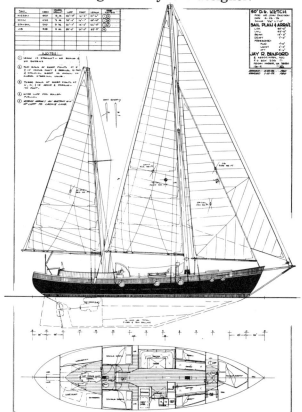

Chapter
8
Custom Yachts
at Stock Boat Prices?

by Frank Madd

Custom yachts at stock boat prices? How can that be? Everyone "knows" that the production line boats are built more efficiently and thus they cost less — right? Is this a trick question? It sounds too good to be true — is it?

Maybe. A very definite maybe. If you're considering a quality cruising boat of, say, 35 to 40' and up. If you're willing to search out the good yards out of the high rent districts. If you can wait while the builder finishes the jobs he has on hand and can then take on doing your boat. If you can find a designer who is clever enough to design a boat that is simple in its construction and concept, yet provides the features you want along with the seaworthiness necessary for how she'll be used.

Even though the stock boat builder may be more efficient, in the sense of using less man hours to build the boat, he has other costs the custom builder does not face. The production builder must amortize the cost of the tooling, molds, and patterns over each boat he builds; must carry on an expensive ad and promotional campaign (ad space does cost money, as do brochures and salesmen); and often must pay a dealer a commission for selling the boat to you.

Thus, the custom builder will save you the costs of the share of the tooling, and ad campaign costs, and the large sales markups (often 25 percent). All these savings can be put into the extra labor it will take to do the one-off's lofting and templating, and the interior detailing that you specifically want in your custom boat.

What types of construction are suited to producing reasonably priced custom yachts? The most economical are those using large sheet stock like plywood or steel, and having hull forms developed for these large sheets to lay on easily. A properly designed hull of this type can be very handsome, with the chines becoming a part of the sculpture of the hull. Also, there can be a topside chine which can provide a reinforcement point for a guard rail.

Paul Miller, who has his boat shop on the north end of Vancouver Island, has put together some pricing that indicates the Benford sailing dory designs can be built for even less than similar sized stock boats. His experience building a small one of these certainly confirms it.

Custom building also gives the owner a chance to become involved in the selection of almost everything that goes into the boat, from the materials for the hull to the hardware. The owner can also save some costs by doing the materials ordering-purchasing through the builder's accounts, if the builder is agreeable. This saves the builder's time, and this cost savings can be passed along to the owner. The owner can also save by acting as the go-fer, going for the supplies and hardware that the builder needs picked up. This gives the owner a chance to look at the things before they're installed on the boat, to be sure it is what he wanted.

The most persuasive advocate of this concept I've talked to is John Guzzwell. His conviction is not lightly founded. He's been making a living as a professional boatbuilder for a score of years, and the quality of his work is recognized worldwide.

When John Guzzwell finished *CORCOVADO* a couple years ago, a review of the accounting revealed that she had indeed been created at the same price as a stock boat of the same size and type. In the process, a boat with several superior features had been created. She had a larger rig than the stock boat and sailed quite well with some of the credit due to the inclusion of the Hundested variable pitch prop that would feather under sail. She was a little lighter than the stock boat, with greater apparent stability. She also had better visibility from inside and a layout custom tailored to the owners.

Not every builder is capable of turning in this sort of performance. The builder must be located in a lower overhead area, have ready access to the supplies needed, and have good mental organizational skills in addition to being efficient in the use of his time. Each part of the job must be done in the proper sequence. Supplies must be ordered in advance so that they are on hand and there is no waiting for them to arrive. Thus, the builder won't have to work around an unfinished part of the job, and lose some time coming back to finish it when the missing part arrives.

This sort of efficiency leads to keeping the building hours in line. Most builders work on a fee of so many dollars per hour. There is very little published information about how long it takes to build a boat. Last fall in an issue of Cruising World magazine, the Pardeys quoted some figures for building times. They noted that the consensus of the builders that they had talked to took one hour to build two to two and a half pounds

of displacement. Thus, a 20,000 pound boat would take 8,000 to 10,000 hours to build.

In talking with several builders in the Pacific Northwest, I found that they could normally build four to five pounds of displacement in one hour. Their effect may have something to do with this being one of the few areas that still has a good deal of custom building activity.

The Pardeys' figure for hours is probably quite valid for the more elaborate forms of construction, or for operations without a lot of power tools and equipment. Also, a proper building in which to build the boats can save a lot of time fighting the elements.

For amateur builders, I would think that even more time should be allowed than the Pardeys indicate, unless the boat is of a simple construction and/or the builder is experienced in the work.

When's The Best Time To Go Cruising?

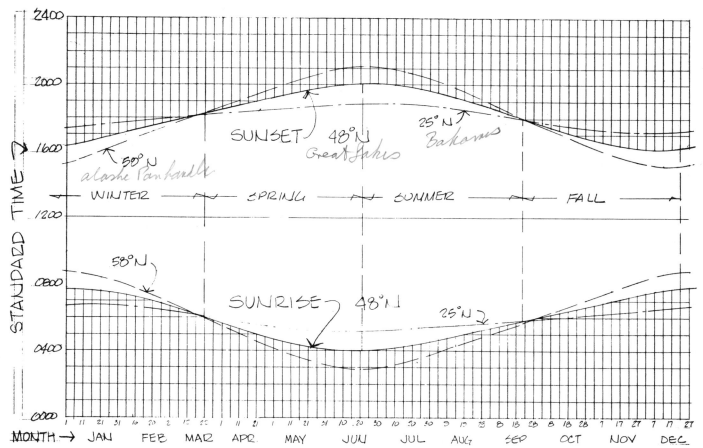

A few years ago, I spent a winter evening looking up data and putting together this graph. I wanted to sort out what was the best time to be out cruising and one of the things we enjoyed while cruising was the long hours of daylight. The longer hours of light gave us more flexibility to go with the tidal currents and still make our passages, especially our landfalls.

The result of doing this research and graphing was that we started taking our cruising time earlier. This year, we're planning to do our first long cruise in June. This gives us both the advantage of long hours of daylight and the chance to be out cruising before school lets out and the anchorages start getting crowded.

(J.R.B.)

Chapter
9

Benford 38

38' Ketch
For: Paul Pfeifer
Design Number 126
1977

In the normal course of our work, we're offered commissions on a vast array of intriguing designs, from a 13'-10" long distance sailing cruiser to a 131' ketch. We are currently working on several different projects averaging about 40', with some as unusual as the 23' long range motorsailer we're doing for an Alaskan. A more common project would be in the 30' to 50' range, and the design we did for Paul Pfeifer on his 38' ketch is a good example.

The 38' ketch resulted from Paul's persistence in seeking out just the right boat for his needs. Several years ago, he set out to find a kit boat he could outfit to his specifications. However, nothing that was available came close enough to being just right to suit him.

As Paul continued his search, he wrote to a number of yacht designers inquiring if they had a stock design that might be something close to his dream vessel. In response to his inquiry, we told him about the Benford 30, and the preliminary work we'd done on a 38' version of it. Paul liked many of the innovative ideas on the Benford 30, such as the roomy and well lit great cabin aft, the possibility of a passageway under the cockpit between the forward and aft accommodations, and the separation and privacy the midships cockpit provided for the quarters aft and forward. (This approach to designing unconventionally commodious cruisers has since been applied to a 34'-6" version with both a cutter and gaff schooner rig.)

Paul's concept was for a boat that would be performance oriented, since most of his sailing had been racing, including a couple of Transpacs. The new boat might be entered in the Ensenada and other Mexican races, since her homeport would be in Southern California. In commissioning us to go ahead with the de-

sign, he gave us an extensive set of notes he'd worked up on all the features he wanted incorporated.

We decided to build the boat in Airex cored fiberglass, to take advantage of the strength and stiffness, as well as the excellent insulation offered with this material. Building in Airex was also a reasonably economical way to achieve the esthetic treatment we wanted, since we were not as restricted in building shapes with this material as we would have been with more traditional wooden construction.

This is an excellent example of the true progress that has been made in yacht design. It is only the advent of new materials and methods of construction that has allowed designers to expand on the shapes and styles that can be economically built. The new technology has also permitted much lighter construction that still will stand up to the stresses at sea. These lighter vessels have also been getting stiffer with the monocoque construction methods now used, which permits setting up the rigging tighter and in turn permits better windward performance. This increased weatherliness of the rigs has directed more work towards refining underwater shapes — boats like the 6 and 12 meters have long incorporated features that promote weatherliness, while fin keels and spade rudders were in use before 1900. But the technology of recent years has led to the current types of underbodies and keels using NACA foil sections. In fact, in the early 1970's, I started adapting the NACA foils to our so-called "full keel" designs with excellent results.

With Paul's desire to maximize performance, and the likelihood of a lot of light air sailing, we decided to use a medium fin keel and skeg/rudder underbody to reduce wetted surface. Both appendages are of NACA foil derivation. Thus, with these changes and the additional 8' of length and 6" additional beam, we created the 38-foot, larger "sister". When I describe one of my designs as being a larger or smaller version of another, perhaps it is with more than due share of poetic license, for the evolution is in fact often quite different. But I would be remiss not to give credit to the new design's starting point.

The earlier design from which the 38 evolved has a long keel, with only the forefoot cut away. Thus, when I referred to this boat having reduced wetted surface, it is in relation to a long keel boat, and not to an IOR racer. The main reason for having a skeg in front of the rudder is to separate the flow to the rudder, allowing a much higher rudder angle before stalling sets in. Also, the skeg adds considerable stiffening to the rudder in supporting it, and its greater strength will make it that much harder to damage.

Like many of our clients, Paul planned to make the boat his home. To this end, the accommodations had to be a balance between comfort for the long periods in port as well as underway. The final layout incorporated the wonderfully roomy great cabin aft of the Benford 30, with the saloon, galley and navigation areas in it. The passage berth and the double berth opposite (fitted with sailcloth leeboards) provide berths amidships for comfort at sea (to leeward on either tack) and in

port. The large head forward has a separate shower stall. The forward cabin also has a large hanging locker, an oilskin locker, and two berths in the bow for occasional guests. Plenty of ports and hatches provide light and air, including ports in the transom. The center cockpit has a partial shelter over the forward end to give protection from the elements. The aft cabin trunk provides 6' 5" headroom in the galley. The headroom reduces to 5' 6" to 5' 8" under the cockpit seat in the passageway. The forward trunk has 6' 5" to 6' 8" headroom.

I've been assured that the liking, or at least acceptance, of a dodger or doghouse is the sign of a sensible man with some real experience in cruising. The hard dodger on the 38' ketch is expendable, for there is a conventional hatch and companionway closure under it. We chose to make it a hard dodger for the simple reason that the fabric ones seem to have a limited life when exposed to the elements, and the hard one also let us put proper handrails on it for the safety of the crew.

Paul wanted a ketch rig to give him more options as to sail combinations, and plenty of sail area for light air sailing. In fact, without the mizzen, she would have the normal sail area for a cutter of her size. Thus, with a mizzen staysail and genoa, she'll be able to keep going even in the lightest conditions. The heavy weather rig for the boat will be the double reefed main and the

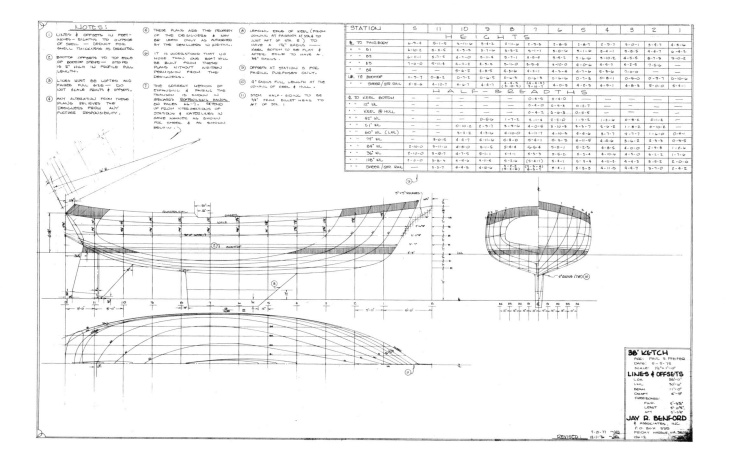

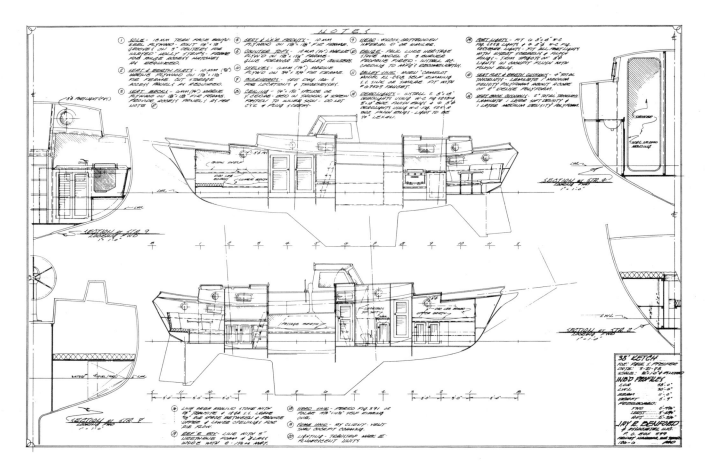

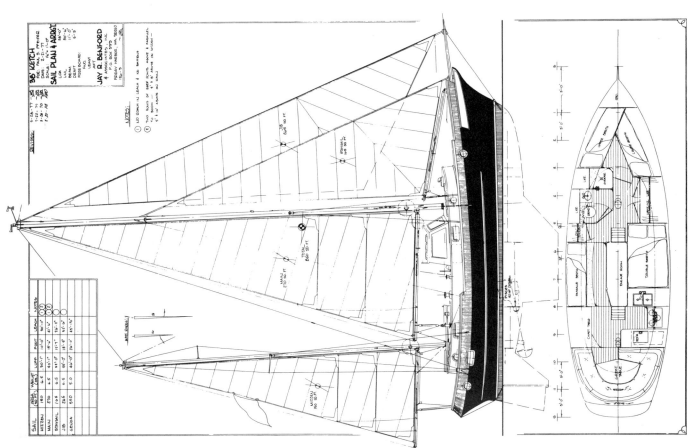

staysail. This puts the upper loading at the upper spreader level. Since there is nothing to keep this point on the mast from bowing lighter airs, the runners will be tied off by the shrouds. However, when the wind pipes up, the runners will be available to help keep the staysail luff tight and keep the mast properly in column.

Paul liked my idea of blending the traditional appearance above the water with the modernized underbody to give the combination of comfort and performance he wanted. The following figures from my calculations and computer design analysis will demonstrate how well I was able to fulfill these criteria:

PARTICULARS:

Item	English	Metric
Length over all	38'-0"	11.58m
Length designed waterline	30'-6"	9.30m
Beam	11'-0"	3.35m
Draft	5'-9"	1.75m
Freeboard:		
Forward	5'-9¾"	1.77m
Least	3'-10¾"	1.19m
Aft	5'-3¼"	1.61m
Displacement, cruising trim*	16,675 lbs.	7,564 kg.
Displacement-length ratio	263	

Ballast	6,200 lbs.	2,812 kg.
Ballast ratio	37%	
Sail area	850 sq. ft.	78.97 sq. m
Sail area-displacement ratio	20.8	
Wetted surface	338 sq. ft.	31.40 sq. m
Sail area-wetted surface ratio	2.51	
Entrance half-angle	21 degrees	
Prismatic coefficient	0.57	
Pounds per inch immersion	1,118	
GM	3.86'	1.18m
Water	110 gals.	416 liters
Fuel	75 gals.	284 liters

*CAUTION: The displacement quoted here is for the boat in cruising trim. That is, with fuel and water in the tanks, the crew on board, as well as the crew's gear and stores in the lockers. This should not be confused with the "shipping weight" often quoted as "displacement" by some manufacturers. This should be taken into account when comparing figures and ratios between this and other designs.

Miller Marine of Bainbridge Island was the successful bidder for building the boat in Airex cored fiberglass. They delivered the boat partially finished to Paul a while ago, and he's been busy outfitting it ever since. His persistence is paying off handsomely in getting a fine ship.

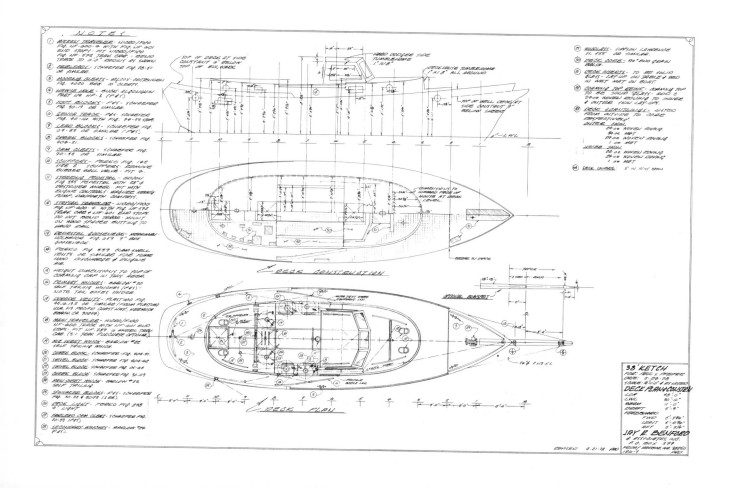

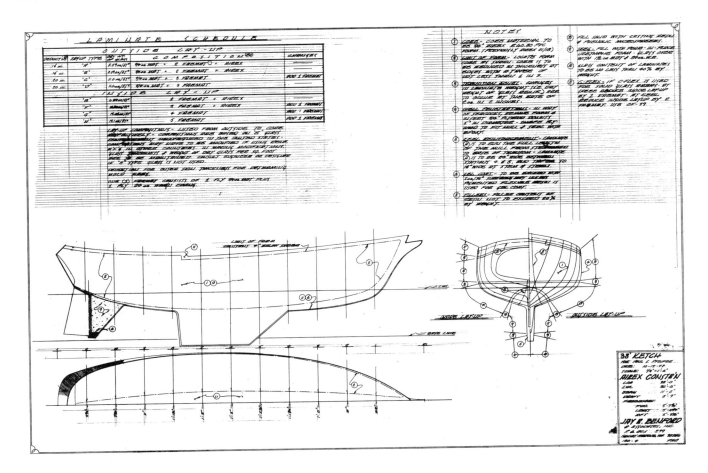

CRUISING WORLD magazine comments on the Benford 38:

"The most impressive feature of the Benford 38, and indeed one of Benford's fortes, is its enormous and original interior and deck/cabin arrangement. Benford has the ability to combine this with a salty and charming appearance. It is hard to imagine any designer fitting more accommodations in a 38-foot waterline boat without transforming the design into a Greyhound bus."

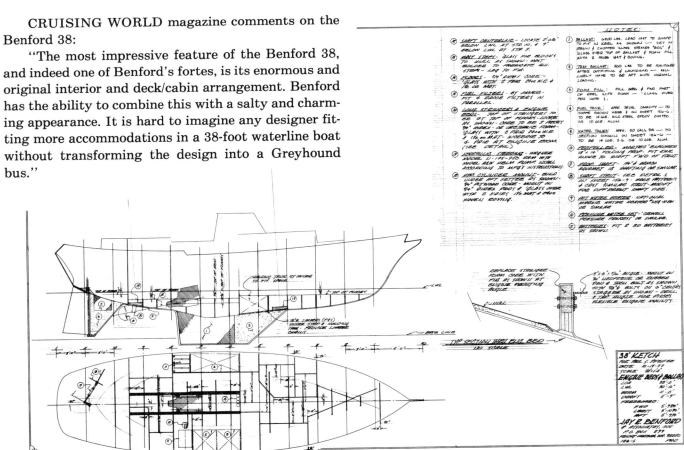

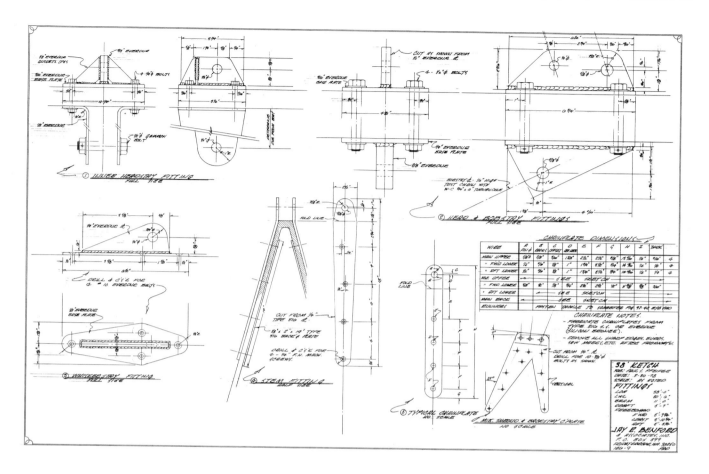

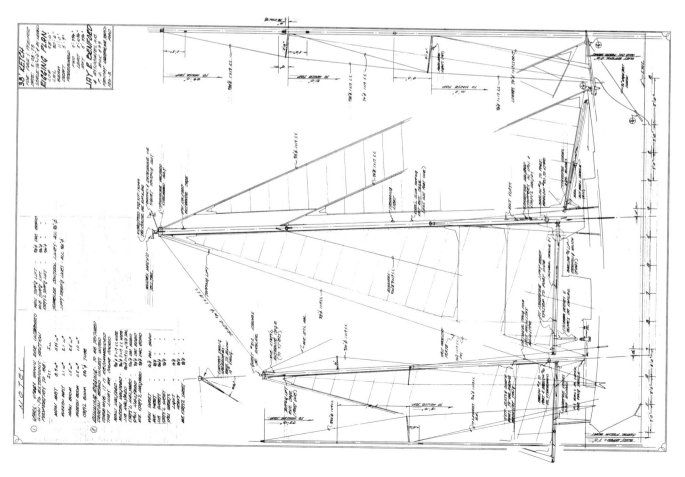

34'-6" Version:

The 34'-6" cutter and schooner are direct descendants of the Benford 30 and 38 designs. The basic layout is directly evolved from *BAKEA*, the first of Benford 30s, and the extra 4½' of length is put to good use in loosening up the layout and providing extra stowage room. The schooner version has a small upright piano in the great cabin, and could be steered from there with the remote controls of an autopilot. The cutter version has *BAKEA*'s inside steering station aft for a more conventional steering operation. The aft cabins are high enough that the helmsman can properly see forward. However, I would still do the close quarters maneouvering from the cockpit helm.

The extra 4½' of length and 6" of beam mean that this boat is relatively narrower, and more easily driven. She will enjoy enhanced windward performance, with the same good stability and sail carrying power that the Benford 30 enjoys.

Construction is Airex foam cored fiberglass, closely following the scantlings for the 38. She could readily be adapted for cold-molded construction.

Particulars

Item	English	Metric
Length over all	34'-6"	10.52m
Length designed waterline	28'-0"	8.53m
Beam	11'-0"	2.55m
Draft	5'-0"	1.52m
Freeboard:		
Forward	5'-3 3/8"	1.61m
Least	3'-6"	1.07m
Aft	4'-9"	1.45m
Displacement, cruising trim*	16,064lbs.	7,287kg.
Ballast	5,000lbs.	2,268kg.
Ballast ratio	31%	
Displacement-length ratio	327	
Sail area:		
Schooner	700 sq. ft.	65.03 sq. m
Cutter	705 sq. ft.	65.50 sq. m
Sail area-displacement ratio:		
Schooner	17.59	
Cutter	17.72	
Entrance half-angle	23¼ °	
Prismatic coefficient	0.56	

*CAUTION: The displacement quoted here is for the boat in cruising trim. That is, with the fuel and water tanks filled, the crew on board, as well as the crews' gear and stores in the lockers. This should not be confused with the "shipping weight" often quoted as "displacement" by some manufacturers. This should be taken into account when comparing figures and ratios between this and other designs.

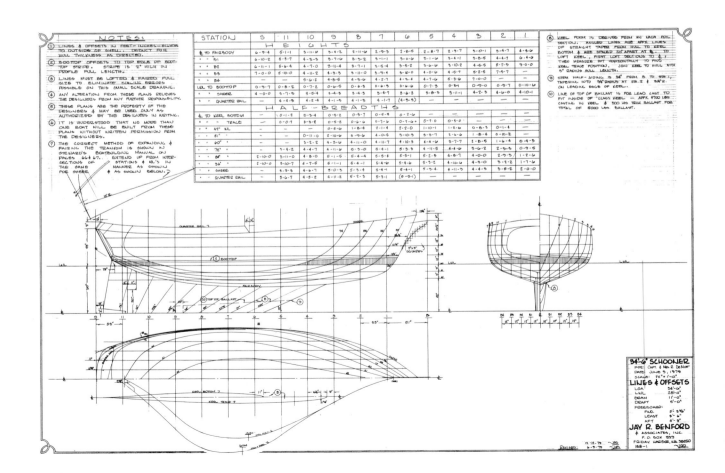

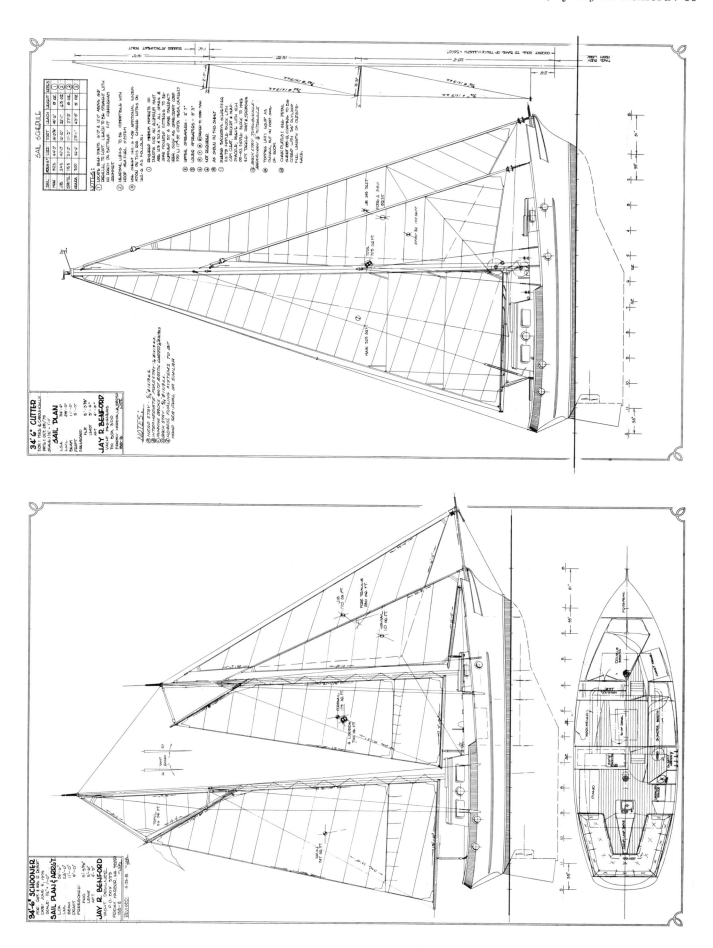

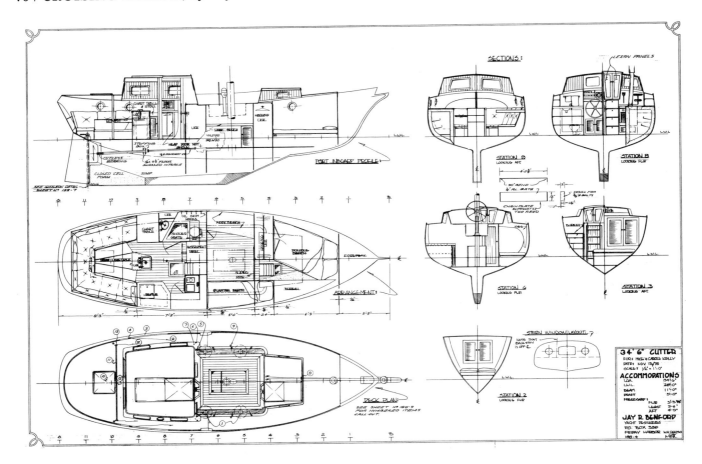

Anchoring

When anchoring, the function of the anchor is to keep the boat from leaving the chosen position. For it to do this, the anchor must be up to the job, and it must be well set. There are a number of published guides to "correct" anchor sizes. Most of them will provide an anchor which will work in average conditions. To be really secure, it is best to go up one or two sizes when buying the main working anchor. This is money much better spent than on elaborate insurance policies, for this is self-insurance at its best.

Setting the anchor is another matter. The anchor rode (chain or chain and rope) must be long enough to give enough scope. A scope of 5 to 1 may be about average, but 7 or 8 to 1 will be even better. If there are too many other boats anchored in the area to swing on that long a scope, set the anchor at the scope and then shorten up a bit.

Setting the anchor is best done under power, slowly backing down as the rode is fed out. When the full scope is out, increasing the power to really dig in the anchor will insure its staying put. To be sure it is not dragging, watch the shore line and be sure the boat does not keep moving aft, but is stopped by the anchor before easing up on the throttle.

When anchoring in an unfamiliar anchorage, we've found it's best to take a slow swing around the pro-posed anchoring site, watching the depths on the depth sounder, to be sure we will not go aground when the tide falls or when the tidal flow reverses.

Tying Up

One of the most common problems cruisers have is establishing a proper technique for tying up the boat. All too often they will just take their lines and tie up straight in to the float. This method does not let the boat move up and down easily enough with the passing waves, and puts extra unnecessary strain and wear on the boat. It is better to angle the lines fore and aft from the bow and stern. This more accurately positions the boat where it is wanted, and the angled lines in the middle (the spring lines) aid this.

The actual tie to the cleat or mooring rail should not be one that takes a long time to undo. The possibility of a speedy departure due to weather changes or anything else make this a point well worth thinking about.

The knot used to tie the mooring line should be simple and easily undone, and yet hold the boat without slipping or letting go ahead of time. It is worth learning the bowline, two half-hitches (clove hitch), and the rolling hitch. These are often the best knots for this duty.

Chapter

10

The Proper Offshore Yacht

Part I: Basic Considerations

THE SELECTION of an offshore cruising vessel should, if anything, be approached more carefully than selecting a partner in marriage. A divorce from your vessel is hard to arrange when you're in mid-ocean; and the selection of the wrong vessel may lead to the more conventional sort of divorce. The practice of "arranged marriages" with the parties meeting for the first time at the ceremony has pretty well died out. So should the practice of letting someone else select your offshore cruiser. Only through long experience in a variety of cruisers can a sailor begin to define his ideal boat.

Careful consideration should be given to why the offshore passage is being undertaken: Is it to go somewhere and back within a specific time frame, such as a vacation? If so, it might be better to cruise local waters, so there are fewer concerns about the vagaries of the weather upsetting the schedule of the cruise. To attempt a long passage and return in a set time frame pressures you into maximizing speed and checking the calendar, instead of enjoying each day spontaneously as it comes.

However, if the voyage is to be a leisurely one, seeking out remote parts of the world at a comfortable pace, and exploring their coastal recesses, then a different type of boat will do. In this case, the offshore cruiser must be suitable for uses as both a floating home and coastal cruiser.

We have had the privilege of designing a number of vessels intended for offshore cruising in the past few years. As our specialty and main interest is cruising boats, we've developed our own approach to the selection and evolution of these craft. This is based on: 1) budget; 2) crew size and relationships; 3) range and cruising ground; 4) potential use of the vessel as a permanent liveaboard; 5) ultimate resale value.

Additionally, the boat must meet certain performance requirements: 1) she must complete each and every voyage she begins (i.e. she must be seaworthy); 2) she must carry out her business in a manner comfortable to her crew; 3) she must be able and behave well on all points of sailing; 4) she must behave satisfactorily with and without a large load of stores.

Since the offshore cruiser is such a specialized craft, and each owner's needs are different, the small percentage cost difference between a stock versus a custom boat is often

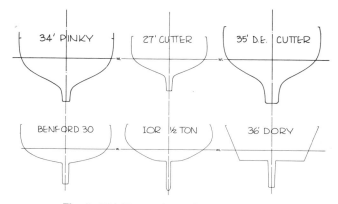

Fig. 1. *Midship sections of several designs*

offset by the custom boat being exactly the boat wanted without any extraneous size, features or equipment.

Fig. 1 shows the midsection of a typical IOR boat and five other midsections from various types of offshore cruising vessels, all drawn to the same scale. Our observations on how well these six meet the basic criteria and performance requirements previously outlined are shown in *Fig. 2*.

As the table shows, the IOR boat doesn't stack up too well as an offshore cruiser. This should come as no surprise though, for she was never designed with this in mind. The IOR boat is intended to get there in the minimum time to collect the maximum trophies.

The trend in racing yachts has been toward less and less lateral plane to minimize wetted surface drag and quicken maneuverability. Based on some lab testing, the keel has been moved forward and further separated from the rudder. This has resulted in some boats being hard to steer off the wind, with some of the smaller rudders causing the boat to stall and broach. Our observations have been that the lateral plane needs to extend aft and the rudder should be large enough to insure good tracking and consistent helm control. Holding a steady course and steering easily are more important in the offshore cruiser than the racer's quick maneuvering, although a properly-designed cruiser

BOAT	IOR 1/2 Ton	27' Cutter	Benford 30	34' Pinky	35' Cutter	36' Dory
RELATIVE COST	High	Low	Moderate	Moderate	Moderate	Low
TYPICAL CREW SIZE	3 to 5	1 to 2	1 to 4	2 to 4	1 to 4	1 to 4
SUITABILITY FOR OFFSHORE CRUISING	Low To Moderate	Moderate To Good	Good	Good	Good	Good
UTILITY AS LIVE-ABOARD	Poor	Good	Good	Excellent	Good	Good
RESALE VALUE	Average[1]	Good	Good	Good	Good	Good
SEAWORTHINESS	Moderate	Good	Good	Excellent	Excellent	Excellent
CREW COMFORT	Fair	Good	Good	Excellent	Excellent	Good
PASSAGE TYPE SAILING ABILITY	Fair To Good[2]	Good	Good	Good To Excellent[3]	Good	Good
LOAD CARRYING ABILITY	Fair	Good	Good	Excellent	Excellent	Good

[1] Dependent upon racing success
[2] Potential speed offsets difficulty of control
[3] Squaresails give advantage for reaching and running

Fig. 2. *Cruising characteristics of various boats*

may still have a short turning radius. The boat that is steady on her helm will make fewer demands on her crew and will be less tiring to handle.

The offshore boat also needs adequate buoyancy in both ends, to keep the boat as dry as possible and to avoid one end being lifted and the other not having sufficient buoyancy to keep from going under, being pooped, or pitchpoling. To minimize rating, IOR boats have increasingly taken on a lean look at the ends, particularly in the bows. This may work in a lightly-loaded boat, but, for the ocean voyager with his vessel laden for a long cruise, it is inadvisable.

Just as there is a continuing development of racing boats, so is there a continuing evolution of cruisers. Those designed this year will be better than those of the preceding generation, but this continuing evolution is dependent on the designer constantly using and trying out his work, with an eye to change that can be incorporated to further improve the design's utility. With the input from use, and first-hand familiarity with modern materials, much improved versions of older, basic type design can be made, without losing the virtues that made the boat a success in the first place.

There are so few people sailing anything other than a marconi rig these days that we are often asked why many of our designs have gaffs and square yards on them. We never discount the esthetic or romantic appeal, but this must take second place to the practical considerations of which is the easiest rig to use and which gives the crew the best control of the sails and the boat.

A properly designed and rigged gaff-rigger will go to windward quite well—we've checked some of our fat little pocket cruisers with gaffs and found they'll tack through 80 degrees, tack to tack. From this, and from following more "modern" vessels in sailing the same courses, we've concluded that much of the rumored lack of windward ability of gaff-riggers is due to the hull form and not to the rig itself. Add to this the safety advantage of being able to get the gaff sail down while off the wind (without having to luff up as with marconi rigs), plus the greater efficiency of the gaff rig off the wind, and you can see why many owners are building new gaffers.

As if this weren't unsettling enough, we are also rigging many of our boats with square sails. Our first-hand acquaintance with square sails began in 1959, and the more we use them and learn about them the more potential we see in them. The 34' Benford pinky *Sunrise*, our current vessel,

has two of them. One is rigged in the traditional manner with the sail furling to the yard with buntlines (led to deck), and the other is rigged with brailing lines that gather the sail to the centerline. The latter method has proven to be the easiest to use, and we're now working on a modification of it with a wire down the center of the sail and using jib furling gear to roll up the sail forward of the mast.

With the rig properly designed, square sails can be comfortably carried on a close reach. Since the square sails are the easiest sails to control off the wind, the fore and aft sails end up being used mostly just for windward work. Thus, our most recent square rig designs have been for a staysail schooner-type fore and aft rig with square sails added on the foremast. This is the brigantine rig. It provides a variety of sails that can be used for just about any wind condition. Modern gear and materials are making the square-rigger a practicality again on a smaller scale. Try it. . . .

Part II: Comparing Six Different Yachts

ONE FEATURE that seems to have passed from the scene, sadly, in the yachting press is the publication of lines drawings. With the increasing accuracy of unauthorized photographic copying of published drawings, there has been an accompanying decrease in the material that has been released by designers and builders. This reluctance to publish is a natural result of seeing so many close copies built and also of a desire to keep dodges of the racing rules under wraps.

This is unfortunate for the potential buyer, for he no longer can see the hull form he's buying, and cannot compare it with others. Nor can the student of yacht design (aren't we all?) find this sort of material to help him to distinguish subtle differences in similar boats.

The data in *Fig. 1* and the stability curves and simplified lines plans opposite provide the student of offshore cruising vessels a chance to see not only their shape but also a great deal of design information not usually made available. Five of these boats are of my design—all different versions of various types of traditional cruising boats. The other represents a modern ocean-racing 30-footer.

A word of caution is in order about the data. It is assumed that the boats are built as designed and calculated. Variances by the builders and owners will modify these figures a bit, and it should not be assumed that all vessels with a similar appearance to those here will behave as indicated. Many subtle variations, not obvious because of unpublished information, will make for differences of performance that may not be what was expected.

The stability curves, drawn from the data on our computerized design analysis, reflect the righting arms in feet at varying angles of heel, in smooth water. The calculations do not include the volume of the deck camber, the deckhouses or anything above the deck line; so from about 75 degrees onward they are a bit low. However, they are all done in the same manner and will thus serve as a basis for comparison of the various hull forms.

The complete righting moment is calculated from these by multiplying the righting arm by the displacement of the vessel. The righting moment for low angles of heel can be calculated by multiplying the sine of the angle of heel times the displacement times the GM. (The GM is the distance from the center of gravity, G, to the metacenter, or the point around which the boat appears to rotate as she starts to heel, M.)

On two boats (my 27' and 35' cutters) there are two stability curves, for there are two different versions of the designs. The original version is the lower curve, which was felt to be suitable for good performance, and the upper

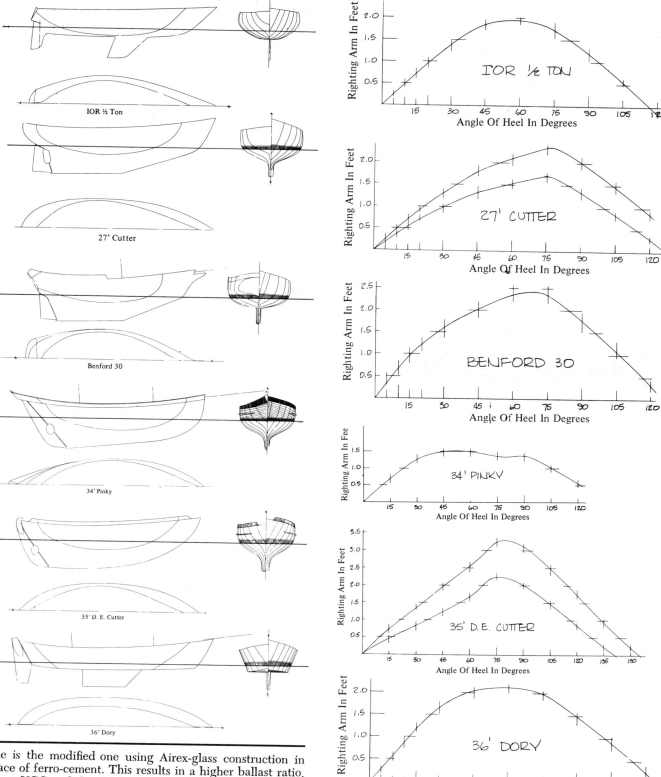

one is the modified one using Airex-glass construction in place of ferro-cement. This results in a higher ballast ratio, lower VCG and thus higher GM and an increased righting moment. These two examples will serve to show the effects of changing weights on a vessel, and how it affects the stability and performance—something to bear in mind when loading for a voyage.

The IOR Half Tonner is a composite of features of these boats that we've observed over the past couple of years, and exhibits some of the rule-induced humps and hollows. It also shows the typical forward placement of the keel mentioned last month. The waterline beam is held down to decrease initial stability and the ends are fine, resulting

in lessened reserve buoyancy. This leads to the stability curve dropping off faster at high angles of heel.

Our most recent little double-ender, the 27' cutter, has enough depth to give 6'2" headroom in the cabin, and has a layout designed for a couple to live aboard. The hull form features good buoyancy in the ends, moderate entrance and easy run. The fairly hard bilges give good form stability, and the freeboard and shape in the topsides carry

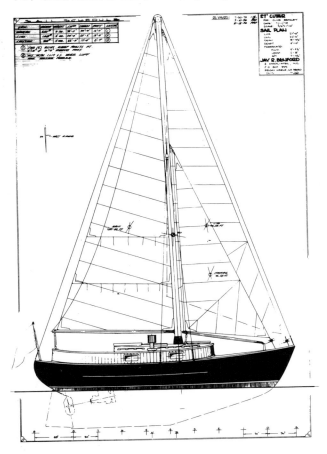

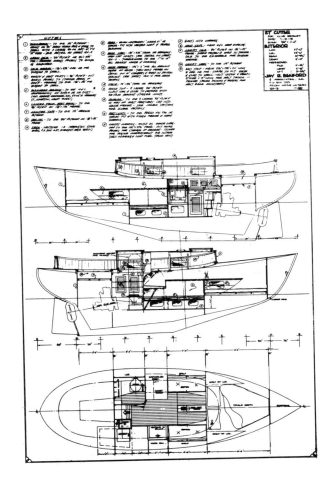

Fig. 1

COMPARING SIX VESSELS

	IOR 1/2 Ton	27' Cutter	Benford 30	34' Pinky	35' Cutter	36' Dory
I.o.a.	30'0″	27'0″	30'0″	34'0″	35'0″	36'0″
l.w.l	23'0″	22'6″	23'6″	30'9″	30'0″	31'0″
Beam	10'2″	8'9″	10'6″	11'3″	11'6″	11'0″
Draft	5'0″	4'0″	4'6″	6'3″	5'6″	4'6″
Freebd.						
FWD	3'10½″	4'4½″	4'9″	4'0″	5'0″	5'0¾″
Least	3'0½″	2'8″	3'0″	2'0″	3'9″	3'0¼″
Aft	3'1½″	3'3½″	4'5¾″	3'0″	3'11″	4'2¾″
Disp.	7280	9235	10,975	31,240	23,240	13,425
Disp./length	243	362	377	479	383	201
Ballast	2900	3080	3300	12,500	6000	5350
			4450		10,000	
Bal./disp.	40%	33%	30%	40%	26%	40%
		48%			43%	
Prismatic coef.	.61	.54	.55	.58	.54	.55
GM	3.35'	2.25'	3.98'	2.67'	1.95'	3.18'
		2.91'			2.92'	
Righting moment at 1 deg. heel (ft./lb.)	425	363	762	1456	791	745
		469			1184	
SA	352	450	560	770	700	700
SA/Disp.	14.99	16.36	18.14	12.42	13.75	19.83
Wet. surf	169	194	254	390	338	296
SA/wetted	2.08	2.32	2.20	1.97	2.07	2.36

the peak of the stability curve well over to about 75 degrees. The keel is well aft, with good length for tracking ability, but the forefoot is cut away to quicken maneuvering.

The Benford 30, a modernized version of the Friendship sloop, is the sixth revision and modification on this basic design we've done in as many years, this one is being built in fiberglass in Seattle. The beamy hull has good form stability, and the long keel is shaped as an elongated airfoil, and properly cut away forward and filled in aft.

Relatively the heaviest of the group of six, the 34' pinky has good sail-carrying power and a pleasant motion. The interesting dip and rise in the stability curve occurs about the time the keel would lift out. The deep deadrise gives generous room inside and good stores carrying ability. This type of hull needs to be well ballasted, as it is (40%), and this, combined with good freeboard, provides fairly dry decks.

The 35' double-ended cutter is an evolutionary development of the Colin Archer types, with finer bow sections to more closely equalize the buoyancy in the ends and let her go to weather more easily, relatively less beam to make her easier to drive, a slightly fuller keel to allow for lower density ballast to be placed low, and a raised flush deck to provide 22' of length with headroom. The raised deck also serves to raise the peak on the stability curve at high angles of heel.

The stability curve for the 36' dory most closely resembles that of the IOR boat, but the greater reserve buoyancy makes for an extended peak on the curve and a greater range of stability. She has a fin keel, but it is well aft and there is a generous-sized rudder to provide good control. The hull of this craft is perhaps best thought of as a combination of the wider bottom of a skiff or sharpie and thus having less flare amidships, but with the depth of the dories providing good freeboard for stability. Even higher stability could be had (if a justification for it could be presented) by replacing the ferro-cement and scrap iron construction of the airfoil fin with lead set below a timber spacer. This would serve to lower the CG of the ballast and increase the GM and the righting arm. However, there's no need to add this expense unless a much heavier rig is to be used.

No one can choose the right boat for you. You must do your own thinking. Articles such as this can only briefly cover one man's philosophy of boating, colored by his experiences and prejudices. The sea demands self-reliance for survival; use it also in choosing your boat. ☐

Chapter
11
Mercedes

35' D.E. Cutter or Ketch
For: Jonathan Graham
Design Number 77
1971

The original version, left, and the revised version, right, for cold-molding.

We are often reminded of the not-so-subtle ironies in life by the saying "Plus ca change; plus c'est la meme chose." Indeed, the more we endeavor to change ourselves and/or our surroundings into something newer or better, the more we find ourselves looking back at the results, shaking our heads in wonder and announcing, "Well, the essence of this is really not so very far removed from Old So-And-So, is it? When will we ever learn?" And indeed, history has so very many lessons for us. However, it does not mean we must stay there mired in cobwebs. It only indicates our forward progress could be ever so much more efficient if we'd cast more than a glance over our shoulder, from time to time.

There are periods of wishing to return to the womb that are a little longer and more compelling than others. Such is the calling many hear from the old Colin Archer lines. The romance attached to the hundreds of heroic stories of those Norwegian rescue boats has little yet to surpass it. The theory clings: if you were to go to sea, what safer boat to go in than a genuine Colin Archer? (Then you wouldn't have to find yourself in a position to be rescued, for you'd already be in a boat intended to *do* the rescuing.)

All this is well and good, but let's move up a century. We keep the essence: the sturdy construction, the core of seaworthiness, the bluewater intentions. Then we create *MERCEDES*. She's narrower so she's easier

to drive. Her bow sections are more refined, so she's more evenly balanced. (Some of the old Colin Archers had been known occasionally to drop their sterns under in extremely heavy going.) The finer forward lines, in combination with her modern cutter rig, give her greater windward ability. We put her well-balanced cutter rig all inboard with roller-furling headsails and all running rigging leading to the cockpit, to keep her crew safer with easier sail handling. The combination of these improvements, together with her long keel, makes her very pleasant on long cruises.

Then there's the considerations for contentment below decks. A century ago, modern creature comforts were not such a high priority as they are now. With increased leisure time, we've learned a little better how to capitalize on our enjoyment of spaces. *MERCEDES* is no exception. We designed her originally for a crew of two, to whom we provided a lovely roomy main saloon more commonly found only on much larger boats.

Because of the ample depth and long keel on this 35-footer, headroom is a comfortable 6'2½" throughout, even with the flush deck. The galley is located in the best position for living aboard, near the companionway where any wet coming aboard with the crew from the cockpit is the least objectionable, and easiest cleaned up. The chart table aft to starboard is also handy to the cockpit, for those long dark nights and necessary moments when the crew on watch must know just what those flashing lights are indicating. Forward of the galley, just in front of the fireplace, is the grand, 13 feet of open lounging area. There is the option of comfortable accommodations to sleep four, if desired, while two could live aboard easily on a longterm basis. The head full forward is well separated from the rest of the vessel, and is roomy enough to contain a shower and larger locker as well.

One of the original design requirements was to keep the cost low, and maintenance straightforward and simple. We aided this by choosing traditional rigging details. The tiller obviates the expense of steering gear. There is no rudder port to build as the rudder is hung outboard on the stern post. An additional benefit of this arrangement is that the rudder can be easily removed for repair while cruising without having to beach the vessel. A short boomkin offcenter to starboard allows easy attachment for the standing backstay while still allowing room for the rudder to swing freely. A number of builders of this vessel raised the rig 12 inches, with our approval, in order to carry a hard dinghy on deck. The engine installation is simplified due to the long, deep keel allowing the engine to be fitted on its beds in a perfectly level position.

Light, so often lacking on older sailboats, is stressed in this modernday version of the Colin Archer type. There are four large, (12'') portlights each side as well as a skylight over the main table. Thusly the caveman days are gone.

As is the nature of the design business, one good basic design led to other variations on the theme, to suit variations in clientelle's needs. The second interior arrangement which we drew up essentially switched the forward berths aft and moved the galley and navigating areas forward a little. More working space was installed forward of the head. The basic soundness of this design underwent quite a test. She was built in Thailand for Cornelia Dellenbaugh, in 1975, and after 2½ years of cruising to Australia and back, *BRILLIG* was preparing for a voyage home to the U.S.A. By

then it was October of 1977, and although they were 95 miles from the nearest land, and well beyond the recommended limits for shipping lanes off Viet Nam, *BRILLIG* was shot at, rammed, boarded and ransacked by Vietnamese who pirated them all ashore. Three months later, they were released from their barren cells and allowed once again to feel the freedom of wind pulling at their sails. Singapore saw them being re-outfitted before sailing finally for home.

The next modification we made to this basic design was a gaff ketch rig for Paul Miller, of Pt. Hardy, B.C. He and subsequent owners of *SIHAYA* sailed her off the Pacific Coast and around Vancouver Island quite handily. We were delighted to learn about a world record which was broken by a sister to *SIHAYA*, and have taken the liberty of quoting our client's letter about it as follows:

"It is my pleasure, to be able to inform you, that I have recently (24 May '82)' successfully completed my non-stop single-handed circumnavigation of the world, from Holland via Cape Good Hope, south of New Zealand, Cape Horn, back to Holland in 286 days. It was the first Dutch attempt and accidentally a world record was broken, held by Mr. Robin Knox Johnston.

"Your 'Benford 35' (ketch rigged) design, built by 'Ferrocem' Schiedam, in Holland, proved to be very much the boat I needed for this (sometimes) spartanic trip.

"Both ship and rigging stood up to my high expectations and in this case one could say: 'You can't argue with success'.

"In some 1973 yachting magazine about the 35' ferrocement cutter by Benford, I read: 'Many sisters to *MERCEDES* are currently under construction now. They'll make comfortable, responsive, safe and seaworthy vessels.'

"I CAN'T AGREE MORE.
　　　　　Yours truly,
　　　　　Pleun van der Lugt.''

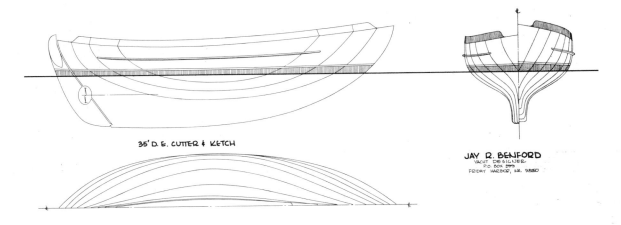

35' D. E. CUTTER & KETCH

JAY R. BENFORD
YACHT DESIGNER
P.O. BOX 399
FRIDAY HARBOR, WA. 98250

The gaff cutter rig drawn up for Frank R. Smith, Jr. also found the hull with a more conventional interior, still roomy, but with her living areas a little more separated. Photos of a sister ship taken off Stockholm, Sweden, show her in wonderful form.

Another optional arrangement forward of the midships settees contains a raised double berth to port and hanging locker and dresser to starboard, with entrance to the head forward and slightly off-center. This area can be open and share in the delights of company and warm fireplace aft, or can be closed off into a completely private stateroom.

MERCEDES was originally designed for ferrocement construction. As she is flush-decked and double-ended, she is among the most straightforward and strongest designs to build for a medium such as this, or such as fiberglass (for which C-Flex and Airex plans are also available). She has also be redesigned for steel construction, but as round bilged vessels are really for the more skilled of steel craftsmen, we would encourage primarily professionals for this medium. This popular design, for which the sale numbers have currently climbed to 75, has most recently also been redesigned for cold molded wood construction, with the draft reduced to 5'-0'' and the displacement reduced to 20,000 pounds.

Thus the options on what started out as a very salty and simple Colin Archer memory have grown. The lessons of learning from history are evident and encapsuled in *MERCEDES* and her sisters. The advantages of current technology, of reports of sailing variations on the original theme, and of different needs by different clients' cruising and construction philosophies, all help us best to capitalize on the essence of something good and make it even better.

SIHAYA photo courtesy Paul Miller

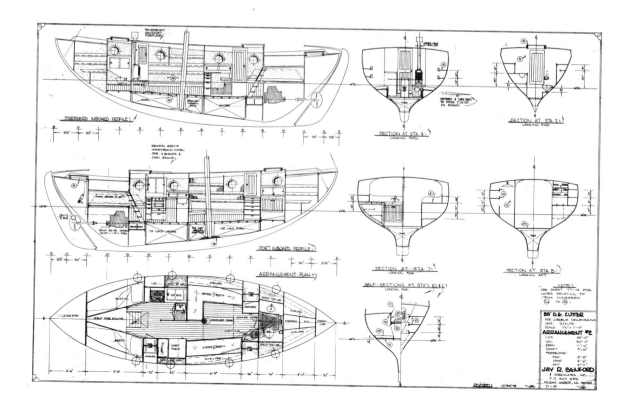

Particulars

Item	English	Metric
Length over all	35'-0"	10.67m
Length designed waterline	30'-0"	9.14m
Beam	11'-6"	3.51m
Draft	5'-6"	1.68m
Freeboard:		
Forward	5'-0"	1.52m
Least	3'-9"	1.14m
Aft	3'-11"	1.19m
Displacement, cruising trim*	23,240 lbs.	10,541 kg.
Ballast:		
Ferro version	6,000 lbs.	2,722 kg.
'Glass version	10,000 lbs.	4,536 kg.
Ballast ratio:		
Ferro	26%	
'Glass	43%	
Displacement-length ratio	383	
Sail area:		
Cutter	700 sq. ft.	65.03 sq. m.
Gaff Cutter	740 sq. ft.	68.75 sq. m.
Ketch	753 sq. ft.	69.96 sq. m.
Sail area-displacement ratio:		
Cutter	13.75	
Gaff Cutter	14.54	
Ketch	14.79	
Wetted surface	338 sq. ft.	31.4 sq. m
Sail area-wetted surface ratio:		
Cutter	2.07	
Gaff Cutter	2.19	
Ketch	2.23	

Entrance half angle	23¾ degrees
Prismatic coefficient	0.538
Pounds per inch immersion	1,035
GM: Ferro	1.95'
'Glass	2.92'

*CAUTION: The displacement quoted here is for the boat in cruising trim. That is, with the fuel and water tanks filled, the crew on board, as well as the crews' gear and stores in the lockers. This should not be confused with the "shipping weight" often quoted as "displacement" by some manufacturers. This should be taken into account when comparing figures and ratios between this and other designs.

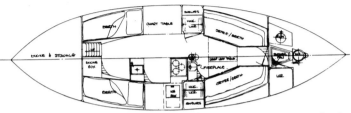

The original layout proposed in our preliminary design in 1971, above, and a later revision of the gaff cutter's layout in 1983, below.

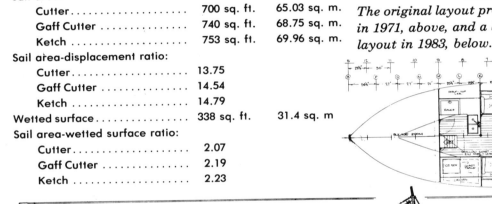

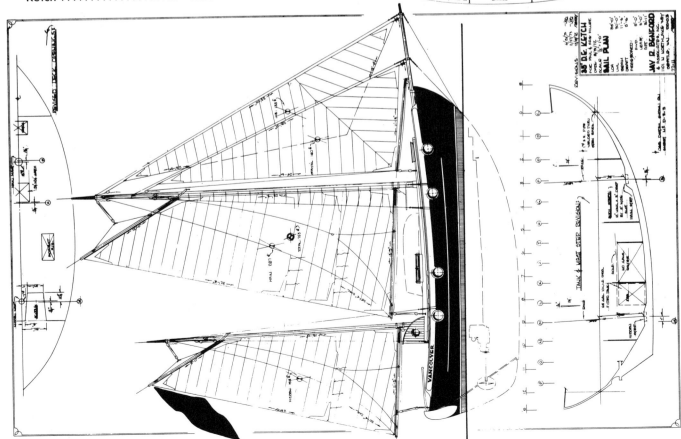

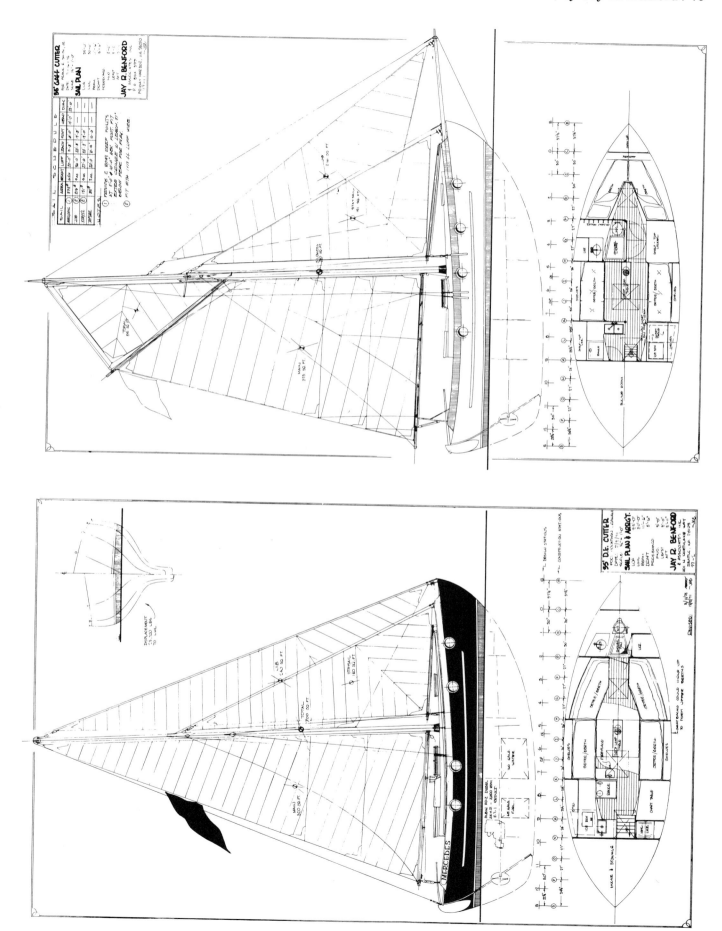

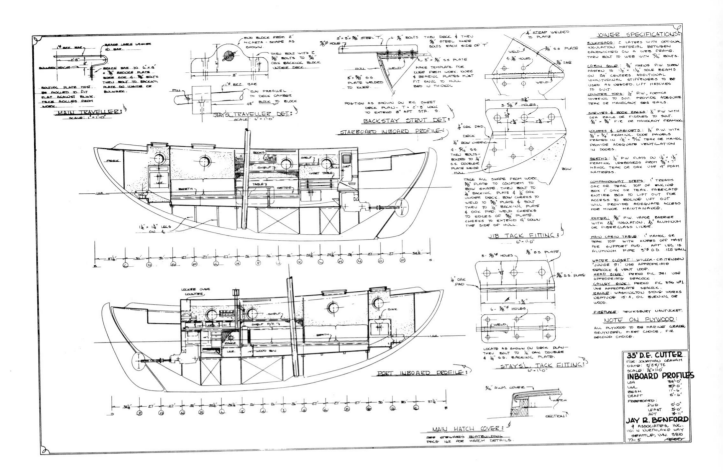

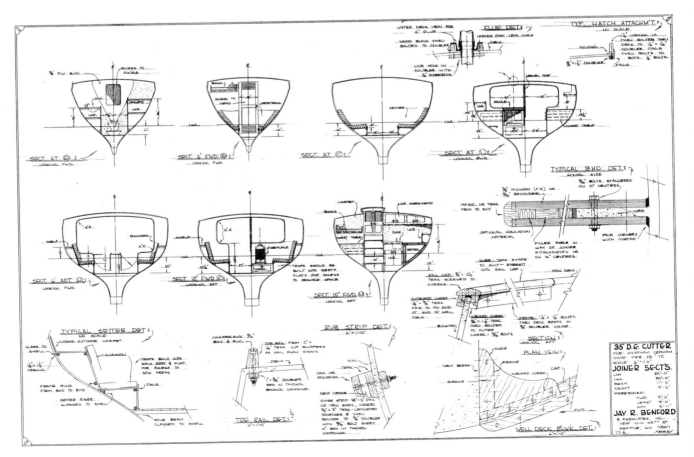

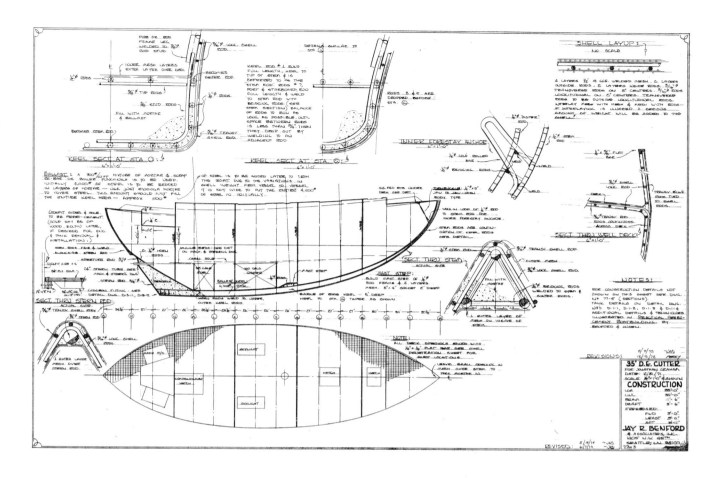

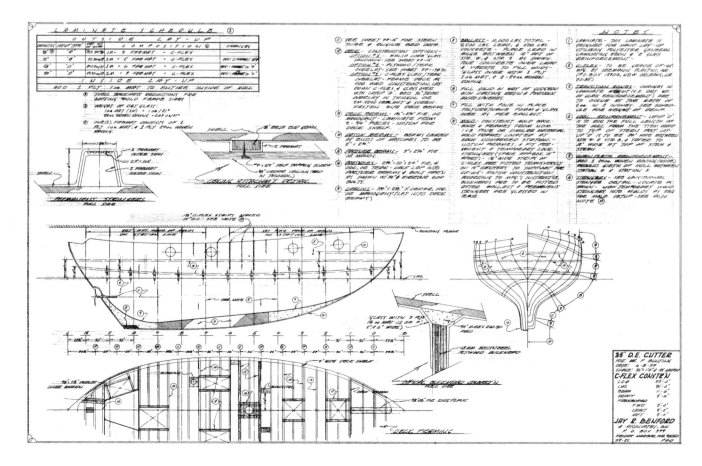

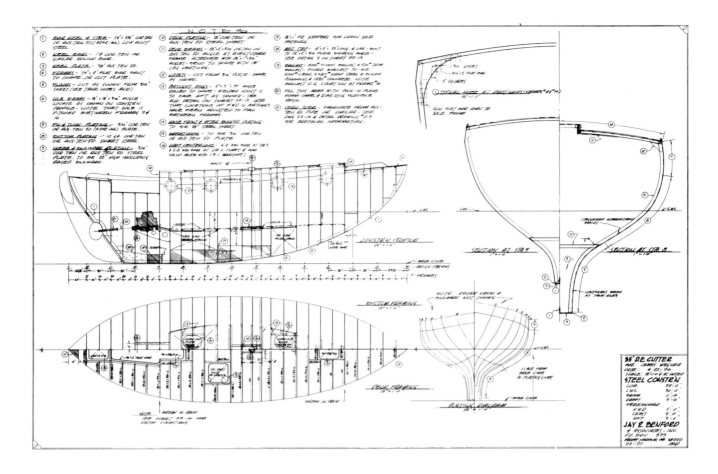

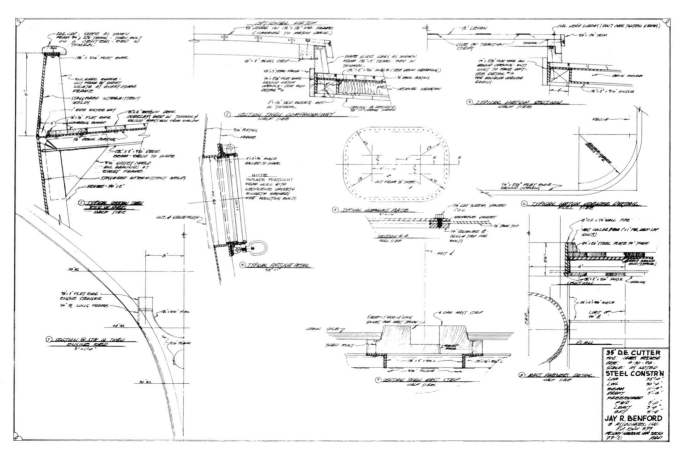

Chapter
12

The Custom Design Process

Who Needs A Custom Design?

Fortunately, there's really no such thing as a "typical" custom design client. As all our clients are very much individuals, their differences and unique requirements are such that the most interesting and widely varying designs can be created. Perhaps some of the most pleasing clients to work with are those who have had a good deal of experience skippering a variety of boats. Such clients have selected aspects from each of their prior vessels to suit their particular, and often evolving, cruising, living, and working philosophy. In the process, they have also learned what they wish to avoid. In working with the individual custom design clients, however, the work flow most often follows a "typical" process, and the description of it here will provide a good idea of what can be expected.

The creation of a new yacht is similar in complexity of materials, equipment and form to the thousands of hours of design and engineering which go into the creation of a new airplane or automobile. A major difference arises, however: the yacht designer and his client are able to afford only a few hundred hours in developing a new design. Thus, the custom yacht design client must be prepared to approach his new design on a somewhat empirical and experimental basis. The yacht designer will bring forth his best efforts, together with his many successful past experiences, to create the finest new design possible to best fit the parameters set out by the client. A client with extensive past experience in boating is the best prepared to venture into the realm of experimental ideas. For the new ideas to have the best chance of working most

successfully in filling the clients' needs, they must be based on tested past experiences.

Those without experience are best off starting with used boats first. This is a much more economical way of breaking into discovering what each cruise, with its varying conditions in weather, waters, locale and crew, will reveal, to help build up a store of ideas of just what their different experiences dictate as necessary for their next vessel.

Most of the inquiries we receive deal with having a new boat custom designed, or with modifying an existing design to meet some specific need and type of service.

How To Choose a Yacht Designer

The creation of a special boat to fill a unique set of requirements can best be accomplished by those with the specialized experience, day in and day out, in doing just this. A prospective client would do well to make an overview of the market with several thoughts in mind. Firstly, which of the many designers available has created yachts which the looker admires and indeed loves? What publications with his designs are available? With what construction materials has he accumulated extensive experience? Next, a closer inspection of this newly narrowed field should include the various designers' experiences. How successful were their yachts? Were they merely handsome in appearance and poor performers in reality? Or were their yachts of high performance in specific areas to the detriment of the enjoyment of the rest of the boat and/or crew? Did their yacht hold together, or were their problems with the construction? If the latter, was it possible to determine whether it was a builder or designer problem? Talking to a number of builders who have constructed a chosen designer's yachts may reveal exhiliarations and/or problems with that designer.

Does the designer really care about his work, or is it just another job? Often a way to tell this is what the designer does with his spare time: does he seem to enjoy cruising and/or racing (thereby accumulating more knowledge to feed into future design work) or does he spend the majority of his time elsewhere, seemingly relieved to be away from the subject? The best designers truly love their work, see it not as a 9:00 to 5:00 job, but as something they would never wish to "retire" from. Those with such an approach to the art will naturaly see their job as one in which they want to do their best effort. They know that future work comes from top present performance. This includes thoughtful consultation during all stages of the boat, from design through construction and into operation of the vessel. The result: a grand yacht and a happy client.

Custom Design Procedure

The custom design process usually begins with the designer receiving a letter or phone call from the client inquiring into the possibility of creating a workable boat out of the ideas and thoughts he's collected over some period of time. From this point, letters are exchanged, or meetings arranged, to review the concept and its feasibility. The client often supplies photos and clippings of boats which appeal to him. Such details as the new vessel's intended use, desired range, speed, and rig, as well as the cruising and working philosophy of those who are to be involved in the new vessel are also discussed. Extent of design detail desired, and construction information required in the plans is also of pertinent interest. Once it's agreed that there is potential merit in the idea, the designer will explain the costs involved in the preliminary drawings.

With the payment of the retainer, the designer sets to work to give the idea some form on paper. When the designer is reasonably pleased with the drawing, two copies are sent to the client so that one can be marked with comments and questions and returned to the designer. The designer will answer the questions and give his opinions on the clients' comments, and then frequently revisions will be made to the drawings. These revised drawings will make the circuit again (sometimes more than once) until both the client and the architect are in agreement that the basic concept is well enough defined to proceed with working drawings. Sometimes, however, the preliminaries are done as exploratory work towards seeing if an unusual idea

will work, and if it is in the range of something near the projected budget. If it is not close enough to the mark, a second (or more) drawings may be made to see if the goals can be achieved by some other route. If, as occasionally happens, on seeing the drawings and quotes, the client decides that the boat is not what was in his mind (or for any other reason decides that he is unable to proceed beyond this stage), he may complete payment for the preliminaries and be under no further obligation to have the design completed.

Many times, the client will want to circulate the preliminaries for bids (also preliminary) to ascertain that the project will be within the budget. The designer usually assists in this, in recommending yards and in commenting on the bids as they are returned. Assuming the bids are reasonably as expected, the next stage in the design process is begun.

The evolution of the working (construction) plans and details involves perhaps the most hours of the total project, due to extensive engineering, calculating, research, computer time, and drawing work which needs to be done. However, this part of the design usually runs more smoothly than the evolution of the preliminary conceptual work, because the gestation period has passed and the work which needs to be done — although innovative in a different way — is relatively straightforward.

However, because the design is an entirely new creation, and as such is as experimental as the previously-mentioned new plane or automobile design, there's always "fine tuning" as the new ideas are tried and fitted into the total concept which is to be brought to life in the boat shop. The yacht designer, with fewer available hours and a much smaller staff, must depend partly on past experience, and even partly on intuition. However, the advances in recent years in the computer industry have eliminated the need for an excessive amount of rule-of-thumb estimating. The result of the need for "fine tuning" of a new design is that there is occasionally the need for changes while the boat is under construction. The client and the yard should be ready and able to accept this sometimes frustrating aspect of what is the natural result of working out the myriad problems inherent in bringing a brand new design to life for the first time. Naturally, the designer will make every effort to foresee as many of these problems as possible before they get to the shop, but often even the client does not realize just what he has asked for, until he sees it in real life. Should he change his mind about any aspect of the design as it comes to life, this of course may affect many other parts of the vessel — all of which will need alteration accordingly, and which usually add time and cost to the project correspondingly.

As a general example, one area which can never be

calculated with complete accuracy is the weights of new vessels; at best, even in the top production yards which may be popping out hundreds of the same units annually, there is some variance in weights and trim between supposedly identical yachts. Each one requires slightly different trim ballasting after launching. To exercise very great accuracy in precalculating weights of a one-off custom yacht is thus, by comparison, almost a black art. Differences between construction practices and biases from one yard to the next are difficult to prejudge on the drawing board. When the designer does know which yard is to build the yacht, he can base his estimates on weights and trim of the vessel with somewhat greater accuracy, based on his knowledge of the particular practices and prejudices of that yard.

Custom Design Fees

The fee for a custom design will vary amongst designers, depending on the extent of detail put on the drawings, the time spent on the project, and the overhead costs of the office. Some designers will charge a percentage of the cost of the construction of the boat, often in the 7 percent to 15 percent range. However, this does not always provide the most incentive for the designer to keep the cost of the boat to the client as low as he can. An alternative method is for the designer to quote a flat fee for the work, after talking over the project with the client and after reviewing the cost records from prior design jobs of similar size and complexity. A third method is for the designer to bill for the time spent on this job at a previously quoted rate, or rates if several staff members will be working on the job. With unusual projects, or highly sophisticated concepts for very simple boats, it is often best to approach the job on an hourly rate basis, with frequent billings so that the client can keep track of the cost of the design work on a current basis.

Delivery Time For Custom Designs

Most small jobs and revision work can be expected to take a minimum of two to three months, and may be as long as six months or more, depending on the size of the yacht. If a specific delivery time is needed to fit a construction schedule, the designer appreciates being advised of this, so that schedules can be coordinated. Most designers have a number of projects "in process" at any one time, and just getting a position on the waiting list may take additional time.

Many custom design jobs, particularly on larger yachts, can be expected to take the best part of a year to gestate smoothly from the original concept into plans for the finished yacht. It is particularly important to allow plenty of planning time during the initial, conceptual work, so that the various new ideas can have the change to be absorbed, develop further, and finally evolve into the best end product. Once the preliminary conceptual work is over, the balance of the construction drawings flow reasonably smoothly.

Models And Tank Testing

Construction of models and arrangements for tank testing can be made through the design office, but are usually billed directly to the client. Thus, only the direct design office costs are charged against the project.

Construction Bid Solicitation And Review

Construction bids can be solicited from recommended yards, if desired, and review and recommendations on them provided. If this service is desired, the designer needs to know of this in advance, so that it may be included in estimating of time and expense.

Material Lists

Most designers do not normally provide separate materials lists as a part of plans for a design, as materials and equipment are already specified throughout the drawings, and the builder can generally best familiarize himself with the design by compiling a materials list as required, upon studying the plans. Should separate materials lists be desired in the plans, the client should mention this in advance, so that it may be included also in estimating of design time and expense.

Inspection

We generally inspect construction progress at the builder's site in our local travel territory. The purpose of these inspection visits is to consult with the builder, to answer any questions or problems which may arise, and to generally spot-check various aspects of the vessel to see that she is coming to life in the manner which we envisaged when we originally created the plans. Some visits also cover minor changes desired by the client and/or builder, and to approve such changes so that they will not drastically affect the successful outcome of the design. It is not the intention of the designer to accept liability for the execution of construction of the vessel in accordance with every detail in the plans, on account of such inspection trips, for the available time and relatively few number of visits make it impossible to accurately determine this. Rather, we rely on the builder to construct the vessel in compliance with the specifications, tolerances and materials designated in the design, so that the designed performance of the vessel can be met, and we are happy to consult with the builder in an effort to best aid him in achieving this end.

We are pleased to inspect vessels which are built outside our generally travelled area for the cost of the travel and living expenses incurred in doing this. However, if it is a large yacht, and/or the time involved in the inspection process is considerable, then in addition, we charge for such consultation time. Quite naturally, such time subtracts from the designer's available time at the boards, but it also continues to give him/her important feedback for ongoing design work. Each designer's policies in this area is quite different from another's.

When The Boat Is Built . . .

After launching, we enjoy, whenever possible, partaking in the builder's sea trials. Our participation thus does not end either at the drawing board or the construction site, for we take the natual extension of our interest in our work which has stimulated this new custom design, by desiring to learn exactly how she reacts to her more demanding testing grounds at sea. Taking this sort of care, we believe that we are contributing to the sort of concern and attention to detail which we expect the builder will also have brought in seeing her come to life. The result is to enhance the yacht's worth, and her future resale value. The continuing success and longevity of our firm depends on our continuing ability to create fine designs. As custom yacht design is our first love and life's work, we want to ensure the continuance of our good name by taking the time and care necessary to see our designs successfully progress from the drawing board into the water.

Reuse Of Plans

Unless otherwise specifically prearranged, building rights for one boat only are included with the design fee or purchase of a set of existing plans. All rights of design ownership remain with the designer, and the designer should be consulted for arrangements for building rights for additional vessels.

Copyright

All designs, whether so marked or not, are protected by international copyright laws, and may be used and/or reproduced only with the permission of the designer.

Expiration Of Quotes

When a designer quotes a fee for design work, quite naturally the quote would be valid for only a limited period of time. In our office, it is good for sixty days, unless otherwise stated. Thus, if a client desires to proceed with work on which a fee was quoted more than sixty days previously, it is advisable to contact us again to reaffirm the price.

Other Design Business Aspects

Beyond the creation of an entirely new design, other aspects of custom design work include modifications to existing designs, consultation on other designs and/or vessels, and production design work.

Such modifications might include new interiors, new rigs, modified profiles, alternate engine-machinery, and/or alternate construction materials and methods. The basic considerations in doing such work are, to a small scale, quite similar to the creation of an entirely new design.

Consultation on such things as construction problems of any vessel, working out a new rig for an older vessel, or offering an opinion on construction method of another boat other than our own design, is usually done on an hourly basis.

Production Designs

Designing for a boat which is to be built in production is another area of custom design. The basic approach is much the same as any other custom design. In addition to the process outlined earlier for proceeding with such work, the designer would also want such information as projected intentions for production quanities, construction schedules, location of construction site and intended or desired builder.

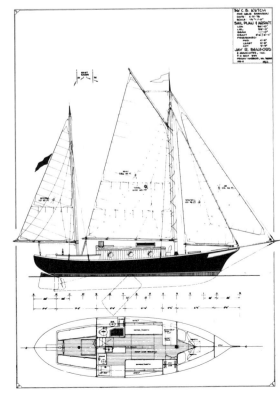

Chapter
13
Sunrise

34' Pinky Ketch
For: Jay & Robin Benford
Design Number 92
1972

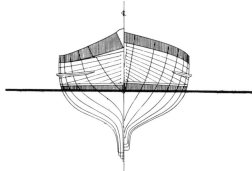

One of the nicest things about the yacht design business is the chances one gets to try out the boats after they come to life. This is not only feeding the ego, but a valuable part of the continuing education that is a must if one is to stay in the field for a lifetime. And, if one is constantly looking for new ideas and better ways of solving old problems, actually living with one's creation under a variety of conditions will help to broaden perspective on the situations encountered.

When the clients this 34' Pinky Ketch was designed for had a change in their personal situation (divorce), the boat became available in a partially completed state. It was not long after being told (say about 15 seconds) that lust for the boat began the wheels turning to scheme to get together enough funding to possess her. Determination must count for something for this did come to pass.

Having been wanting to be living aboard again, after being in various shoreside accommodations for three years, we now have SUNRISE set up to make life aboard very pleasant. Her hull, deck, cabin, engine room and galley were built by Tripple and Everett Marine Ways, Inc., and she's been outfitted by Mantra Marine and Vic Franck's Boat Co., Inc., all of Seattle.

West Coasters are not well acquainted with the hull type of our SUNRISE, and she often raises questions along this vein. New Englanders will more readily recognize her as being a pinky, dating back to earlier days when pink sterns proved handy for the East Coast fishermen. The pink stern is particular to a double-ended craft which has its bulwarks carried abaft the sternpost, giving additional deck space not usually available on the typical double-ended stern. The uses of the pink stern for the fishermen included added deck space for working the nets, boom crutch and support for the main sheet horse, and protection for the rudder. In the earlier days, as this area is not always planked over, it also doubled as an extra head. From an aesthetic point of view, a pink stern also helps sweep the eye along the sheer and aids in the graceful overall effect of this line.

The rig has gone through several evolutions, seeking the most practical setup for ease of handling and getting enough sail area to keep her moving in light airs. The fore and aft rig now consists of four roller furled sails: the jib or genoa, the staysail, the main trysail, and the mizzen staysail. All the operation of these sails is controlled from the cockpit, with the furling lines and sheets led there. (The former gaff main and mizzen and original square rig have been sold to the owners of SMAUG, a sistership built at Paul Miller's shop at Port Hardy, B.C. They plan more ocean sailing than SUNRISE has been doing, so this size rig will work quite nicely for them.)

The new square rig has one longer yard, with a triangular topsail set flying above it. This sail has a downhaul and is readily doused in front of the course, and then hauled down on deck to stow. The new course is also triangular, with the point down at the base of the mast, so there are no sheets to tend with these two sails set. For added area in lighter winds, there are two studding sails set from the yardarms and held out with whisker poles, with sheets leading aft to the cockpit and tack lines led forward and then aft so they can be carried on a reach. All these sails are triangular, made of heavy nylon spinnaker cloth — the topsail gold, the

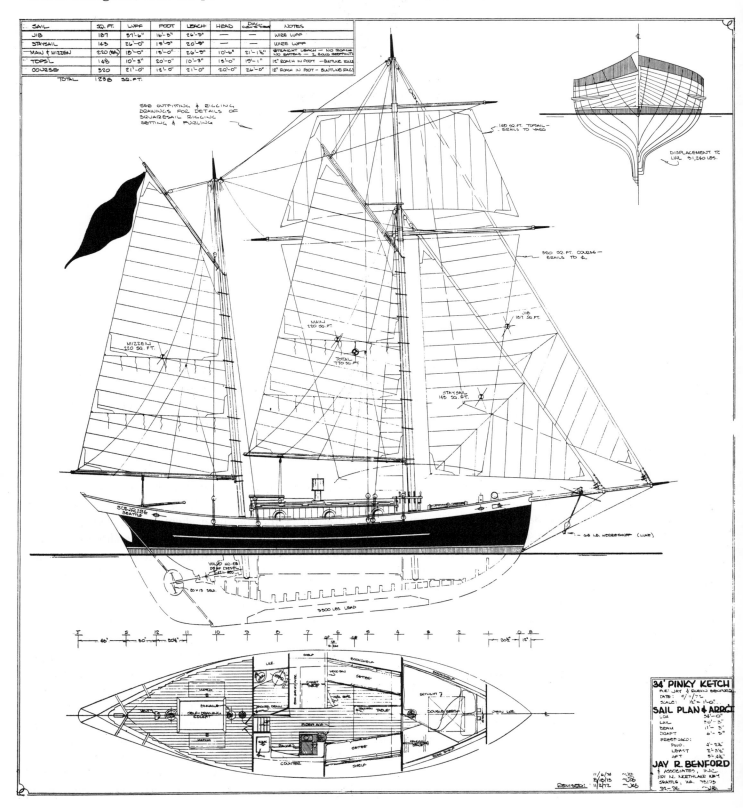

course orange, and the stuns'ls red and green, of course — and all set flying, so all sail handling is done from on deck. (For a more complete description of this rig and its operation, see the section in this book on The Great Pyramid Rig.)

The rig is easily handled by a couple, and can be singlehanded with practice on the part of the skipper. With all the various combinations of sails available, it's easy to add or take off sail area to give her just the right amount of power.

Sailing this vessel is most enjoyable, for the variations in sails to set make her quite handy, and in most normal sailing conditions, reefing need not be done. Instead, a different sail combination is set, and she's on her way in good fashion. We have been very well pleased

with how light SUNRISE is at the helm. She has a little weather helm, enough to make one feel secure should the wind become gruffer. She goes to weather smartly with the fore and aft rig, and can close reach with the squaresails. In 16 to 20 knots of wind, she will close reach with the squaresails, jib and mizzen, moving along at a steady 6½ knots, surging to 7½ knots. In the same winds, on a run, she does a steady 7½, with surges as high as 8½ knots. She doesn't need much wind to move her along, nor does she put up any fuss cutting through the water, for her wake is pleasantly smooth. With 25 horsepower from her Volvo MD 2B diesel, she'll motor at 6 5/8 knots, with better fuel economy at 6 knots, our common cruising speed under power alone.

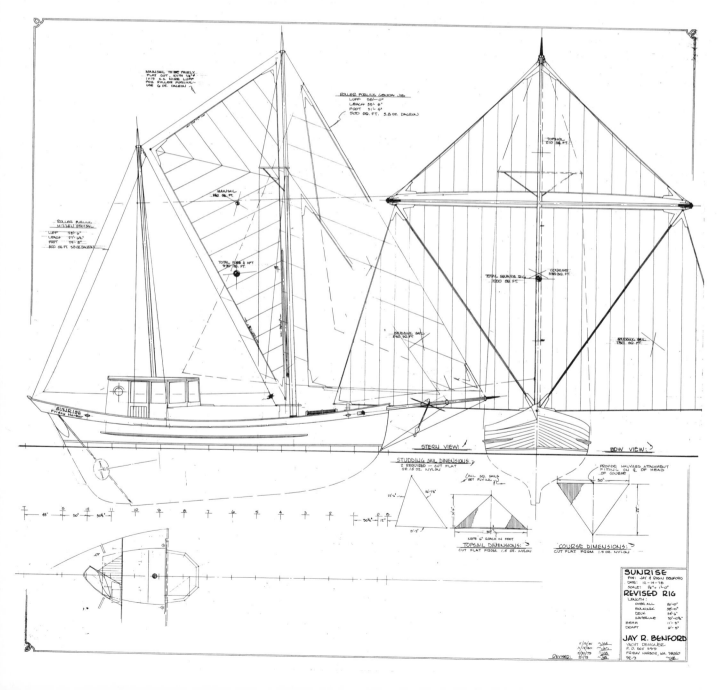

The interior makes for a very workable, open living arrangement. The after part of the hull is taken by the engine room, allowing a lot of comfortable area around which to work on the Volvo and check her health. The engine room is also home to one, 35-gallon water tank (aft of the engine) and two, 54-gallon fuel tanks (forward and outboard of the engine.) There is considerable space for stores, boat tools, batteries, hot water tank and engine accessories in this engine room — in addition to comfortable elbow room. A glass portlight is inserted in the deck aft of the cockpit to add light to the engine room below, in addition to the 12-volt light aft of the mizzen mast in the engine room. The cockpit is recessed over the engine itself, and the cockpit sole can easily be removed should the engine ever have to be hauled. Entrance is either through cockpit hatches or through a door in the bulkhead between the engine room and the main living quarters. Thus, any noise, dirt, smell and/or vibration of the engine is separate from the cleaner living area forward.

Entering the main cabin, one finds a head with shower to port, conveniently close to the cockpit for access to dripping rain gear. The galley to starboard opposite is also handy to the cockpit for that warming cup of coffee. In addition, the electrical panels are mounted on the cabin's aft bulkhead over the sink,

handy to the cockpit. Back to back with the galley's wood stove is a Tewkesbury Nantucket fireplace which renders cheer to the lounging/dining area. Opposite to port, is an enormous chart table (built to house charts laying flat), with bookshelves and stereo over, and with a 12-volt DC/110-volt AC refrigerator and large wood bin under. Settee/berths provide the main social area to port and starboard amidships. Both settees have ample shelf space above and lockers below. The port settee has a folding detachable extension which forms a double berth for guests when in use, yet stows compactly when not required. A second water tank, housing 82 gallons, is beneath the cabin sole in this area. An enormous, hinged dining table betweeen the two settees can seat six for meals. This whole area is well lit with large portlights port, starboard and forward. In addition, there is a beautiful, large, brass kerosene lamp over the table, with a smaller one in the galley, and several, 12-volt, flourescent lights for more concentrated work in the galley, over the chart table, and for reading at the settees.

Forward of the main cabin, the foc'sle with its double berth under the large teak skylight provides a delightfully private area for star gazing and admiring the rigging overhead. Outboard to port and starboard, pocketbook-size bookshelves make midnight and early

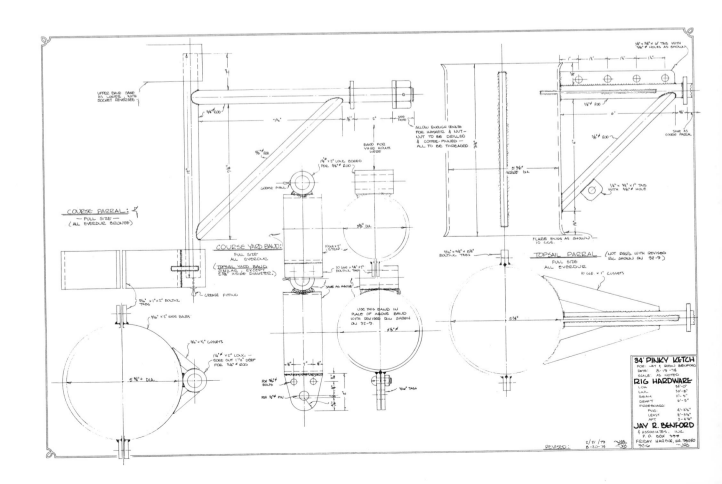

morning reading convenient. A hanging rod near the entrance way to starboard places clothes within berth's reach. A shelf flat along the head of the berth leads to a further stowage locker forward of the head of the berth, where two, flourescent lights are well placed for reading; if one person wishes to sleep while the other reads, one light may be turned off on the side of the mooring bits, leaving half the berth in shadow, and the other light on the other side of the mooring bits still sheds light well on the other half of the berth.

Being in the yacht design business can be quite hazardous to the pocketbook. The rate at which design ideas evolve rarely seems to match the rate at which the dollars revolve. When we are not in a position to jump from one new boat into another (i.e., our usual condition), we limit our playing to producing new ways to improve our present boat. SUNRISE has been in this wonderful position for a number of years now. She has numerous items of new gear and lovely little homey improvements belowdecks that make her more comfortable for everyday living, but the biggest change is the Great Pyramid rig shown on the drawing on page 89 and detailed more elaborately in the next chapter. In addition, the fore-and-aft rig was changed from matching gaff main and mizzen to completely

PARTICULARS:

Item	English	Metric
Length over all (incl. bowsprit) ..	50'-0"	15.24m
(on bulwarks, w/pink stern)	38'-0"	11.58m
(sternpost to stem)	34'-6"	10.52m
Waterline length:.............	30'-8"	9.35m
Beam	11'-3"	3.43m
Draft (fully loaded)	6'-3"	1.91m
Displacement, cruising trim*	31,240 lbs.	14,170 kg.
In current trim	27,000 lbs.	12,247 kg.
Freeboard:		
Forward	4'-2½"	1.28m
Least	2'-3½"	0.70m
Aft	3'-4½"	1.03m
Sail area:		
Fore & Aft — working sails .	750 sq. ft.	69.68 sq. m
— with genoa ...	1063 sq.ft.	98.76 sq. m
Squaresails	1000 sq. ft.	92.90 sq. m
Storm Trysail	68 sq. ft.	6.32 sq. m
Lbs. per inch immersion @ LWL..	1,200	
Ballast:		
Outside (lead)	9,300 lbs.	4,218 kg.
Inside (lead)	1,000 lbs.	454 kg.
Power: Volvo MD 2B, 25 hp @ 2500 rpm,		
3.42:1 Reduction/Reverse gear		
Water tankage	125 gals.	473 liters
(including one, 8-gal. hot water tank)		
Fuel tankage..................	108 gals.	409 liters
(two, 54-gal. tanks in engine room)		
Headroom (under cabin beams) .	6'-2"	1.88m
Displacement-length ratio	479	
Wetted surface................	390 sq. ft.	36.25 sq. m
Prismatic coefficient	.577	

*CAUTION: The displacement quoted here is for the boat in cruising trim. That is, with fuel and water in the tanks, the crew on board, as well as the crew's gear and stores in the lockers. This should not be confused with the "shipping weight" often quoted as "displacement" by some manufacturers. This should be taken into account when comparing figures and ratios between this and other designs.

Roy Montgomery Photo

SUNRISE when she was originally for sale, with two Benford pocket cruisers ahead of her — a 20' gaff sloop under her bowsprit and an 18' canoe yawl next ahead.

roller furled main trysail, mizzen staysail, large overlapping genoa and staysail. This is extremely handy and can be set completely from the aft deck. It also allows more sail to be set for the lesser winds of our coastal cruising grounds.

The next major change we'd like to incorporate on *SUNRISE* is a pilothouse, shown in the same drawing as the Great Pyramid Rig. If *SUNRISE* had been designed originally for us, she definitely would have been a pilothouse vessel. We like to cruise all year round, and especially enjoy the peacefulness to be found in cruising without crowds. This, of course, means much winter time cruising. We aren't masochists, and have no need to prove to anyone how hardy we are. We do appreciate creature comforts. These do not include making long (or short) passages while shivering in the cockpit in stinging cold winter rains, which we've been doing anyway for nine years. It only makes the thought of a pilothouse all the more tantalizing. Thus, we've had plenty of time to figure out just how handsome (and cozy) such a pilothouse could be. There would be plenty of windows for good lighting and excellent all-around visibility. A five-foot quarter-berth will even fit in nicely under the aft deck, thus allowing our young son, Joshua, his own private nook. (Presently, his bunk is the starboard settee in the main saloon.)

Should a future owner of *SUNRISE* wish to cruise her in more tropical climates, a pilothouse would have the alternative advantage of shelter from blistering sun. Numerous clients have adamantly stated their preference for a good shelter from cool, wet and/or sunny weather. For the latter, the pilothouse needs to have good ventilation. Sliding doors port and starboard and opening ports and/or overhead hatch all help accommodate these needs.

To date, I have had the pleasure of owning four of my own designs, and I am looking forward to many more. As the yacht designer is his own most difficult client (with ever evolving ideas in his mind as to what is the "ideal yacht" for himself), I will no doubt have the continuing pleasure of experiencing a variety of vessels as the years pass. At present, I'm very much enamored with SUNRISE, and hope some day to find just the right sort of people who'll be proud to take good care of her in future.

* * * *

Scantlings:
  1-3/8" Red Cedar Planking
  1-3/8" x 1-3/4" Bent Oak Frames
  Fir & Gumwood Backbone
  3/4" Red Cedar Ceiling
  1-1/2" x 3-1/2" Fir Stringers
  Guard: Yellow Cedar with Iron Bark over
  Bronze Keel Bolts
  Galvanized floor drift bolts
  1" Red Cedar cabin sides
  1-1/8" laid fir decks
  1" Red Cedar bulwarks
  7/8" x 3-1/2" Teak caprail
  1-3/8" x 2-7/8" Yellow Cedar deck beams
  3/4" Laid fir planked cabin top over 3/4" Red Cedar
    (total: 1-1/2")
  7/8" Fir Cabin Sole
  Fir rudder
  Teak skylight over foc'sle
  Planking is bronze fastened
  Six, 10" opening bronze ports on cabin sides
  Two, 8" non-opening bronze portlights on cabin front
Finish:
  All exterior and interior wood is finished with Deks Olje. No painting, no varnishing. She looks like she's varnished, only she has an oil finish.
Accommodations:
  Owner's Stateroom:
    Double berth
    Hanging rod
    Two bookshelves full length port and starboard

  Two reading lights (12 volts) mounted on mooring bits at head of berth plus 4-plug 110v outlet on shelf-flat.
  Stowage forward of, and under berth
  Beautiful teak skylight — raises wing and wing — over berth
Main Cabin:
  Two settee/berths, 1 each port and starboard, port settee has extension for double berth, shelves outboard
  Stowage behind and under settees port and starboard
  Large, hinged, folding dining table with bronze stanchion; this has fed nine at one sitting, although four to six is most comfortable.
  Large chart table holds more than 100 charts, laying flat
  Narrow shelf outboard & 2 large bookshelves over chart table
  Large wood bin outboard under chart table
  Refrigerator midships under chart table — opens forward — Norcold 12V.
  Tewkesbury Fireplace at aft end of starboard settee, facing diagonally forward
  Two reading lights provide indirect lighting from under cabin front beam (over forward end of settees and table)
  Four-plug 110V outlet outboard of chart table, & light over chart table
  Kerosene, brass lamp over dining table
  Kerosene lamp in galley, plus two 12-volt lights overhead
  Brass clock and barometer on forward, cabin bulkhead
  Neptune 2A stove/oven, back-to-back with Tewkesbury Nantucket fireplace
  Solid teak galley counter, L-shaped with sink in aft end of "L"
  Large locker beneath stove, and two, 2-shelf lockers beneath starboard side of galley counter and
  locker   beneath sink
  Manual sink pumps for fresh & sea water
  Three-shelf teak spice rack above galley counter
  Four-plug 110V outlet at forward end of galley counter
  Companionway ladder forward of opening door to engine room
  12 volt electric panels on aft bulkhead above sink
  110 volt circuit breaker panel on locker bulkhead on inboard side of sink

Head:
  Stainless steel sink set in tall counter/locker
  Wilcox Crittenden model junior #51 marine toilet
  Two door, two shelf locker outboard of toilet
  Foot pump pressure water shower on telephone style nozzle, with cord long enough to reach around to galley sink by opening head door
  Two-plug 110 volt outlet on locker face
Engine Room:
  Two, 54 gallon fuel tanks, port and starboard forward
  Three, 240-amp/hr. batteries in fiberglass battery boxes
  National 8-gallon hot water tank, heated by 110-volt A.C., and/or engine cooling water
  PAR 12V bilge pump with float switch and whale 25 Gusher manual pump
  Volvo MD 2B 25 hp diesel engine; 3.42:1 reduction gear
  20 x 19 3-blade bronze propeller
  35-gallon water tank aft of engine
  Stowage space aft of water tank
  Good room around engine port and starboard for maintenance
  Good storage space for fenders, spare lines, life cushions, tool box, etc.
  Well lit by deadlight in aft deck plus 12-volt light

SUNRISE ready for launching. Visible are the gammon iron over the bowsprit onto the stem, the shoulders on the bowsprit for the eyebands, the catheads, the chocks in the bulwarks, and the generous scuppers formed by the bulwark planking being held clear of the deck through the midships area.

over engine.

Access either through door from main cabin, or through port and/or starboard cockpit hatches

Sails and Rigging:

Type: Tops'l Ketch

Spar Material: Sitka Spruce, oiled with Deks Olje

Roller Furling: On jib, staysail, mizzen staysail, and main trysail — entirely controlled from cockpit

Bowsprit: 12 feet, fir, oiled with Deks Olje

Sail Inventory:

Sail	Area
Main trysail	240 sq. ft.
Genoa	500 sq. ft.
Staysail	143 sq. ft.
Jib	187 sq. ft.
Course	330 sq. ft.
Tops'l	210 sq. ft.
Storm trysail	68 sq. ft.
Mizzen staysail	180 sq. ft.
(2) Studding Sails	230 sq. ft. each

Material: Dacron fore and aft sails, and nylon squaresails

Notes: All sails can be set and furled from on deck.

Standing rigging: Stainless Steel

Running rigging: Dacron

Deadeyes: Lignum Vitae, made in Nova Scotia

Blocks: Teak shell, s.s. strap and pin, bronze sheave with bronze roller bearing

Winches: Two bronze, Barlow #20 & one bronze, Barlow #16

Electronics and Electrics:

Knotmeter: Kenyon, KS-100

Log: Kenyon, KL-100

Compass: 5" Sea Master with Brass Binnacle with light

Depth Sounder: Coastal Navigator 200 ft/60 meters

FM Stereo/Tape Deck: Sony Cassettee & FM Radio-Stereo

Nine Flourescent Lights

Ship's Power: 12 volts/480 Amp-Hr

Shore Power: 110 Volt. (4, plug outlets)

Starting Battery: 12 volts/240 Amp-Hr

Circuit Breakers: Marinetics Panel, with voltmeter and ampmeter

Battery Charger: Sentry Charger with remote control switch-

Roy Montgomery Photos

Left: The original rig on SUNRISE, with the course brailing to the centerline.

Below: Reaching in the Straights of Juan de Fuca off Victoria with the Olympic Mountains in the background. This shows the second evolution of the square rig with the wire down the centerline of the course and the roller furling gear on it. The buntlines on the topsail also show well — there were seven of them used to hold the topsail loosely furled onto the topsail yard when it was lowered. Then someone would go aloft and put the gaskets (sail ties) on it making it a tight furl. The 65 pound Herreshoff (Luke) anchor is pulled up to the bowsprit roller and tied back to the catheads. Note the crew member with the proper cruising spirit in the midships hammock.

ing and charge meter, 20 amps
Alternator
MECA 2400 VHF Radio
Seascan 16-mile Radar
Equipment:
    Life lines & netting all around
    3 fire extinguishers

Steering: tiller
Anchors: 65 pound Herreshoff; 35 pound plow
Rode: 300' 3/4" nylon, 100' 3/4" nylon, each with a length of chain
Anchor Windlass: Ideal electric; Chain Wildcat and Rope Drum
Guest Searchlight: 200,000 candlepower
Brass Salem clock and barometer
One large kerosene lamp and two smaller kerosene brass lamps
Custom settee and berth cushions
Docking lines and fenders
Kerosene anchor light
Electric anchor light
Electric spreader lights and running lights
Six life jackets
Four buoyant cushions

Roy Montgomery Photos

Above: The wonderful skylight over the double berth. It provides excellent light and air, and gives extra headroom in the forward stateroom. We're able to lie in the berth and look up the skylight and see what the weather is doing before arising.

Below: Master shipwright Bill Modrell celebrating the launching while his friend serenades us on the bagpipes.

Roy Montgomery Photos

Above and below: The knees reinforcing the pink stern and the overhanging deck are shown clearly here. Note also the substantial pintle and gudgeon arrangement and the protected propellor in the aperture. The channel holding out the chainplate is typical of those onboard. They keep the deadeyes and lanyards clear of the bulwarks and give a bit wider angle to the shrouds.

Jay R. Benford, Photo

Chart Tables:

With a bit of forethought, a designer can provide a really practical chart table in almost any boat. Doing a bit of design work on mine, I enjoy having what I call a "no-fold" chart table.

Since the largest of the over 100 U.S. and Canadian charts I use is 36" by 48", I made the chart storage bin on SUNRISE 37" by 49" clear inside dimensions and a minimum of 1½" deep. Thus I don't have to fold any of the charts on board, and the source of the "no-fold" name.

The next logical step down from this size is a "one-fold". This would mean storing 36" by 24" sized charts, and I usually specify a minimum of 37" by 25" clear inside dimensions for the chart box or drawer.

A "two-fold" chart table should be the minimum used on the smallest boats. This means the charts would be folded twice down to 18" by 24" size, and the minimum box for storing them would be 19" by 25" clear inside.

The simplest chart tables have a hinged lid over the chart storage box that becomes the chart table. On my "no-fold" chart table, I've mounted a 48" Mayline parallel rule. I use this for design work on the chart table, and have found it handy for just keeping the charts in place on the table as well as facilitating a navigation work style making use of the other drafting tools on board. The lid/board is 3/4" plywood covered with K&E Laminene drawing board surface material with an 1/8" grid. This has a plastic surface and is easily wiped clean. As it is a little slippery for charts, the parallel rule and its wires are appreciated in keeping the charts in place.

Good lighting is also important to the navigator. I've taken a flexible arm drafting lamp and mounted it over my chart table. I cut off the plug and wired it into the lighting circuit on board. I replaced the 110V bulb with a 12V 15 watt bulb, and have been very pleased with the result. The 15 watt bulb is plenty of light for most all the work done there. It will reach out to the edge of the board and makes for a great reading light when sitting on the settee alongside. For drafting work on brighter days, I have a 25 watt bulb I can put in its place, but this is hardly ever used.

The arrangement of my chart table also has bookshelves over the back of the board as well as outboard of it. The VHF radio and radar viewer are both mounted over the table, so they're handy to the charts of the area in question.

There's no excuse to build a new boat and not include a proper chart table. A good work area for the navigator can make the navigation easier, contributing to the safety and enjoyment of all aboard.

Roy Montgomery Photo

The Great Pyramid Rig

A naval architect's solution to the paradox of the ideal cruising sail system: How to add sail but keep the rig easily manageable.

By JAY BENFORD

WE CRUISED *Sunrise* with her original square rig for about five years, learning how best to handle it and making evolutionary changes before developing the Great Pyramid Rig as a solution to several thorny problems.

The course (the bottom square sail) was originally fitted with horizontal brailing lines. There were seven of them on about three-foot centers. They ran completely around the sail and came down to the deck in a bundle which I would grasp and haul on to furl the sail. This was a simple and very functional system. The only problem we had with it was that the brailing lines occasionally hung up on another part of the rig as they were swaying about in the breeze.

When the course was brailed up, it was about the same diameter as the mast, creating a fair bit of wind resistance. In an effort to reduce that, and to eliminate the bits of line in the brailing bundle, we had the course fitted with a stainless steel wire down its centerline, parallel to the mast. We attached conventional jib-furling gear to roll up the sail vertically, directly in front of the mast. This worked nicely, but one had to be sure the downhaul tackle was well set up for the furling operation to proceed smoothly. It cut the diameter of

the furled sail in half, too.

However, two problems remained that I wanted to solve. One was that the rig, as originally designed for long passages, was conservative in area—just about right for regular Tradewind passage-making. We had bought the boat

from the original client only half completed, but with sails and spars already made. As an economy move, we decided to go ahead with the original rig. We found out later that most of our sailing was in light conditions and more sail area would be needed to increase her speed in those conditions.

The second problem was not quite as easy to solve. The original topsail was rigged in the traditional manner. The yard was hoisted about eight feet to set the sail; dousing the sail meant lowering it that same distance and tightening up on the buntlines to gather the sail up under the yard. However, I seemed to be the only one willing to go aloft to put the gaskets on to make it a tight furl, especially in any kind of sea. In light conditions, or in a protected harbor, this was a rather simple operation. At sea, when shortening sail as the wind increased, going aloft became more of an adventure. High wind velocities could flog the sail and cause chafe if it wasn't tightly furled and secured to the yard.

The solution came only gradually. I began by sketching methods of increasing the sail area. It was soon apparent that a yard long enough to permit setting two sails with enough area was just too big for the boat. That led me to thinking

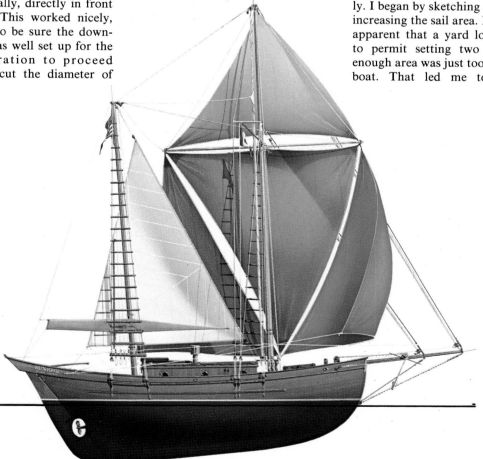

about studding sails, in the manner of the old clipper ships. I sketched a rig I liked, formalized it with a drawing and circulated a couple of copies to get quotes on sails. With this rig, the topsail and two stuns'ls were set flying, each with a four-foot yard at its head. This eliminated the need to go aloft by bringing the sail down on deck, and the additional sails gave us the extra area wanted.

However, the quotes from the sailmakers sent me back to the drawing board to come up with a way to make it an affordable project. The price lists for the sails made it immediately evident that the route to lower prices was with lighter weight sail cloth. I had started out specifying Dacron of conservative weight in keeping with the character of the design. In reviewing things, I thought that the stuns'ls were certainly light-weather sails, so why not go very light on those two, say to 1.5-oz. nylon? A quick trip through the calculator brought such interesting savings that I decided to figure how low I could get the price of the sails if all the squaresails were of the lighter cloth. That just about sold me on the idea of trying the lighter cloth; it was certainly more affordable.

However, the nylon cloth would stretch more than the Dacron originally specified, and that might not work well on the four-foot yards. Also, those little yards might have a tendency to get hooked in other parts of the rigging. Could I work out a way to eliminate them? Could I spread enough sail area and yet keep control of it?

The Great Pyramid Rig is the result of these ruminations. It consists of four triangular sails—thus the name—that are all set flying from on deck. It has significantly reduced the weight of the rig aloft and eliminated a great deal of windage too.

We have 20 feet of spread between eyebands on the yard—up from 22 feet on the original yard. The original topsail and course rig had 468 sq. ft. of sail area. The new rig has 1,000. The biggest sail, still the course, is only ten square feet bigger than the old one, and I can

Top: The course has just been set, and preparation is being made to hoist the tops'l. The day after these photos were shot, a halyard was rigged to the center-line of the head of the course, facilitating hoisting the sail. The procedure now is to fasten the foot of the sail to the downhauls to haul out both of the upper corners of the sail.

Photo also shows the lifts from each end of the yard to the masthead. These lifts allow us to control the angle of the yard—horizontal or vertical—for clearance when rafting or passing through locks. The braces from the ends of the yards to the mizzen masthead allow us to control the horizontal rotation of the yard; there is approximately 40 degrees fore and aft rotation possible due to the way the yard is rigged. Note also, the spreaders are raked well aft, so that the upper shrouds are kept clear of the yard.

Above: The tops'l has now been set, and the lines are being coiled onto the pinrail at the base of the mast.

set and douse it myself. All four sails are set flying, with the halyards, outhauls and sheets led to the pinrail at the base of the mainmast. Once set, the yard is revolved from one reach to the other by the braces, which lead aft to the cockpit. If the stuns'ls are set, their sheets lead aft, as do the tack lines for hauling them forward on a reach.

The lifts on the yards run from the yardarms to the masthead and then down to the pinrail on deck. These lines control the yard when it is set horizontally at rest. They also allow the yard to be cocked up at an angle almost paralleling the mast. Cocking the yard like this permits laying alongside other vessels, lock walls or tall piers without worrying about fouling the rig.

Incidentally, we've found that it's easy to foul one rig, and we've had quite a few cases of boats snagging the yards in close quarters. Thus, it is up to the crew on the boat with the yard to warn others of it, in self-defense.

When I originally worked out the rig, I thought I would need or want a whisker pole to hold each of the stuns'ls in place. It turned out that we got delivery of the sails well ahead of the poles and decided to try flying the sails anyway, being too curious to wait longer to see if the whole thing worked as planned. Once out in San Juan Channel, we started hoisting away, soon having all four sails set and drawing. After the general hilarity died down and we got over referring to the rig as the "circus tent," we realized it was working very well. In fairly light conditions, we were quickly overhauling a ketch half again our size. This first trial sail immediately brought home the point that the poles for the stuns'ls would not be required for most of our sailing. The sails set and drew quite nicely without the poles. Later trials indicated the poles would really be required only for poling the weather stuns'l forward on a close reach. This proved to be such a nuisance for our normal lazy style of cruising that we have taken to dropping the weather stuns'l on a close reach and setting a jib instead.

I'm often asked if this rig would

Above left: The port stuns'l has been set (note advantages of color coding to determining which sail flies where). The downhaul from the head of the tops'l is visible in this shot, where it leads down in front of the course. The technique for dousing the tops'l is to let fly the halyard and haul on the downhaul to pull the sail down to a position where it is blanketed by the course. Then the sheets are eased off as the sail is hauled down onto the foredeck. We have rigged the halyard and the downhaul as one line, with a shackle at each end, one for the halyard operation and one for the downhaul operation. The rig with the yard braced around and the stuns'l sheeted in well aft, with the vessel sailing between a reach and a broad reach. **Above right:** The starboard stuns'l has now been set, and the yard squared around so that we are now on a run. The "bone in her teeth" is evidence of her approaching hull speed, and the lack of whitecaps all around indicates the modest wind strength required to achieve this. **Below:** The downhaul tackle for the course has since been revised, and now has three snap shackles attached to its upper end.

work on other boats. My answer is a qualified yes. The qualifications are that the boat should be able to carry the weight aloft without impairing her stability, and that her spreaders need to be raked aft to allow the yard to revolve at least 30 degrees each way. Doing this makes the sails useful from at least one reach to the other reach, and *Sunrise*'s spreaders are so designed that we can carry the sails on either close reach.

I've tried to work out just why the rig does work so well by analyzing its performance. With the yard to hold the sail out in the proper position, we've eliminated the typical problem of a spinnaker collapsing and scraping the headstay. The fixed yard also eliminates the rythmic rolling so often seen with a spinnaker, since the sails cannot oscillate. One of the main virtues of this rig, other than its ease of setting sails and control, is the ease of reducing sail. The ability to quickly take down one or more of the sails and to keep the right amount of sail set for varying wind conditions, makes for great peace of mind when shorthanded. This ability to use just part of the rig was pleasantly brought home last December, as we started our annual Christmas cruise. There was a 25-plus-knot southerly blowing, and we were doing over seven knots (hull speed) and having a great sail. The rig is truly versatile and a great source of pleasure and fun to all aboard. □

Jay Benford, of Friday Harbor, Wash., is a designer of imaginative cruising boats, power and sail.

Two corrections to this article should be noted:

(1) The spread between the eyebands on our new yard is 30', not the 20' as noted on page 98.

(2) The last sentence on the first paragraph of the top photo's caption on page 98 should read: "The procedure now is to fasten the foot of the sail to the downhaul tackle, hoist the centerline halyard up snug, and then haul on the outhauls to haul out both of the upper corners of the sail."

Rachel Adams, Photos

Rachel Adams, Photo

The 20' Supply Boat, BATEN, above and the 14' Tug/
Cruiser, GRIVIT, below are two of the Benford designed pocket cruisers to be included in a subsequent
volume devoted completely to small cruising yachts.

The 32' Trawler Yacht, LADYBUG, at right, is shown
in more detail on pages 118 and 119. She was splendid-
ly built by Joe Proulx in San Diego.

Gene Coan, Photo

Jay R. Benford, Photo

STRUMPET, at right, was designed for Dodie and Ernest K. Gann. They cruised her for five years in the Pacific Northwest. More information about her is in chapter 16, beginning on page 109.

Roy Montgomery Photo

The 60' ketch, HARAMBEE, was built by Herman and Gail Husen. She has become a familiar sight in the San Juan Islands, carrying paying guests for several years. The Husens live aboard year 'round on their lovely vessel.

Jay R. Benford, Photo

RAGNAR, upper left, is a 20' smaller sister to the Benford 30, AFFINITY, above. The upper center sailing shot, opposite, is of RUNAWAY GIRL as is the upper right construction photo. The balance of that page shows BAKEA in more detail and the plug for the mold, upper left.

The above two photos and the sailing shot of RUNAWAY GIRL, opposite, are by Roy Montgomery. Other photos opposite by Jay R. Benford.

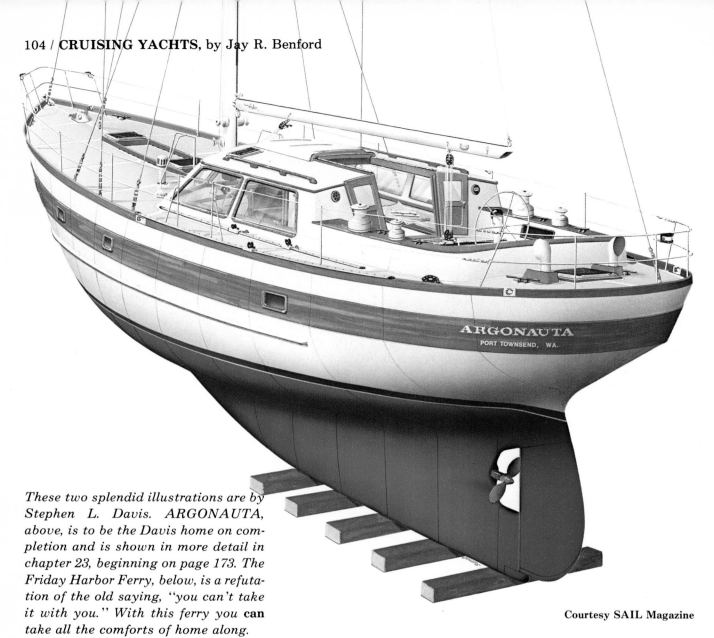

*These two splendid illustrations are by Stephen L. Davis. ARGONAUTA, above, is to be the Davis home on completion and is shown in more detail in chapter 23, beginning on page 173. The Friday Harbor Ferry, below, is a refutation of the old saying, "you can't take it with you." With this ferry you **can** take all the comforts of home along.*

Courtesy SAIL Magazine

Chapter
15

Friday Harbor Ferry

For: Jay R. Benford
Design Number 183
1979

By Frank Madd

Illustration by Stephen L. Davis

WHAT IF?

Ten years ago, during one of our regular office "what if" sessions, we got into discussing the sad state of what was being offered in the way of houseboats. People who wished a mobile liveaboard boat were offered only one kind of boat. Since several of us live aboard, we have a special interest in this lifestyle. The ability to tow waterskiers and consume a gallon or two per mile to go cruising seemed the antithesis of what was really required. What were being called houseboats were really house trailers with a box underneath to keep them afloat. The only quality control seemed to be in getting good four-color printing jobs for the sales brochures.

THE BETTER MOUSETRAP.

Starting with a clean sheet of paper and open minds, we analyzed the requirements of the liveaboard. From this, we laid out the parameters of the ideal houseboat. It would have maximized living accommodations, operate at economical displacement hull speeds, and be built in a manner that would make it a good investment. Also, it must look like it belonged on the water; not like something styled in Detroit for cruising the Interstate highways.

THE STROKE OF GENIUS!

What finally got the project launched was Jay's idea to make it a small ferry boat in style and design. This gave us a boat that looked like a proper little ship, and one that would give the same feeling to those aboard. It also gave great accommodations, by making the cabin practically the full width of the hull. But, most importantly, it was an easily driven hull form that would provide very economical operation. One that could be cruised through the thousands of miles of semi-protected waterways where most people do all their cruising, and one that would have tremendous room for her size and all the features to make her an economical vessel to operate.

THE GOOD FERRY.

The result of following these thoughts to their logical conclusion was the Waterbed 30. After Jay designed her in 1973, she was published in quite a number of magazines, and generated more mail than any other design Jay has had published. Thinking we were really onto something, we approached a number of production builders to see about putting her into production. Uniformly, their reaction was negative, ranging from a polite "no thank-you" to loud guffaws.

To us, this seemed a sad commentary on the state of the boating business — no one was willing to do something that was somewhat different than his competitors. Here was a whole segment of the market that was being virtually ignored. No wonder so many builders folded during the recent recession; they had no idea how to innovate and offer different products that would set them apart from their competitors and give them a market all to themselves. Since those early negatives from shortsighted builders, we have had a gradually increasing amount of interest in the ferryboat style houseboat idea. A 34' version of the original Waterbed 30 was drawn up for one group. The resulting design has 50 to 100% more living room inside than most 40' houseboats. Her twin skegs protect the props and rudders, and make for graceful, upright groundings. The twin screws make for good maneuvering and the two small diesels provide safe and very economical operation. I think it's the most practical cruising boat I've seen in decades and I hope to live aboard one myself someday.

Jay has also drawn up what he calls the "office version" of the Friday Harbor Ferry. In it, he's got two staterooms, a roomy head with five foot long tub and shower unit and washer and dryer stack set, a good sized office, a large galley and dining and living room combination, and a cozy pilothouse. This has 320 square feet of enclosed living space on the lower deck, and 170 in the upper house and 30 in the pilothouse for

a total of 520 square feet. (The yacht version has 320 plus 80 on the upper deck for a total of 400 square feet.) If the office version was used for just living aboard, the space the office uses could be added to the living quarters, making it even roomier.

Discussions have ensued with a number of other people interested in a variety of sizes, including a 60-footer, all of which would be most delightful. However, action is what is now needed: bold, fearless and resolute. I am convinced that once this houseboat is built and marketed by a quality-oriented, efficient sales team, we will see this boom into an around-the-world solution for everything from housing shortages to co-op condominiums to charter boat dealers on lake and island resorts to straightforward boating buffs. Our conclusion is simply this: the design came in before its time. The market responded with resounding glee. The builders, mired in "the known market", cowered in their corners. After a decade of unwavering and increasing enthusiasm by clientelle wanting this lovely gem, the builders are creeping out of their pubescent closets. We are ready and waiting. If you are a builder who wants to build a delightful, practical, roomy packet, and you can handle the avalanche of waiting sales, the Good Ferry is here. Don't be hesitant or fumblefooted: the lion has been flexing his muscles for ten years and when he leaps, it will be high.

Illustration by Stephen L. Davis

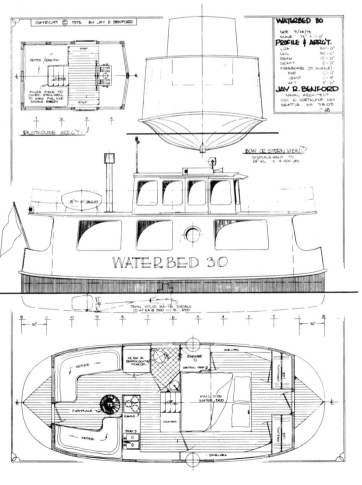

Particulars of FRIDAY HARBOR FERRY
Design No. 183

Item	English	Metric
Length — over guards	34'-7½"	10.55m
molded hull	34'-0"	10.36m
waterline	34'-0"	10.36m
Beam — over guards	14'-7½"	4.46m
molded hull	14'-0"	4.27m
waterline	13'-0"	3.96m
Draft, cruising trim*	2'-3"	0.69m
Displacement, cruising trim*	23,000lbs.	10,432kg.
Displacement-length ratio	261	
Prismatic coefficient	0.54	
Pounds per inch immersion	1635	
Water tankage	300 gals.	1135 l.
Fuel tankage	200 gals.	757 l.
Power	twin 20 hp	diesels
Headroom	6'-5"	1.96m
Enclosed living spaces —		
lower house	320 sq. ft.	29.73 sq. m
upper house	170 sq. ft.	15.79 sq. m
pilothouse	30 sq. ft.	2.79 sq. m
total	520 sq. ft.	48.31 sq. m
GM (est. — very stiff)**	5'	1.52m

*CAUTION: The displacement quoted here is for the boat in cruising trim. That is, with the fuel and water tanks filled, the crew on board, as well as the crews' gear and stores in the lockers. This should not be confused with the "shipping weight" often quoted as "displacement" by some manufacturers. This should be taken into account when comparing figures and ratios between this and other designs.

**Stability on this boat is excellent. It would take about 40 knots of side wind to heel her to her guard rail. Two adults stepping aboard at her side door should heel her just one degree.

Illustration by Stephen L. Davis

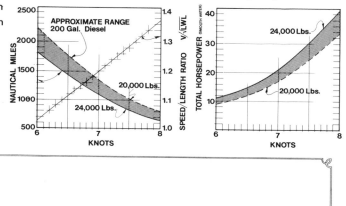

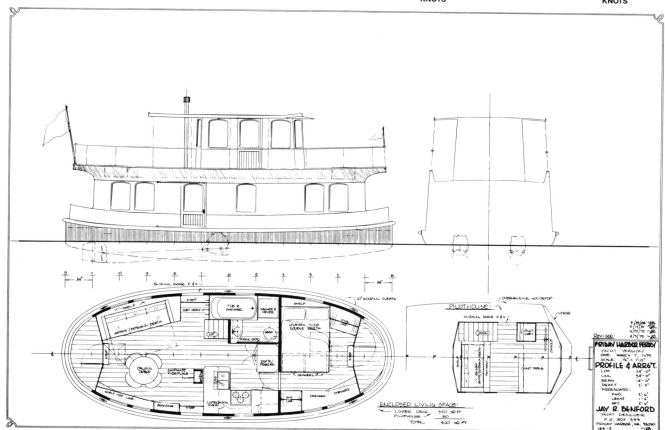

Choice Waterfront Homes

Available with panoramic marine views from Puget Sound to Alaska or Florida to Maine. An ideal liveaboard or retirement home or vacation home, the 34' Friday Harbor Ferry offers a majestic variety of unique marine park settings, each available without ever leaving home. These luxury homes offer low maintenance fiberglass and teak exterior and warm wood interior with all utilities installed, including washer, dryer, bathtub and fireplace. Two bedrooms, complete kitchen, large sundeck, and two viewing porches. Economical diesel power and large tanks provide for safe and low-cost operation. Neighbors too noisy? Move your house. Tired of mowing the lawn and raking leaves? Try ferry boat living for fast relief.

FRIDAY HARBOR FERRY
FOR: JAY R. BENFORD
DATE: DEC. 16, 1979
SCALE: 1/4" = 1'-0"

OFFICE VERSION

LOA	34'-0"
LWL	34'-0"
BEAM	14'-0"
DRAFT	2'-8"
FREEBOARD: (TOP OF GUARD)	
FWD.	2'-6"
LEAST	1'-6"
AFT	2'-6"

JAY R. BENFORD
YACHT DESIGNER
P.O. BOX 399
FRIDAY HARBOR, WA. 98250
183-9

REVISIONS: 3/24/81

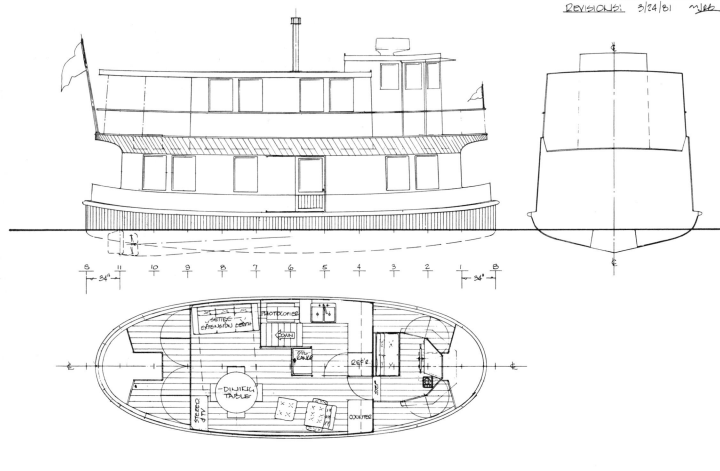

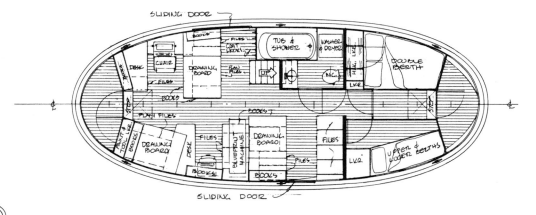

Caution: The Sturgeon Genial warns that Friday Harbor Ferry living may be addictive and habit forming.

Chapter

16

Strumpet

35' Trawler Yacht
For: Ernest K. & Dodie Gann
Design Number 66
1970

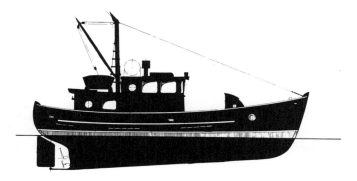

Designers need to learn as much as possible about the personal cruising and living philosophy of their clients in order to create the most effective boat for them. The end result is that each of these custom designed boats makes a strong individual statement. The 35' Trawler Yacht, *STRUMPET,* is a very outspoken example of this phenomenon.

To look at *STRUMPET* is to see strength, sturdiness, an appreciation for history, grace, purposefulness and privacy. It is no coincidence that these qualities are also outstanding characteristics of the people for whom she was created: Ernest K. and Dodie Gann. Knowing of the impressive background of experience of these two fine people (a dozen and a half commands, including the 117' brigantine, *ALBATROS* and the 60' ketch, *BLACKWATCH),* and understanding some of the desires the Ganns had in mind for *STRUMPET,* where does a designer start?

The husky Scottish fishing trawlers were the leaping-off point, as they were then of greatest appeal to the Ganns. They contacted Jay after seeing his 30' Deadrise Boat, *PETREL,* published in NATIONAL FISHERMAN. The preliminaries for *STRUMPET* thus started with a 30-footer on the boards, for this little packet was to be a personal boat, one about which

Gann was later quoted as saying she "was laid out to drink six, eat four, and sleep two. And no more." But moving from a 60-footer to a smaller cruiser (even given the 22' Bartender in between) can be a difficult adjustment and *STRUMPET* soon grew to 32'. Completed plans were even drawn up at this point, and later stock plans for her were sold; that one became the lovely *LADYBUG.* However, her transom stern was soon changed to a handsome, canoe-sterned double-ender and she was drawn out to 35'. After five or six quite complete preliminary studies, she was finally built at that length.

In her 27" high, wraparound bulwarks, *STRUMPET* really captures some of the big ship feeling of the Ganns' larger sirens. Because of these high bulwarks, being on deck gives one a secure feeling of being IN (as opposed to on) a real boat. Because the layout of the vessel is concentrated on just two people, there is a good deal of space left for operating the boat, or for moving about on deck.

A sense of sturdiness is exuded by the air of her lines. It is backed up by the strength in her construction of over one-inch Philippine mahogany and Alaskan cedar planking on steam bent white oak, 1-3/8" x 2-1/4" frames on 10" centers, over a stout backbone

Roy Montgomery Photos

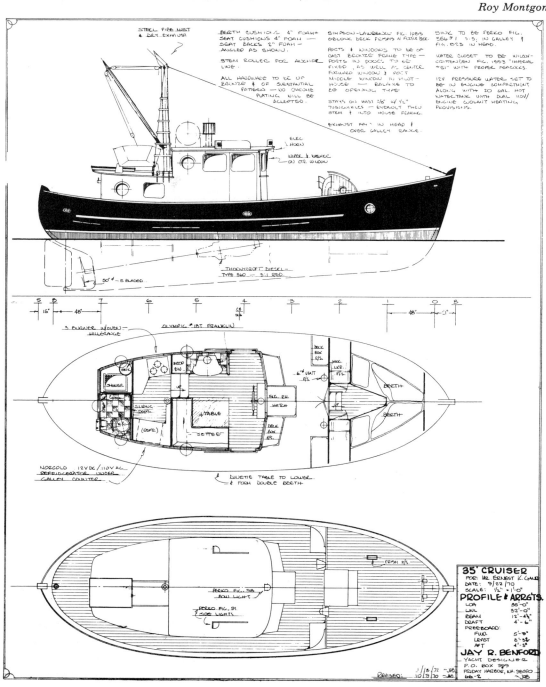

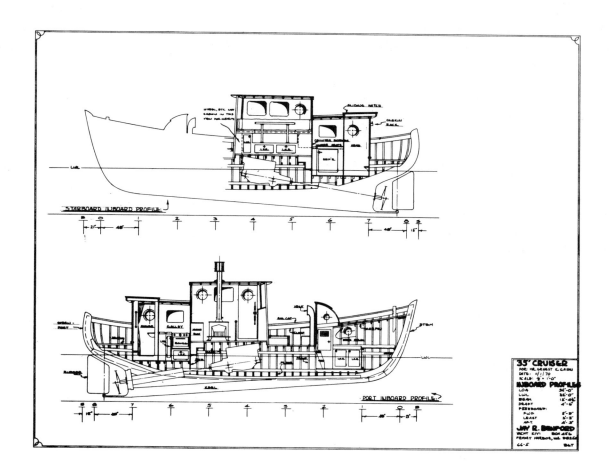

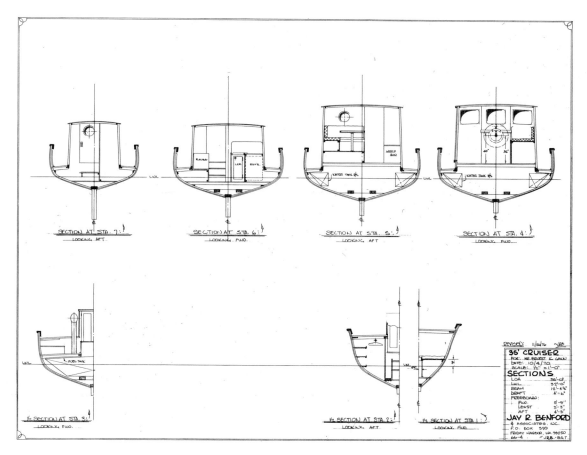

consisting of gumwood stem and sternpost, fir keel, all sided 5½". The six-cylinder Ford diesel, when geared down to a low revolution, hums along in her well insulated quarters. Access to her engine is sensible and workable. With a cruising speed of 1000 to 1200 rpm, she's guaranteed a long service life. Her easy pace also extends the enjoyment of those aboard.

There is grace in her sheer and in her simplicity of outfitting detail. But it doesn't stop there, for *STRUMPET* is extremely stable, and unlike most cruisers, she does not "crouch" down aft, digging her stern in like a timorous puppy caught in the tulip patch. Instead, she requires almost no effort to move forward, sitting atop the water with pride, level, gliding elegantly and proudly along, not unlike a sailboat. The very small wake she leaves behind allows her to slip by without any disturbance to those around her. Even at her top speed of 8.57 knots (higher than any displacement boats have a "right" to be), she maintains the same, steady, seaworthy aura. Her grace commands respect on passing — and well she should!

STRUMPET's interior layout emphasizes the privacy, comfort and practicality that appeal to the Ganns. The steering station is sensibly laid out for maximum visibility, accessibility and ease of movement for the pilot. Sliding doors port and starboard, large windows and portlights all the way around, including a portlight in the aft end of the pilothouse, make the cabin not only airy but safe for the crew who wishes to see out well. The folding table nestles next to a settee which makes it comfortable for the crew to see and keep the captain company. The galley with its ample stowage space, is only a step down aft, but with pass-through bulkheads, and is open to communication as well as warmth from the diesel stove. (At a later point, the Ganns realized the fireplace in the main saloon was superfluous, and replaced it with a large chart table and stowage drawers.) The head fully aft is large and with ample hot water for a comfortable shower. It is also convenient to a crew coming in the aft door, should wet raingear wish to be hung up first before being paraded through the living quarters. The foc'sle is cosily laid out for two, and was at one point modified to include a Tiny Tot heater and a double instead of single berths. A second head was not desired forward, so there is very ample room to move a body about in this stateroom.

Creating *STRUMPET* was indeed a very satisfying series of evolutions in a design process. Experiencing her cruising was pure cream. For as Eileen Crimmin commented in NAUTICAL QUARTERLY's summer, 1980, issue, "Seeing her at anchor or underway causes any knowledgeable sailor to sense immediately that, if this external view is the setting, then surely the rest of her is the jewel. . . . A jewel indeed."

Particulars of STRUMPET

Item	English	Metric
Length over all	35'-0"	10.67m
Length designed waterline	32'-0"	9.75m
Beam	12'-4½"	3.77m
Draft	4'-6"	1.37m
Freeboard:		
Forward	5'-9"	1.75m
Least	3'-3"	0.99m
Aft	4'-3"	1.30m
Displacement, cruising trim*	24,600 lbs.	11,158 kg.
Ballast	3,000 lbs.	1,361 kg.
Displacement-length ratio	335	
Prismatic coefficient	0.628	
Pounds per inch immersion	1420	
Water	190 gals.	719 litres
Fuel	285 gals.	1079 litres

Particulars of 35' Motorsailer

Item	English	Metric
Length over all	35'-0"	10.67m
Length designed waterline	32'-0"	9.75m
Beam	12'-4½"	3.77m
Draft	4'-6"	1.37m
Freeboard:		
Forward	5'-9"	1.75m
Least	3'-3"	0.99m
Aft	6'-0"	1.83m
Displacement, cruising trim*	27,900 lbs.	12,655 kg.
Displacement-length ratio	380	
Sail area	600 sq. ft.	55.74 sq. m.
Sail area-displacement ratio	10.44	
Prismatic coefficient	0.634	
Water	200 gals.	757 litres
Fuel	600 gals.	2271 litres

*CAUTION: The displacement quoted here is for the boat in cruising trim. That is, with the fuel and water tanks filled, the crew on board, as well as the crews' gear and stores in the lockers. This should not be confused with the "shipping weight" often quoted as "displacement" by some manufacturers. This should be taken into account when comparing figures and ratios between this and other designs.

Roy Montgomery Photo

STRUMPET having a gam with RAGNAR, our 20' Gaff Sloop, in Roche Harbor.

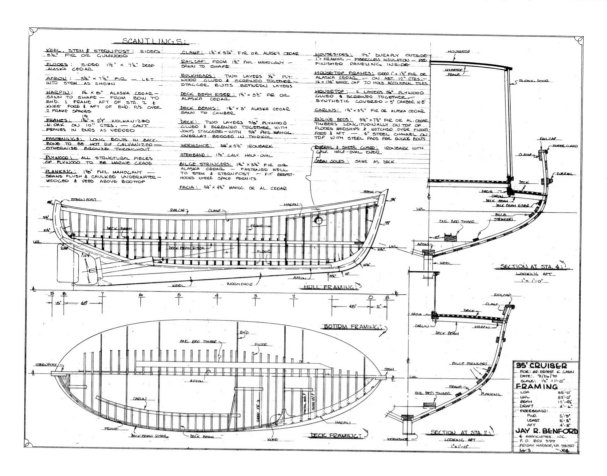

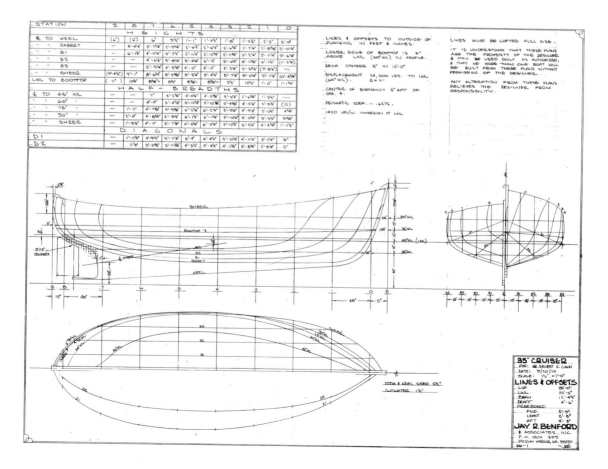

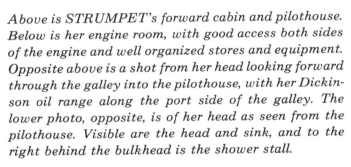

Above is STRUMPET's forward cabin and pilothouse. Below is her engine room, with good access both sides of the engine and well organized stores and equipment. Opposite above is a shot from her head looking forward through the galley into the pilothouse, with her Dickinson oil range along the port side of the galley. The lower photo, opposite, is of her head as seen from the pilothouse. Visible are the head and sink, and to the right behind the bulkhead is the shower stall.

Roy Montgomery Photos

Motorsailer Version:

The motorsailer version of *STRUMPET* was created for a client that wanted the character and charm of *STRUMPET,* with the addition of increased accommodations aft and an auxiliary sailing rig. A head tucks under a seat in the forward cabin. There's a larger chart table in the pilothouse, and the aft cabin is the social area. The settees in the stern convert to uppers and lowers and surround a large drop-leaf table. Part of the galley is tucked under the chart table, increasing the counter space available. The head is quite roomy, and has a separate shower stall.

With a variable pitch prop hooked to a small diesel, she can have a cruising range of about 4,000 miles at 6 knots. This can make her a real passagemaker, and for more information about this type of boat, Robert P. Beebe's book, **Voyaging Under Power,** is the best source of information.

Sukekazu Nagata's 35' Motorsailer, DAI SAN KURO-SHIO MARU (which means BLACK CURRENT CIRCLE III), gliding gracefully along. She was built in Himeji City, Japan, and with the exception of the stern pulpit, her exterior appears to be built faithfully to the original design.

Photo courtesy S. Nagata

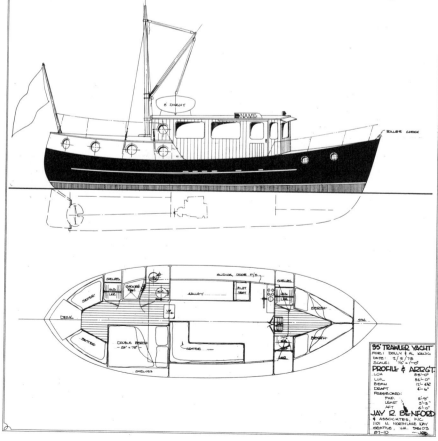

Bill Beers built COMFORT, below, to the 35' motorsailer design, but without the rig. She makes a good, economical motor yacht. The version shown on the drawing at left is based on this same design with a longer deckhouse and revised interior accommodations, having two separate staterooms with the galley and social area in the deckhouse.

COMFORT photo courtesy Bill Beers

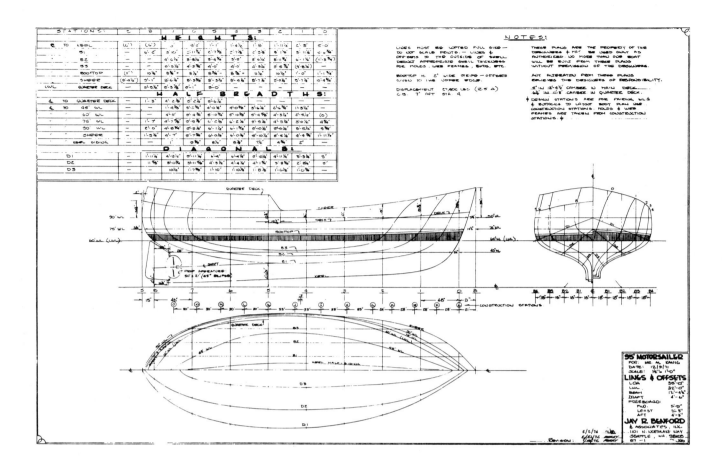

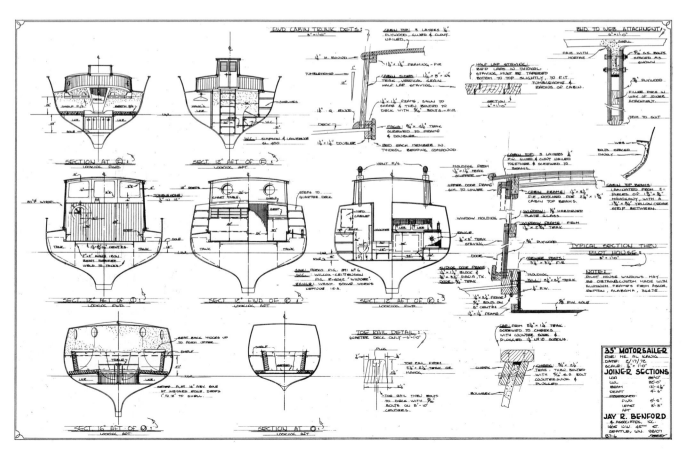

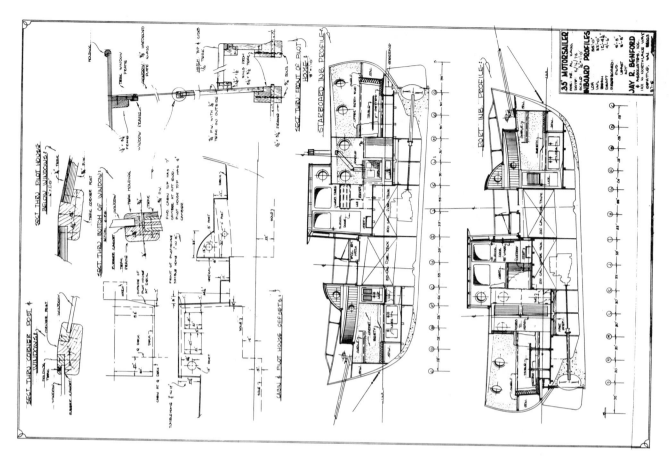

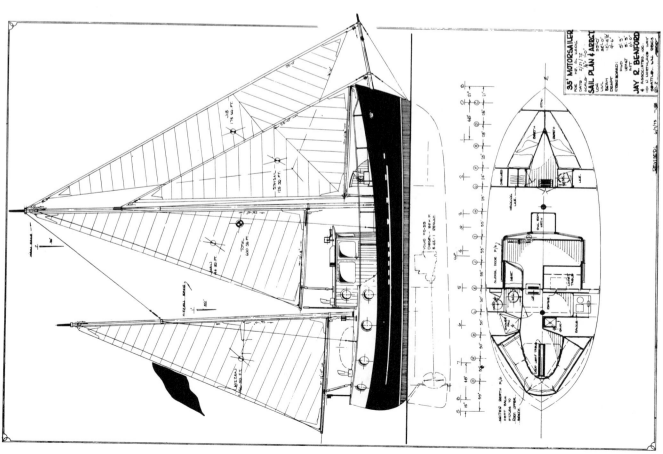

Ladybug

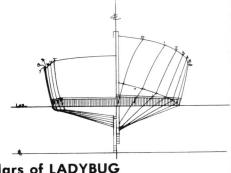

Designed in the fall of 1969, for Mr. Joseph Proulx of San Diego, the 32' LADYBUG is an evolutionary step from our 30' Deadrise Boat, *PETREL*, on the way to the creation of our 35' Trawler Yacht, *STRUMPET*. She's a good illustration of the several steps in the design process which connects one boat to another, in that she shows the definite individuality of her owner, yet the unmistakeable relation to other sisters' basic premises.

She's a comfortable cruising home for one couple, with occasional visits from guests who wish to bunk on the convertible dinette. The foc'sle is completely self-contained and luxuriously appointed. A second head, with shower, is located aft to port. The main cabin contains the control station, dinette and a fireplace for cheer. Aft to starboard is the roomy galley.

One of the great security features of LADYBUG is the deep well deck (about a foot above the waterline), with a minimum of 27'' of solid bulwark, raising to 36'' at the ends. The result is a feeling of really being **in** a little ship and not on a cockleshell: wonderful for cruising with children, as well. A boarding platform and ladder are provided at the stern.

The steadying sail rig helps reduce motion in mixed wave action, and also eases fuel consumption in reaching and running conditions.

Construction is strip planking over bulkheads and longitudinals. *LADYBUG* herself was built over a 4½ year period by Joe Proulx, a professional yacht skipper and boatbuilder. He lavished every detail of attention and love on her, and we are all proud of the results.

Particulars of LADYBUG

Item	English	Metric
Length over all	32'-0''	9.75m
Length designed waterline	30'-0''	9.14m
Beam	12'-0''	3.66m
Draft	3'-6''	1.07m
Freeboard:		
Forward	5'-11''	1.80m
Least	3'-3''	0.99m
Aft	3'-11''	1.19m
Displacement, cruising trim*	15,100 lbs.	6,849 kg.
Displacement-length ratio	250	
Prismatic coefficient	0.695	

*CAUTION: The displacement quoted here is for the boat in cruising trim. That is, with the fuel and water tanks filled, the crew on board, as well as the crews' gear and stores in the lockers. This should not be confused with the ''shipping weight'' often quoted as ''displacement'' by some manufacturers. This should be taken into account when comparing figures and ratios between this and other designs.

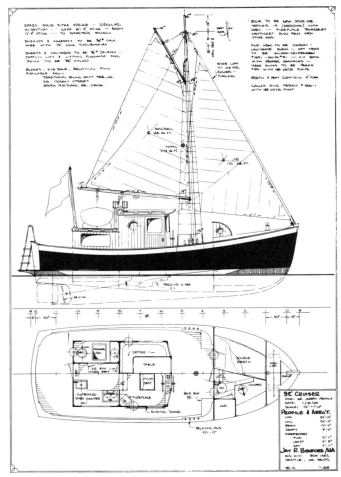

LADYBUG

LADYBUG photos reprinted from SEA, July, 1974; copyright 1974, Petersen Publishing Co.

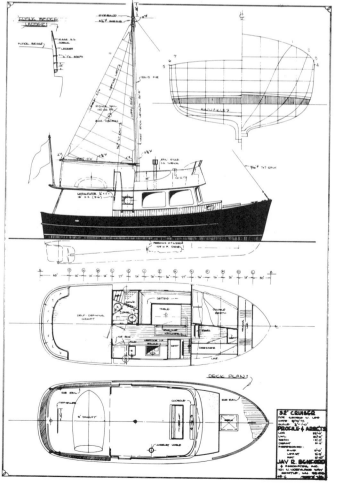

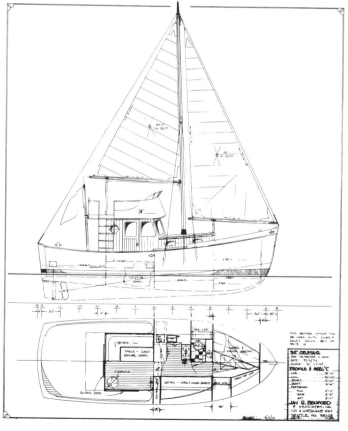

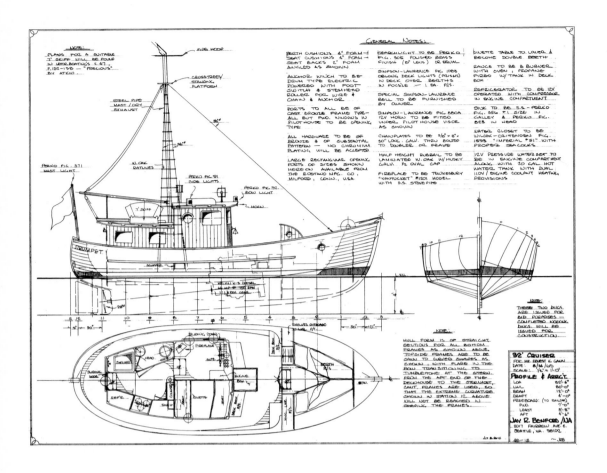

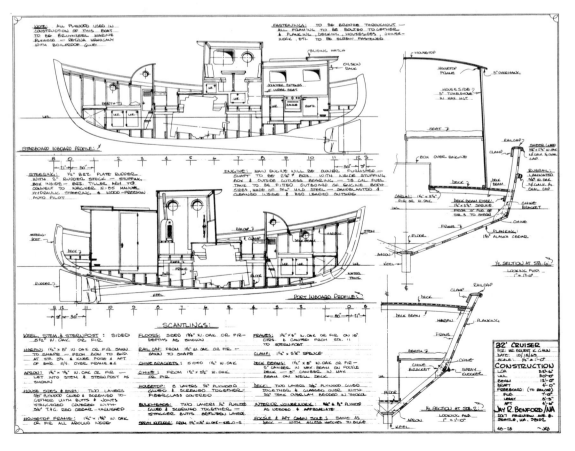

This 32' cruiser is the last preliminary study we did for the Ganns before the final, round-bilged 35-footer. The builders, Jensen Shipyard in Friday Harbor, suggested that there would be no real labor savings in building the chine hull as opposed to the round-bilged one.

So we took the same concept and drew up the larger boat. It was decided that the small additional amount of material in building the extra three feet of length would be only a small change in cost, since all the outfitting and equipment would be the same.

I've included this version here to show the evolution of ideas as well as to show an interesting boat. This design could be completed with only a little more work on our part. She could be done carvel planked, as designed, or in plywood, steel, or aluminum with a little revision to the lines.

Chapter
17

Corcovado

37' Pilothouse Cutter or Ketch
Design Number 125
1975

When we designed *STRUMPET,* Ernest K. Gann's very successful 35' Trawler Yacht, there were only two improvements which Mr. Gann later remarked he would have liked to made to his fine little yacht. The first was that he'd liked to have made her about five feet longer, for the difference in cost would have been minimal in the overall picture (with the same accommodation) and the additional room would always have been able to be used without making the vessel too big to comfortably singlehand. (However, as he had started off with ideas for having us design a 30-footer,

the 35-footer was as large at the time as we all felt comfortable bringing to life and still fit his original intentions.) The second "improvement" on *STRUMPET* which Mr. Gann felt he'd have liked, came about after he'd had several cruises aboard her, during which he realized how easily she slipped through the water. She moves efficiently, with very little wake, readily beating the traditional "1.33" speed-length ratio for displacement-type hulls, by coming up handsomely to 1.52 times the square root of her waterline length (i.e., 8.57 knots at 2375 rpm). Because of this, the Ganns

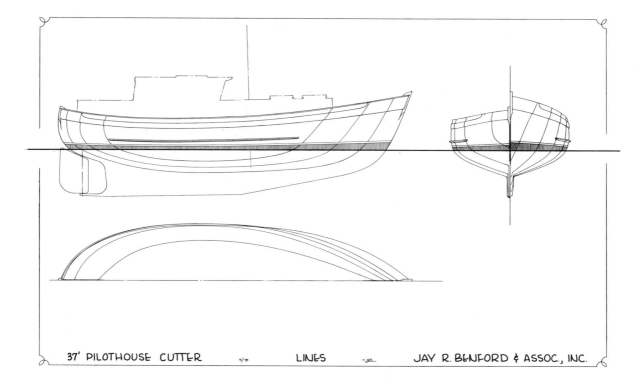

37' PILOTHOUSE CUTTER   LINES   JAY R. BENFORD & ASSOC. INC.

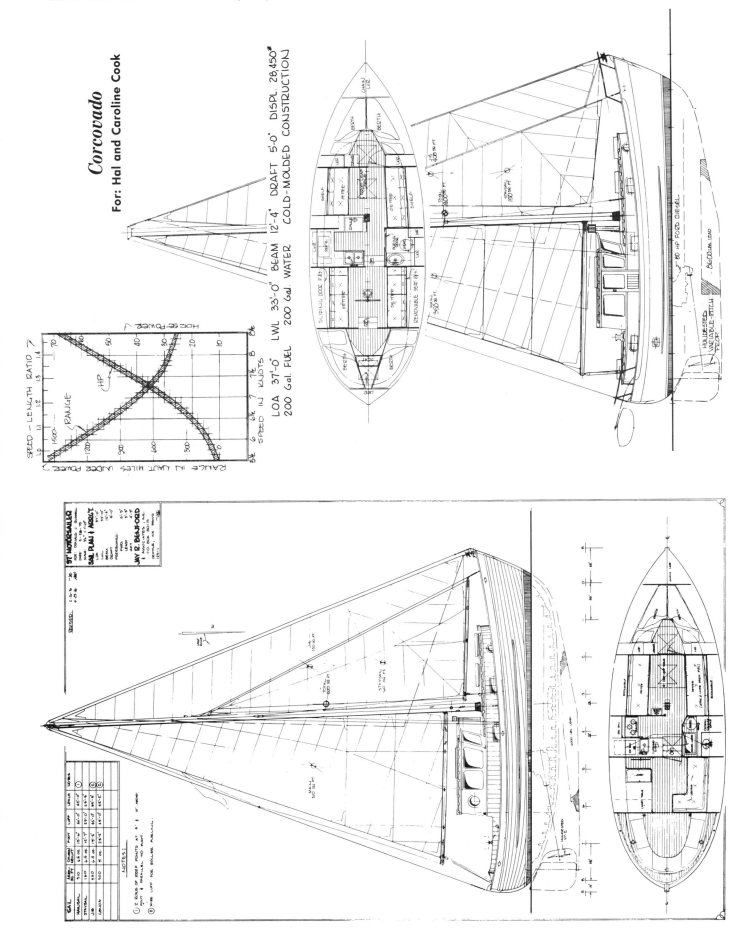

Corcovado

For: Hal and Caroline Cook

LOA 37'-0"   DISPL. 28,450#
LWL 33'-0"   DRAFT 5'-0"
BEAM 12'-4"   WATER 200 Gal.
FUEL 200 Gal.   COLD-MOLDED CONSTRUCTION

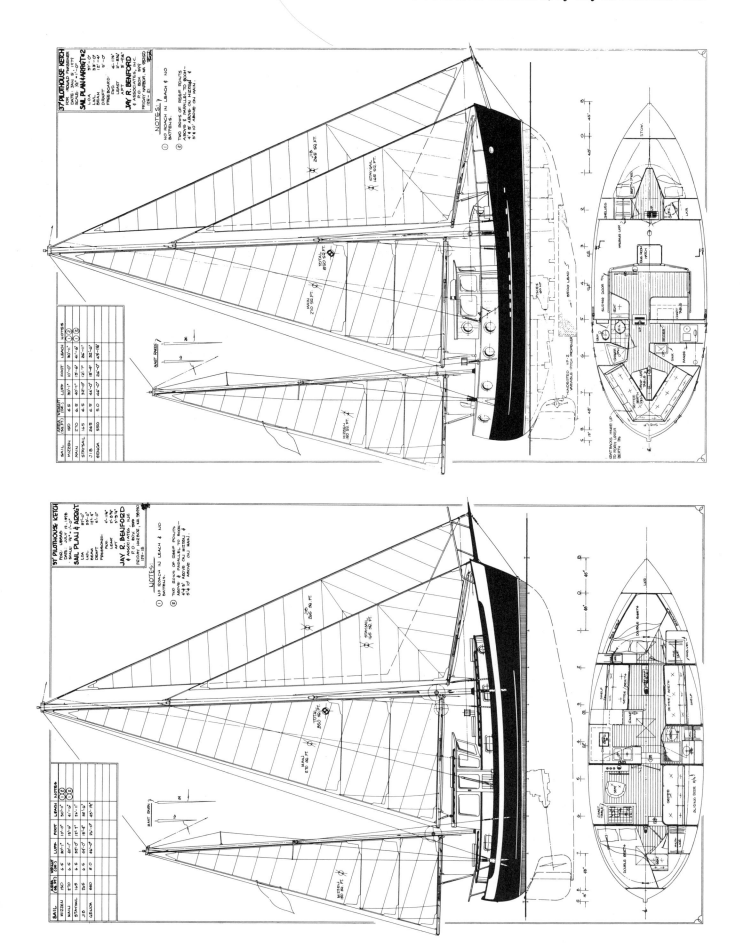

thought the second "improvement" (should they redo her) would be to add a sailing rig to her. As she is now, *STRUMPET* is truly a sailer's powerboat: she's efficient, smooth, responsive, dry, comfortable in a seaway, pleasing to look at, and moves through the water without any fuss.

We were later to have another client, Donald J. Russell, of Tacoma, Washington, who was also enamored with the *STRUMPET* sort of vessel, and who wished to have her endearing qualities combined with a simpler modification of the two "improvements" which the Ganns would have made in *STRUMPET*. To increase her in size, yes — but only to 37 feet, and to add a cutter rig.

The result is an extremely practical and ruggedly handsome vessel. *STRUMPET*'s lines have been refined a bit further to maximize sailing efficiency. The pilothouse has been extended into a trunk cabin to join the foc's'le to the main social areas. An aft cockpit has been added, giving more room for fishing, and/or for tending the lines of the new sailing rig. The rig itself is very straightforward, being all inboard, with all lines led back to the cockpit for ease of tending sail, yet with sail area sufficient to move her to hull speed should the powerboatman find himself ensnared in the taunting clutches of a good breeze. Closer examination of the details of the 37-footer will reveal the great practicality of her design.

The idea of a pilothouse is one which most experienced offshore skippers would not do without. Certainly in the Pacific Northwest, in the Scandinavian fjords, and in most areas with seemingly more than their share of rain, the value of a dry, sheltered steering station cannot be disputed. What most armchair pilots don't think about when they make their fantasy voyages to the South Seas, is that the tropical sun is more violent than most people would care to stay out in, and those who have come to us for a new design, after extensive cruising in the Tropics, have always specified a pilothouse or hard dodger to protect themselves from the harsh sun's rays. The option of having outside steering in the large cockpit is always available with this 37' Motorsailer, however, but one needn't flog himself trying to prove he's a hearty outdoorsman by ignoring the virtues of a pilothouse.

The liveability of this 37' Motorsailer is very fine indeed. The foc's'le, with two V-berths (or optional double) has good space for two hanging lockers port and starboard, aft of the berths. Drawers in the dresser to port, and lockers beneath the settees add to the good stowage capacity here. The area is well lit by the overhead skylight of the forward end of the trunk cabin, with round portlights port and starboard in the trunk cabin as well. This stateroom is capable of being totally closed off by a door in the aft bulkhead, allowing maximum privacy at any time.

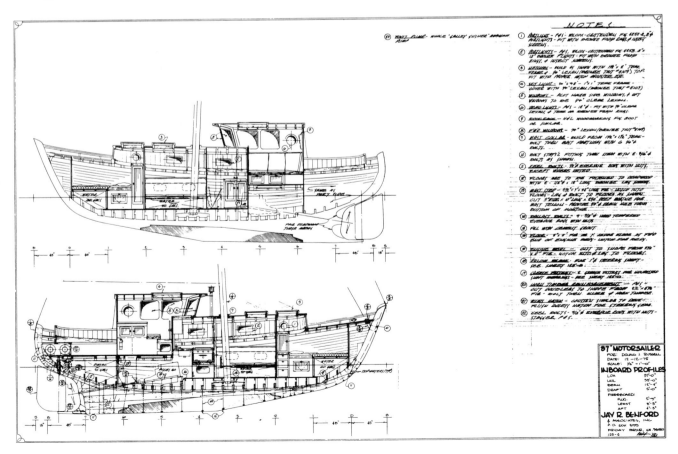

There are two, very comfortable social areas below decks in this little ship. One of these is in the pilothouse itself, with the other being two steps lower: the galley and dining area. The latter, aft of the foc's'le, is home to 6'6'' settees port and starboard, between which is a large folding table which will feed six in comfort. Outboard of the settees are wide bookshelves, with stowage outboard of the settee backs. Upper (Root) berths are comfortably accommodated over the port and starboard settees, as well. There is good pitch in the settee backs, so that the crew can relax in comfort. Again, the area is well lit, with a skylight over the table, and rectangular ports in the trunk cabin sides. A bulkhead fireplace near the port settee adds cheer, particularly in cool evenings.

The galley, aft of the port settee, has a propane range (or optional diesel range) with icebox aft and outboard of it, while sink, with both fresh and salt water brought to it efficiently via a foot-pump pressure water system, is slightly more amidships next to a wide counter. Stowage is good in the galley area, with a bin over the stove, long cupboards over the counter, sink, and icebox, and drawers — locker under the counter and stove. The cook can be entertained while below, for the large rectangular port is thoughtfully located over the stove. To starboard, opposite the galley, is a large, centrally located head, including a sink, shower and

oilskin locker, all being handy to the pilothouse and cockpit area.

The second comfortable social area aboard is the pilothouse, access from below to which is up two steps, and through a door from the main saloon. The purpose of the door in this location, which is built in combination with a hatch, is to keep out unwanted galley or saloon light from the pilot's eyes while the vessel is underway. The L-shaped, starboard settee is at a comfortable height to see out the large pilothouse windows, and roomy enough to keep the skipper company at any time. The helmsman's seat is back-to-back with the very large chart table. Again, stowage space is maximized, both beneath the chart table and outboard and beneath the starboard settee. Visibility is tremendous, maximizing safety in the pilothouse, with windows and ports on all sides. The sun visor and forward slanted windows help to cut the glare and reflections, again adding to safety, and as a result comfort. As is almost a theme throughout the vessel, light in this area is further emphasized by an overhead skylight in the pilothouse, and from here, the skipper can additionally supervise most all aspects of the rig, should sail be set while he is comfortably ensconced inside.

Aft of the pilothouse, there's a large, self-draining cockpit, where, with the aid of self-tailing sheet winches, the crew can readily handle all sails from within the

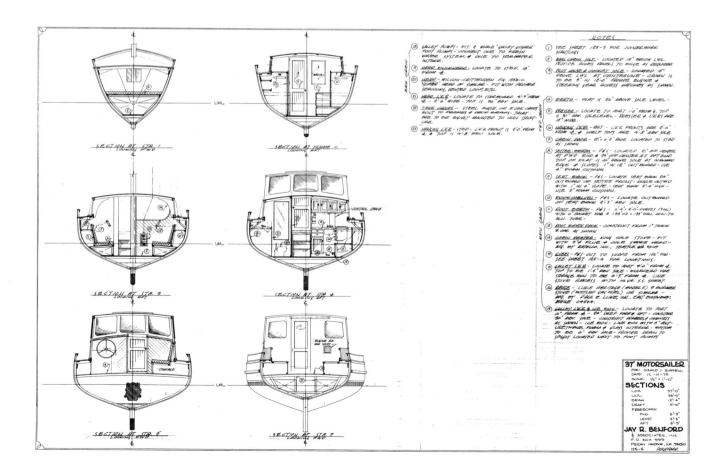

safe recesses of the encompassing cockpit well and high coaming. An emergency tiller can be set up here at a moment's notice, or for those times when the weather is conducive to staying on deck.

The propane gas bottles are safely stowed in a locker in the aft part of the cockpit, and with their own outboard drains, help ensure that propane does not settle in any undesireable location within the ship's recesses. Stowage capacity is once more emphasized in this vessel, with extra space being available in the cockpit lockers.

With all the comforts available below decks, there is still room for extending the comfort above decks, not only in the way of the pleasant cockpit area, but also in the way of clear side decks which extend from the cockpit to the expansive foredeck. Chainplates for the rig are located inboard next to the house, so there's easy access between them and the bulwarks and lifelines on the way forward. The teak overlaid deck adds not only to the beauty, but ensures that good footing is available.

Handling the 37-footer while she's underway is quite a dream. With her jib on roller furling gear, and each of the sheets for the three sails led back to the cockpit, she's quick to get under sail. For the man who prefers powerboating, only one of the sails could be set when the seas get to be a bit rough, and this will slow

down any untoward rolling motion by gently holding her at one angle of heel. She's a very comfortable seaboat, and stiff, as evidenced by the table of design data included here. (Sisters can be built without sails, if preferred).

The 800 square feet of sail area is quite sufficient to give her good speed, yet the center of the sail area is set low enough to keep her quite comfortable with all sails set, up to quite an increase in wind velocity. She has both form and ballast stability, with a GM (metacentric height) of 4.3', and with 6,000 pounds of lead fixed on her keel, and 1,100 pounds of lead inside for trim ballast.

The ruggedly built, 26'' diameter, variable-pitch propeller gives maximum efficiency over a wide range of engine speeds, and permits feathering of the blades under sail, for minimum drag. The 60 h.p. diesel engine housed beneath the pilothouse sole will move her along quietly at a good cruising speed.

Like *STRUMPET*, this 37' Motorsailer is a dry boat. She's responsive to the helm, yet holds her course without complaint. She's fast without seeming to fuss about it, slipping by her cousins who may have a similar outward air, but little of her inward charm. A true sailing vessel, yet at the same time equally comfortable as a pure powerboat, this 37' Motorsailer certainly makes a happy marriage for any who put respon-

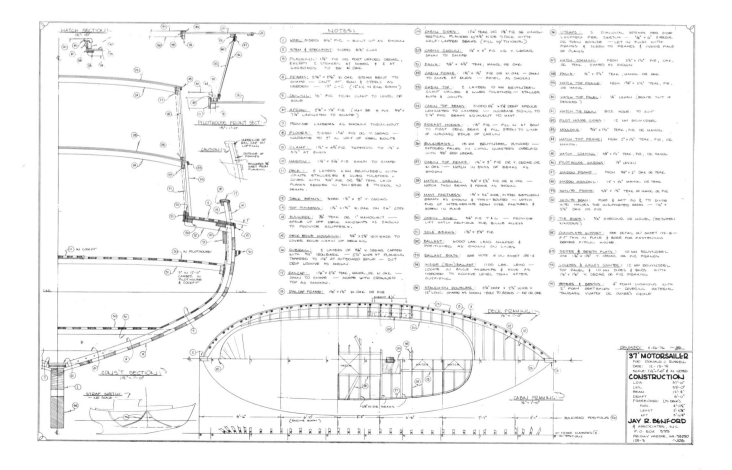

siveness, practicality and handsomeness above any other considerations in their honest choice of a boat. And for those who would like to move gracefully from the rigors of cockpit-type sailboats into the comfort and practicality of a fine pilothouse auxiliary, this 37-footer can't be beat.

Corcovado
For: Hal and Caroline Cook

The first of these handsome pilothouse cutters to be built was CORCOVADO, designed in cold molded wood construction for Hal and Caroline Cook of Orcas Island, Washington. Her pilothouse interior arrangement was altered with the steering pedestal located midships. Bulkheads below were moved slightly to accommodate a larger, U-shaped galley and slightly shortened port settee. An extra stateroom was added aft with a raised trunk cabin. She was superlatively built by John Guzzwell, also of Orcas Island, and launched September 15, 1979. CORCOVADO and SUNRISE were two out of five boats which were awarded judges' prizes at the annual Pt. Townsend Wooden Boat Festival in September, 1981.

Jay R. Benford, Photo

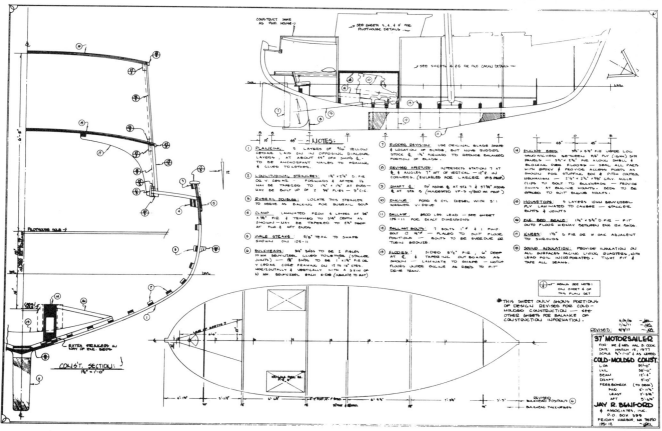

PARTICULARS:

Item	English	Metric
Length over all	37'-0"	11.28m
Length designed waterline	33'-0"	10.06m
Beam	12'-4"	3.76m
Draft	5'-0"	1.52m
Freeboard:		
Forward	5'-9"	1.75m
Least	3'-3"	0.99m
Aft	4'-3"	1.30m
Displacement, cruising trim*	28,450 lbs.	12,905 kg.
Displacement-length ratio	353	
Ballast:		
Fixed on keel	6,000 lbs.	2,722 kg.
Trim	1,100 lbs.	499 kg.
Ballast ratio	25%	
Sail area	800 sq. ft.	74.32 sq. m
Center of bouyancy	52½ % Aft	
Prismatic coefficient	0.619	
Sail area-displacement ratio	13.73	
Center of gravity (G)	3" below LWL	
Metacenter (M)	49" above LWL	
GM	4.3'	
Pounds per inch immersion	1,468	
Moment to trim 1"	2,513 ft.-lbs.	
Righting moment at 1 degree	2,138 ft.-lbs.	
Water capacity	180 gals.	681 liters
Fuel capacity	200 gals.	757 liters

*CAUTION: The displacement quoted here is for the boat in cruising trim. That is, with the fuel and water tanks filled, the crew on board, as well as the crews' gear and stores in the lockers. This should not be confused with the "shipping weight" often quoted as "displacement" by some manufacturers. This should be taken into account when comparing figures and ratios between this and other designs.

During a trip to Alaska and back in the summer of 1980, Hal had this to say:

"The design you did on CORCOVADO pleases us very much. We have used the auto pilot a great deal. It keeps us on a very straight course. . . . We cruise at 7 knots, 1500 rpm. We have sailed with jib, staysail and main and have hit as high as 8½ knots. I feather the prop and can pick up another knot or two if we are moving in a 20 to 25 mph wind. . . . With all gear and supplies on board our waterline is right on as computed by you. Love the self tailing two speed winches. The Hood gear is great too."

Later on, an exhaust pyrometer was added, and we had a chance to check speed and engine loading with varying pitch on the prop. We found that we could get nominal hull speed (1.33) of 7.75 to 8 knots with 1150 to 1200 rpm and not quite ¾ load on the engine.

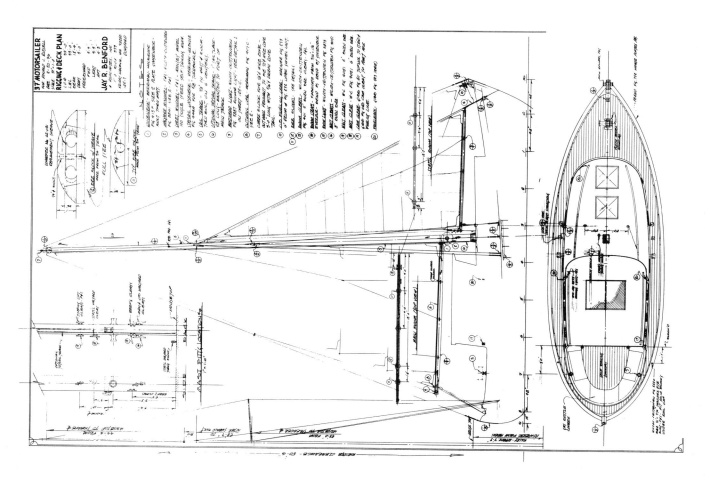

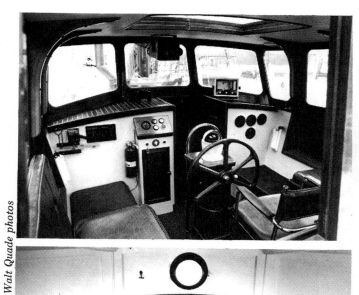

CORCOVADO carries a Benford designed 8' Portland Yawlboat, built by John and James Guzzwell.

Walt Quade photos

Jay R. Benford, Photo

Chapter
18
K'AN

40' Pilothouse Sloop
For: Marshall & Cobanli
Design Number 147
1977

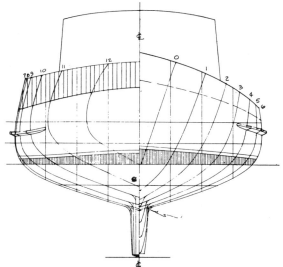

We were pleased to attend the launching of K'AN at noon on December 29th, 1981, at Vancouver, B.C. The boat was launched with the accompaniment of a band, Haida Indian songs, and commentary by the owner. The name is the Haida word for dolphin, and the brief runs she made under power after the launching indicate the name is well chosen. She has a very clean wake. The work was almost completed on her, needing only a little bit of interior detailing and the rigging. Some of those attending did not realize she was a one-off, thinking that the fine finish on her hull meant she'd come out of a mold. The shipwright who completed her intends to build sisterships to order, and quoted attractive prices. (F.M.)

The first one of these 40' Pilothouse Sloops, K'AN, built of C-Flex fiberglass, was launched in Vancouver, B.C., for Don Marshall. The second, strip-planked in wood, is being built by Brian Collett in Cairns, Australia. Plans for other sisterships have gone to such varying locales as Hawaii, Portugal and Maine.

The basic design is an evolutionary development from STRUMPET, the 35' trawler yacht we designed for Ernest K. Gann in 1970. The interest in STRUMPET led to the commission for the motorsailer version of her in 1972. This was then the basis for a 37 footer in 1975 for some other clients. The 37 footer has been quite popular, and John Guzzwell built the first one in his shop on Orcas Island.

When we undertook the design of this 40 footer in 1977, we had first gone over the 37 footer with the clients and determined that it wasn't quite big enough for what they wanted. Thus, we expanded the concept to create this vessel.

Unlike the typical wineglass sectioned long keel yachts, this hull has a distinct keel below the hull. This can be seen on the Arrg't. & Interior sheet of the plans, and on the body plan. The keel form is one we have used with great success on prior designs. It is essentially an elongated NACA foil section, fitted to the hull. The last one we did like this would easily hold 30 to 35 degrees to apparent wind and tack through 80 to 90

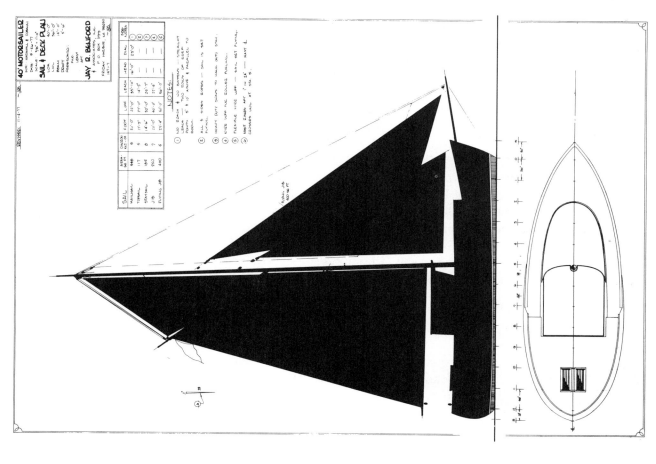

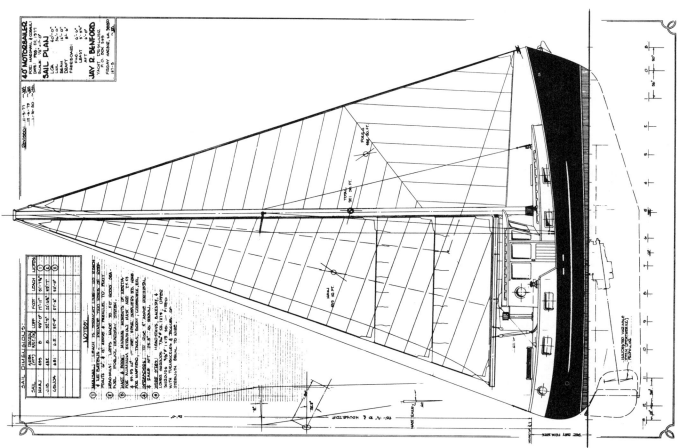

degrees tack to tack.

The propulsion system uses a Gardner 4LW diesel coupled to a Hundested variable pitch propeller. With a conventional reverse and reduction gear, we use the approximately 90 degrees of blade rotation to go from full neutral to full feathered. Using gauges on the engine, we are able to tell when the engine is loaded to full power at any given rpm, and adjust the pitch to suit. This gives excellent economy of operation, as well as minimizing the drag of the prop under sail. The owner of CORCOVADO, the first 37 that John Guzzwell built, emphatically states that this prop system is the key to the great success of his boat. It gives the versatility to be an excellent sailer as well as having a prop big enough to power efficiently.

The stemhead sloop (knockabout) rig was designed to be both very simple to build and to sail. The shrouds come down inboard for a narrow sheeting angle on the headsails. Rather than add knees to take the chainplates, the spreaders are angled a bit aft, and this puts the upper and lower shroud onto the heavy bulkhead at the forward end of the engine room. This, and the foc'sle bulkhead where the inner headstay lands, are locally reinforced to take the loads from the chainplates.

There is an optional gaff sloop rig, with bowsprit and topsail. This is shown in silhouette on sheet 147-7.

On deck, there are bulwarks from alongside the pilothouse to the bow. They rise from 9 inches amidships to 18 inches in height at the bow. All the sailhandling lines are lead to within one step of the pilothouse doors. This makes it handy for shorthanded sailing, as well as for keeping the crew from getting too far removed from the comfort of the pilothouse. Don Marshall commented that he'd had a delightful winter's day sail by wearing just his T-shirt. The cozy warmth of the pilothouse from where he could dart for a moment's sailtrim, as the very easy handling ability of the boat enhanced the use of her in what others might have deemed harsh sailing weather. For those who would like to enjoy their cruising grounds when they're less crowded, this would be an excellent way to do it.

The accommodations are fairly self explanatory. The seatbacks on the aft settees could be hinged to make upper and lower berths port and starboard in the aft cabin, if someone really wanted that many people along on a cruise. There is also plenty of room in the aft cabin to modify the layout a bit and add a second head.

In addition to the doors giving access port and starboard of the engine, there is a section of the pilothouse sole that can be unbolted for major work on the engine. However, with that Gardner diesel, it is unlikely this will be required for quite some time.

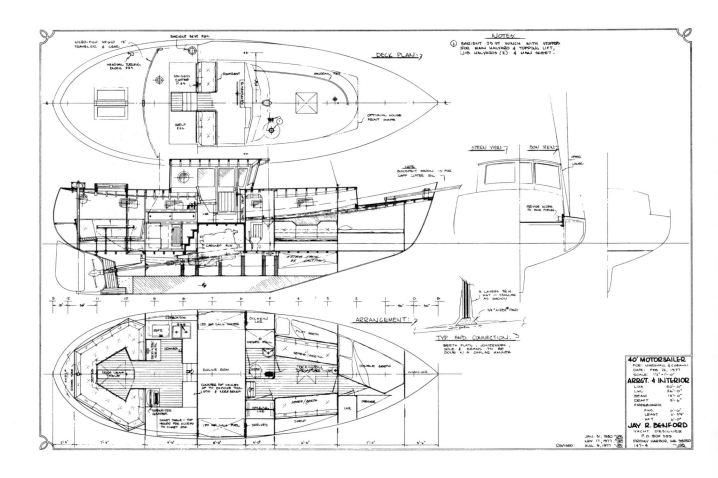

PARTICULARS:

Item	English	Metric
Length over all	40'-0"	12.19m
Length designed waterline	36'-0"	10.97m
Beam	14'-0"	4.27m
Draft	5'-6"	1.68m
Displacement, cruising trim*	30,795 lbs.	13,968 kg.
Ballast	7,700 lbs.	3,493 kg.
Displacement-length ratio	295	
Prismatic coefficient	.56	
Pounds per inch immersion	1,658	
Sail area	921 sq. ft.	85.56 sq. m
Sail area-displacement ratio	15.0	
Entrance half-angle	25 degrees	
Headroom:		
Forward cabin	6'-3" to 6'-6"	1.91 to 1.98m
Pilothouse	6'-6"	1.98m
Aft (Great) cabin	6'-2½"	1.89m
Wetted surface	482 sq. ft.	44.77 sq. m
Sail area-wetted surface ratio	1.91	
GM	4.14'	1.26 m
Righting arm at 30 degrees	1.51'	0.46 m
Water tankage (imperial)	205 gals.	931 liters
Fuel tankage (imperial)	120 gals.	545 liters

*CAUTION: The displacement quoted here is for the boat in cruising trim. That is, with the fuel and water tanks filled, the crew on board, as well as the crews' gear and stores in the lockers. This should not be confused with the "shipping weight" often quoted as "displacement" by some manufacturers. This should be taken into account when comparing figures and ratios between this and other designs.

K'AN photo courtesy Don Marshall

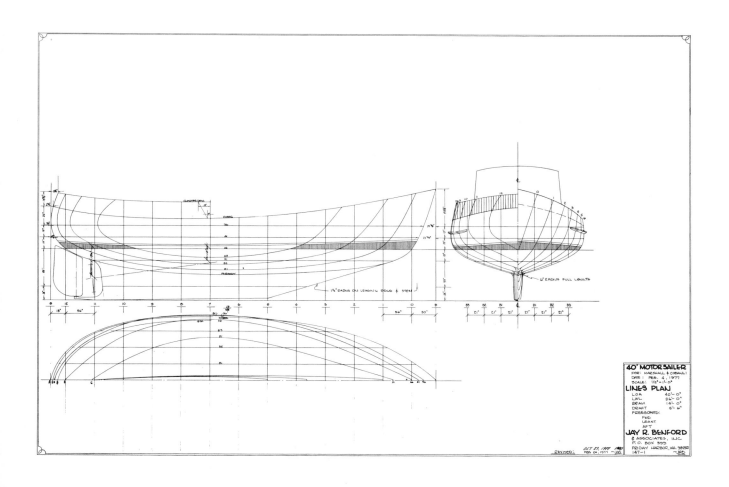

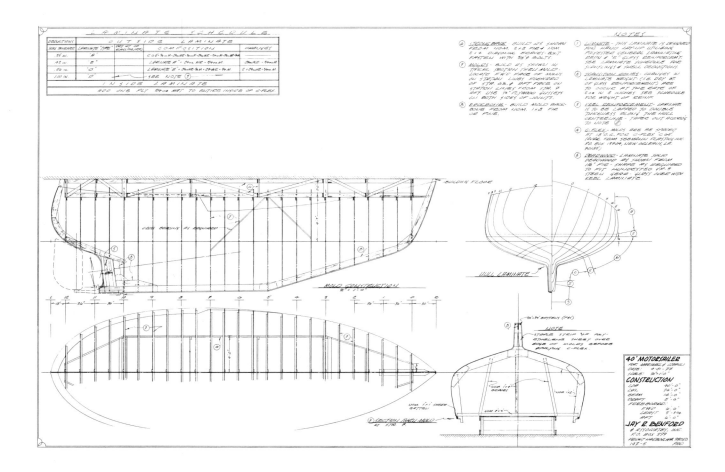

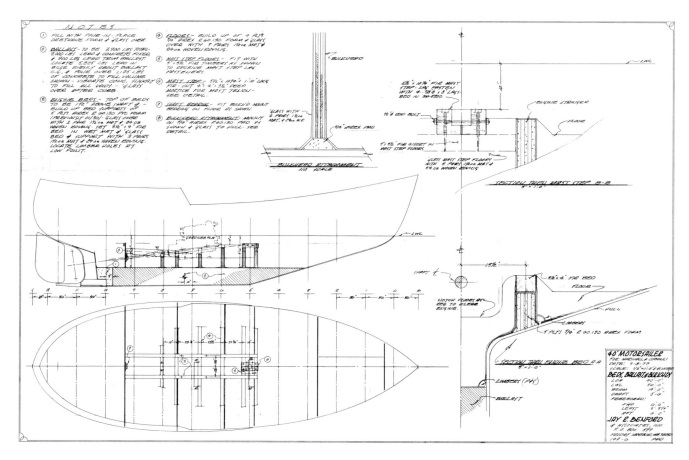

Chapter
19

Orient Express

39' Cutter
Design Number 167
1978

Several years ago we were commissioned to do some preliminary design work on a 39' cutter. The client was a Taiwanese yard that built heavy displacement cruising yachts. They wanted to branch out and offer something different under their own name instead of just building to orders for their existing boats.

We produced a series of profile/sail plan studies ranging from the very racy (167-3B) through the racer-cruiser type (167-3) to a classic appearing fantail sterned cutter (167-3C) with a modern underbody. I liked the latter concept so well that I did up the lines plan for it, even though the client became so busy he was unable

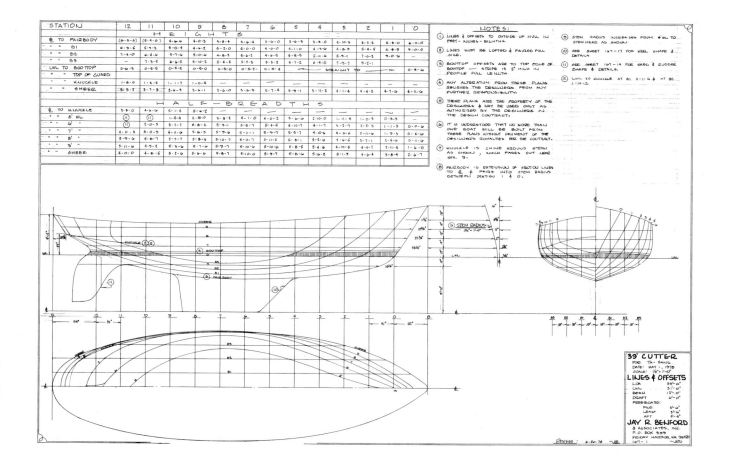

to pursue the project any further. The resulting lines have great appeal to me, and I'm very pleased with the way they turned out.

The accommodation plan would work very nicely for having two couples on board, with a spacious private double berth stateroom at each end of the boat. The settee berths in the main saloon make a nice social area as well as a place for guests or for use as seaberths. The galley, head, and chart table are all close to the companionway. Thus, the traffic from the cockpit will not have to go far forward, and the saloon can be kept drier.

There is a generous lazarette and sail bin in the stern. Under the cockpit and starboard cockpit seat is the engine room, with sitting headroom and a workbench. Engine room access is by hinging up the companionway ladder and opening the door behind the ladder.

The cutter rig has reasonably sized sails and gives a variety of options in shortening down. The genoa and a whisker pole would be the basic additions for a simple cruising outfit. The forepeak bulkhead is sloped to pick up the staysail stay loads, keeping the deck from being lifted there, as well as maximizing the room in the forward stateroom.

The design was done with the thought that she would be built in fiberglass. She could be done as a one-off in Airex, C-Flex, or cold-molded, and I would be pleased to work with anyone interested in seeing this lovely vessel completed.

Particulars

Item	English	Metric
Length overall	39'-0"	11.89m
Length designed waterline	31'-0"	9.45m
Beam	12'-0"	3.66m
Draft	6'-0"	1.83m
Freeboard:		
Forward	5'-6"	1.68m
Least	3'-6"	1.07m
Aft	4'-4"	1.32m
Displacement, cruising trim*	18,750 lbs.	8,505kg.
Ballast	6,500 lbs.	2,948kg.
Ballast ratio	35%	
Displacement-length ratio	281	
Sail area	767 sq. ft.	71.26 sq. m
Sail area-displacement ratio	17.39	
Entrance half-angle	22½ °	
Prismatic coefficient	0.53	

*CAUTION: The displacement quoted here is for the boat in cruising trim. That is, with the fuel and water tanks filled, the crew on board, as well as the crews' gear and stores in the lockers. This should not be confused with the "shipping weight" often quoted as "displacement" by some manufacturers. This should be taken into account when comparing figures and ratios between this and other designs.

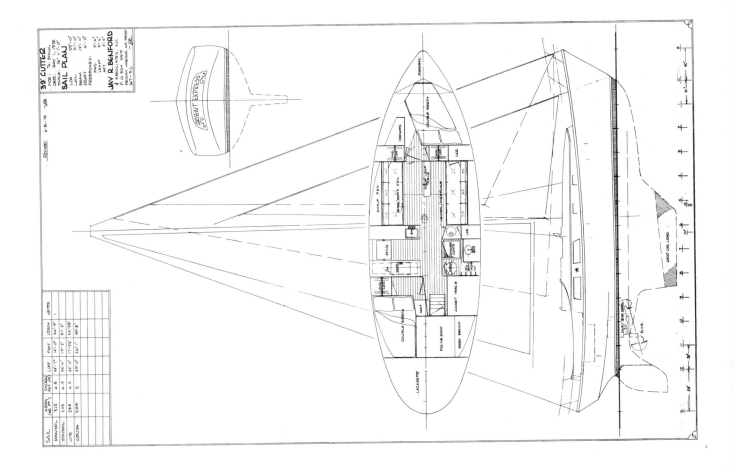

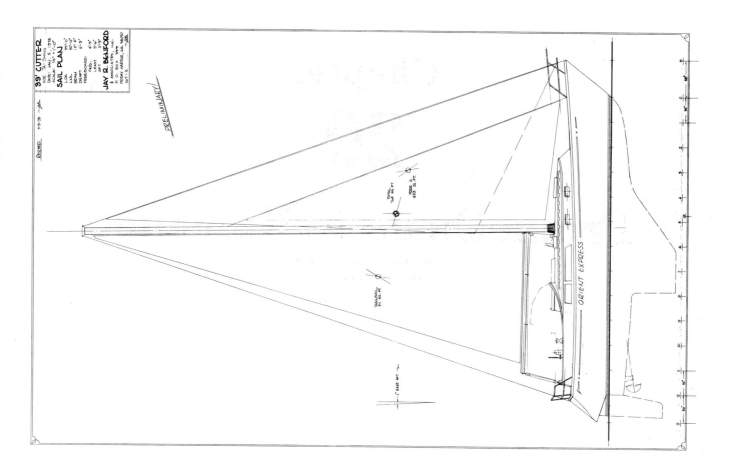

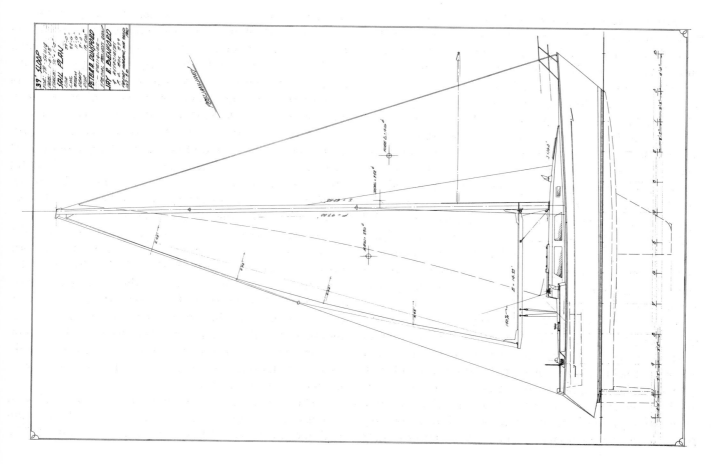

Chapter
20

Prometheus & Ransome

39' Double-ended Cutter
Design Number 159
1977

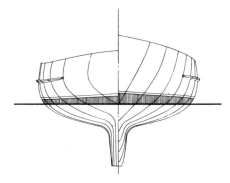

The *Prometheus* design is the result of a commission from David Lowry for a modern offshore cruising boat that would be a fast passagemaker and comfortable home afloat. From all the reports' we get about her as well as our own experiences cruising her, she fulfills these requirements handsomely. She is fast, stiff, weatherly, and comfortable to be aboard.

The hull form is an evolutionary development of a series I have been developing since apprenticing with Atkin & Company in 1963 and '64. At Atkin's, I was involved in the design of a variety of double enders. The Atkins had been developing these designs for half a century, and their seaworthiness and sailing ability had earned them world reknown. My current designs are done with this background, but with each being an effort to improve on what has gone before and also to make best use of the modern materials and equipment available to us today.

With a displacement-length ratio of 264, she is light enough to perform well in all conditions. Thanks to the lightness and stiffness of the Airex core in the laminate, the boat is well insulated and sound deadened, as well as being able to carry the rig well set up for good windward performance. Note also that the displacement quoted is with the tanks full and the crew and average stores aboard — not the shipping weight

frequently quoted by some builders as "displacement".

The draft of five feet was chosen to provide the best balance between good lateral plane for windward ability and reasonable keel depth for getting into shallower anchorages. Of this five feet, only two feet is hull depth (as can be seen from the body plan sections). The balance is all keel, designed in the form of a long NACA foil section. The forefoot is well cutaway, providing good maneuverability, yet the length of keel aft provides for very good tracking and course holding ability. A bonus provided by this design is the ability to place the center of gravity of the ballast as low or lower than most finkeelers of this size.

In keeping with our practice, we've designed the *Prometheus* with generous rudder area, to provide good control in heavy weather. This also provides response at low speeds with slight rudder angles, minimizing the braking effect common to small rudders. Under sail, she steers very easily and can be balanced to sail herself to weather with the helm free. Under power, the propeller torque on the rudder only takes a light touch to balance out and she is easy to maneuver when docking.

The *Prometheus* is easily driven to hull speed with the standard engine. At hull speed, the wake is minimal and indicative of the modest power required. The engine installation is such that the engine is quickly and readily accessible for inspection and maintenance.

The cutter rig was chosen to provide for a variety of sail combinations. With 848 square feet in the three working sails, she has a sail area-displacement ratio of 16.64. Thus, she will only need a genoa for the real light air work. With a GM of 4 feet, she has a Dellenbaugh Angle of 13.4 degrees and a wind pressure coefficient of 1.46. All these number indicate she is quite stiff, and sailing aboard her confirms this nicely. She carries sail well and we found she readily tacked through 80 degrees, tack to tack, or 40 degrees to the true wind.

The accommodations provide comfortable double berth staterooms forward and aft, with settee berths in the main cabin for occasional overflow. At sea, a divider would be fitted to the aft double to provide two sea berths in addition to the settees in the saloon. There is generous drawer and locker storage throughout. In fact, one of the large drawers in the aft cabin worked quite nicely for a crib for our new crew member while we were aboard. The lazarette is huge for a 39-footer: walk-in space for work bench, stowing bicycles and all manner of gear. We've joked about it being an on-board basement, when seven of us had the delight of a ten-day cruise aboard *Alexis,* a sistership to *Prometheus* in Glacier Bay, Alaska.

All in all, I've been very pleased with the results of the design — both in how well she performs and also

the attention to detail on the part of the builders in putting together a handsome yacht we can all be proud of and which is certainly a good investment.

Bob Vollmer, Photo

The shelf-top locker is handy in the fo-c'sle.

The PROMETHEUS galley is roomy, well lit, sociable and workable with many stowage lockers, double sinks, garbage locker, and plentiful counter space, all open to the main saloon.

Reprinted from PACIFIC SKIPPER, January, 1980, copyright 1980, Petersen Publishing Co.

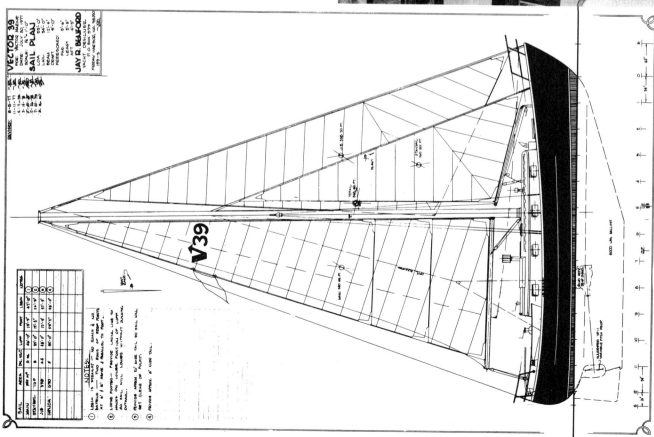

PARTICULARS:

Item	English	Metric
Length over all	39'-0"	11.89m
Length designed waterline	34'-0"	10.36m
Beam	12'-4"	3.76m
Draft.........................	5'-0"	1.52m
Freeboard:		
Forward................	5'-6"	1.68m
Least	3'-3"	0.99m
Aft	4'-3"	1.30m
Displacement, cruising trim* ...	23,275 lbs.	10,557 kg.
Ballast	8,000 lbs.	3,629 kg.
Ballast ratio	34%	
Displacement-length ratio	264	
Sail area	848 sq. ft.	78.78 sq. m
Sail area-displacement ratio	16.64	
Wetted surface................	409 sq. ft.	38.00 sq. m
Sail area-wetted surface ratio...	2.07	
Entrance half-angle	24¼°	
Prismatic coefficient	0.557	
Pounds per inch immersion	1,367	
Water tankage	200 gals.	757 liters
Fuel tankage.................	100 gals.	378 liters
Headroom	6'-8"	2.03m
Moment to trim 1"	2,278 ft-lbs.	

*CAUTION: The displacement quoted here is for the boat in cruising trim. That is, with the fuel and water tanks filled, the crew on board, as well as the crews' gear and stores in the lockers. This should not be confused with the "shipping weight" often quoted as "displacement" by some manufacturers. This should be taken into account when comparing figures and ratios between this and other designs.

PROMETHEUS exceeded all our expectations in her performance. She proved to be a true performance cruiser; fast, stiff, and weatherly.

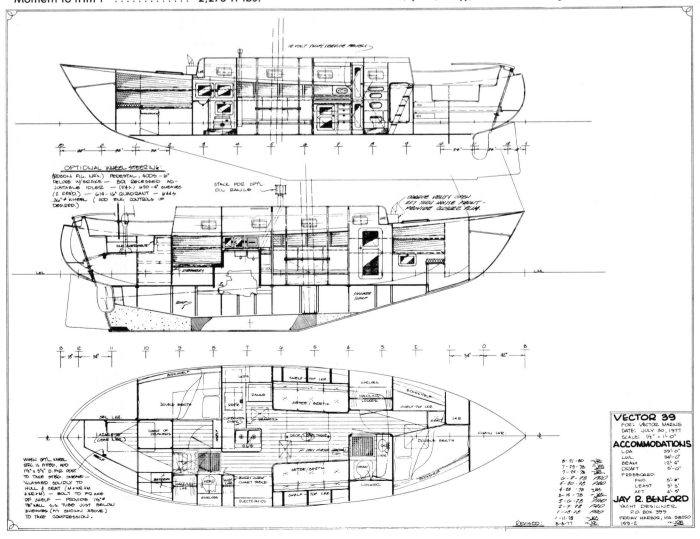

Quotes about Vector Marine boats

Vector Marine, who built *Prometheus* and several sisterships, declared: "3 bedrooms, 2 baths, fireplace, gourmet kitchen, spectacular water view. When you want all that, as well as excellent sea-going characteristics, you've got to perform some real magic to make it work.

Years of research and sailing experience, and the magic of talented designers and craftsmen have produced her. A true live-aboard with every feature this designation implies. Privacy spaces, walk-in storage, and convenient traffic patterns are integral to her design — and seldom found on a vessel this size.

It works. Because design is dictated by function. And every cubic foot is fully utilized.

Prometheus' accommodations include very private fore and aft double staterooms with hanging lockers and chests of drawers. The complete head, with hot pressure water, shower, and linen hamper is large, yet comfortable underway. And her main saloon, with fireplace, settee berths, and folding table for six makes the exchange of sea stories, no matter how wild, a most hospitable experience.

Her galley, open to the saloon and still convenient to the cockpit, is as efficient at sea as it is dockside. With a deep sink, refrigeration area, daylite hatch over the stove, ample storage, even a garbage bin.

Also handy to the helmsman is the chart table, optional at-sea head, and wet locker. A drain pan beneath the cabin sole at the foot of the companionway ladder permits a drenched navigator to come below and use the nav-station without soaking the entire cabin.

She has a large, watertight space for ship stores (nine feet deep, and over four feet high!) just aft of the main companionway. A four by six foot sail locker and lazarette, accessible from topside round out the available storage. Anchor and anchor windlass with anchor rode storage has been provided on the foredeck. One hundred gallons of fuel and two hundred gallons of water give sufficient range for vessel and crew to make long passages without concern."

Jay R. Benford, Photos

"Hey, Mom, RANSOME has REALLY deep sinks in the galley, and the drawers in the aft stateroom are so big I've got a great bed in one!"

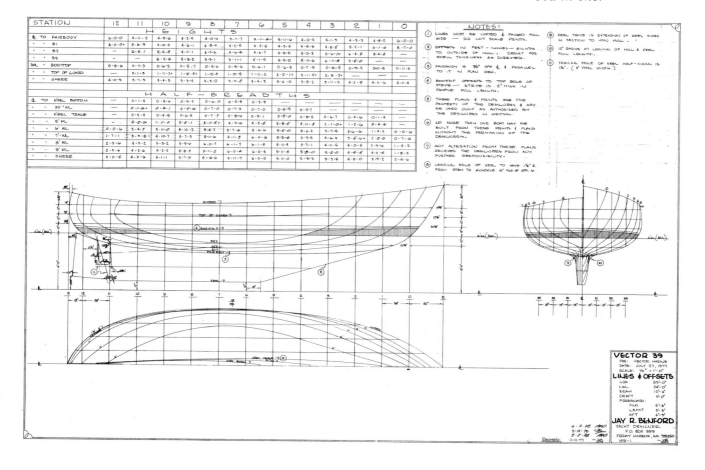

Robert Weiss, in writing for PACIFIC SKIP-PER magazine in January of 1980, described his cruise aboard Prometheus thusly:

"With her engine shut down the pure and confident sailing capabilities of the Prometheus were immediately apparent — a most well-balanced vessel. Her helm was easily managed with an agile response that was not anticipated for a full-keel vessel. This agility is due to her cutaway forefoot and moderate displacement. The bow rose and dipped, splitting a large on-coming wave. The spray went neatly in opposite directions, leaving the deck aft of the mast completely dry. . . .

"I asked Dave why he had chosen this design by Jay Benford. 'It boils down to a lot of frustrations that many sailors go through,' he said. 'I was unable to find what I wanted on the market. The boat I was really going to need just didn't seem to exist for the dollar I was willing to pay. So, I decided to build a custom one-off. I wanted a world class live-aboard cruiser. I do not believe in racer/cruisers, but I do believe that a cruising boat can perform well. I think we have developed this in the Prometheus and all of our experience to date has proven it.

'When I first came to Seattle, I had a pretty fixed idea in mind. She had to be a world class cruising yacht for four with comfortable live-aboard conditions for two. I went to Jay as a result of prior readings that showed his experience in designing cruising sailboats. I was impressed with his use of interior space.'. . .

"The Prometheus proved her builder's claim as she sailed well to half of the true wind speed. When coming about, you could easily make a complete tack within 75°. Her directional stability on a run was admirable with minimal weather helm. . . .

"This expansive interior would be impressive alone, but I would be remiss if I didn't comment on the execution of the superb wood joinery and overall quality of the finish and fabrics. . . .

"The Prometheus would seem to be as the builder claims: 'A world class cruising yacht.' I for one would like to sail a little more of this world aboard her broad and secure decks."

Anne Fleck, an ocean sailor and interior decorator who chose the interior coloring and made the upholstery on several of these cutters, exclaimed:
"I've seen all the top of the line boats. I can't think of a better design, and I don't think there's better quality. The division of space is so nice. They've really thought about how four or six people would live and work and function on this boat. And there's loads of storage. I love it — I'd enjoy owning one myself."

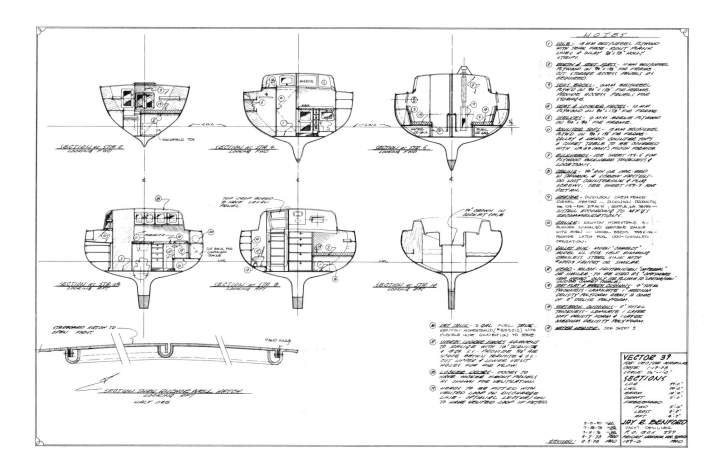

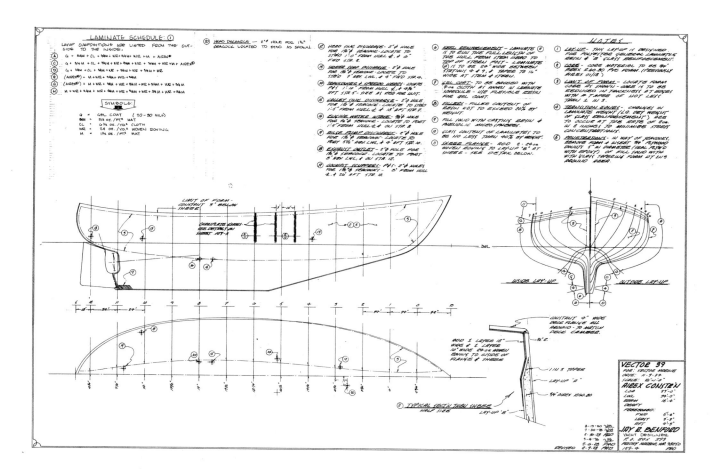

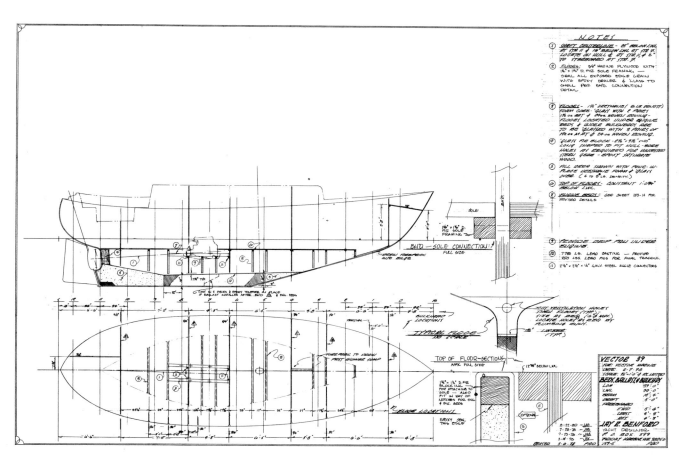

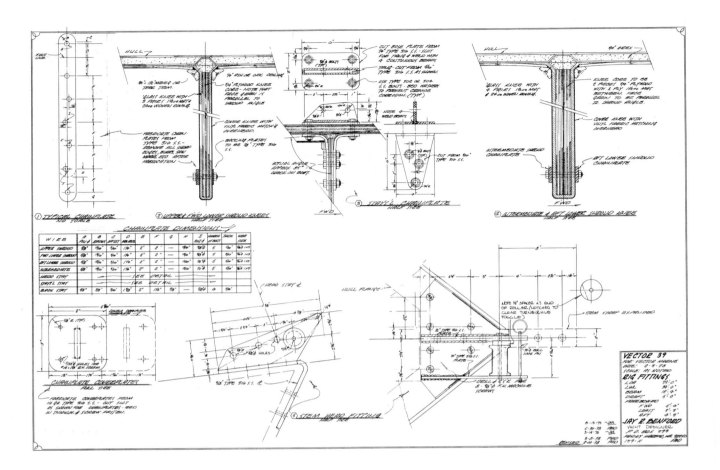

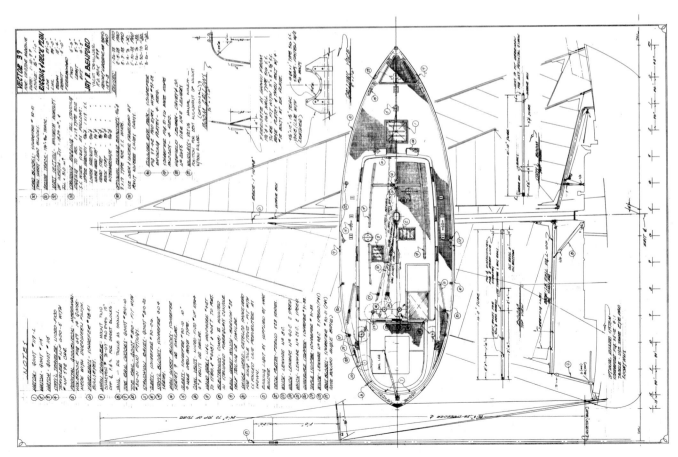

"Houses are but badly built boats so firmly aground that you cannot think of moving them. They are definitely inferior things, belonging to the vegetable not the animal world, rooted and stationary, incapable of gay transition. I admit, doubtfully, as exceptions, snail-shells and caravans. The desire to build a house is the tired wish of a man content thenceforward with a single anchorage. The desire to build a boat is the desire of youth, unwilling yet to accept the idea of a final resting-place.

It is for that reason, perhaps, that, when it comes, the desire to build a boat is one of those that cannot be resisted. It begins as a little cloud on a serene horizon. It ends by covering the whole sky, so that you can think of nothing else. You must build to regain your freedom. And always you comfort yourself with the thought that yours will be the perfect boat, the boat that you may search the harbours of the world for and not find."

Arthur Ransome
'Racundra's' First Cruise, 1923

Bob Vollmer, Photos

40 Foot Version:

Like most of our designs for production boats, the 39 originally had a clause in the contract saying the builders had exclusive rights to build the boat, as long as they build a certain number per year and paid us the royalties for them. Since this clause was still in effect in 1977 when we were approached by Rudy Parenteau about building one in wood, I suggested that we slightly modify and stretch the boat for his clients.

The result is this 40 foot double ended cutter design. The accommodations are the same as in the 39, with the extra foot of length added in the galley and chart table area. The extra length also made for slightly finer lines, particularly in the bow. We reduced the entrance half-angle from 24¼° to 22°. This gives her a little benefit in driving through a short, steep chop. The 39's did so well at this, that this is a minor point at best.

I also gave the stem a little bit different shape in profile, and I found the end result quite pleasing.

The first boat, built for Bob and Nancy Willard, headed south down the coast a couple of years ago. From the cruisers' grapevine, we hear they've gotten well afield in their cruising adventures.

The original version of this 40 footer had a concrete and scrap metal ballast keel, with a draft of 5'-6''. Later clients liked the idea of less draft, and I felt that the 39 had performed so well that I had no reluctance to put the lead keel and 5'-0'' draft on her.

The builders of the 39 made one serious error in getting their business started. They got a loan guarantee from the Small Business Association (the SBA). As boatbuilders often do, they got in over their heads financially for a time. At this point, the SBA moved in and asserted claim to the tooling (molds) and everything else they could find. A few months later, the builders had gotten their act back together, and made several tries to reach an agreement with the SBA. In doing this, they found that the average settlement rate on the loan defaults on SBA loans is 18% — or 18 cents on the dollar. By contrast, these builders were offering 100% repayment over a period of years at an interest rate that seemed fair.

Over a period of months, they had a number of conferences with the SBA. At each of these, they would reach a verbal agreement as to how to proceed to be able to put the boat back in production. Then the builders would write up the verbal agreement and ask the SBA to sign it. Every time they would reach a stone wall at signature time. I told them it was the classic bureaucrat's defense: bureaucrats lose their jobs by making mistakes. The only way they can avoid making mistakes is by doing nothing. This is exactly what they were doing. They were spending the builders' time and emotional energy by letting the builders pursue their dream, but when it came time actually to do something — like signing the agreement — no one in the SBA was willing to take the responsibility for making a decision. After all, if they made the wrong decision, it could be a mark against them and their gathering of points toward retirement. However, if they made no decision, the bureaucracy would not hold it against them. The real world might, but that doesn't count in the bureaucracy.

Vector Marine did a first-rate job of building the tooling, and was constantly being complimented on the quality of their work, both on the tooling and the building of the boats.

Just as this book was in the printer's hands, we received word that the 39' molds were actually sold, so a new negative was made of this page in order to convey the good news. In typical SBA fashion, no one involved with the project was notified in advance as to the actual auction date. By a stroke of good luck, Heritage Boat Works (builders of 20', 22' and 30' boats of our design) heard about the auction, and we were able to see that the molds got into good hands once again. As the design is still timely, and is conservative enough that it will not go out of style, she'll make a good investment not only for the builder but — more importantly — also for the owners. We look forward to seeing more of the 39's slide down the ways once again.

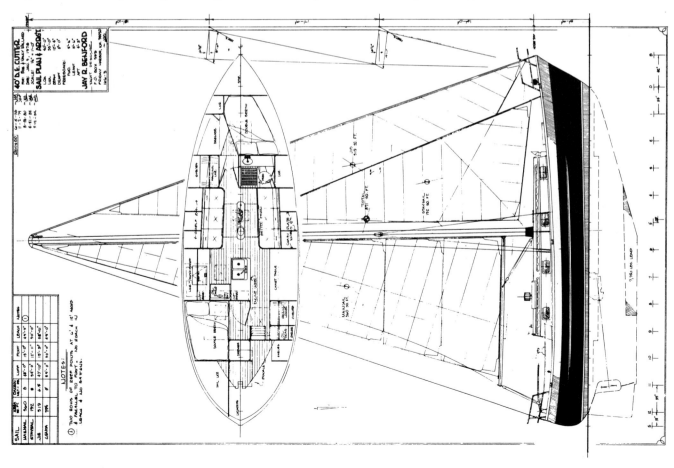

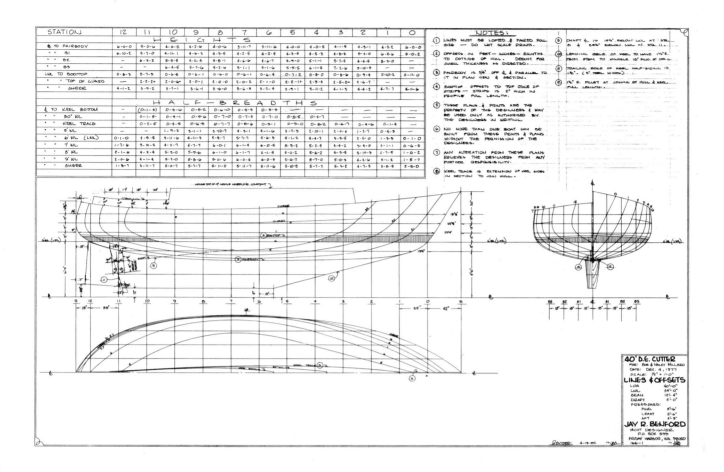

40' D.E. CUTTER
FOR: Bob & Nancy Willard
DATE: Dec. 4, 1977
SCALE: 1½" = 1'-0"

LINES & OFFSETS

LOA — 40'-0"
LWL — 35'-0"
BEAM — 12'-6"
DRAFT — 5'-0"
FREEBOARD:
FWD. — 5'-6"
LEAST — 3'-6"
AFT — 4'-3"

JAY R. BENFORD
YACHT DESIGNER
P.O. BOX 399
FRIDAY HARBOR, WA. 98250
166-1

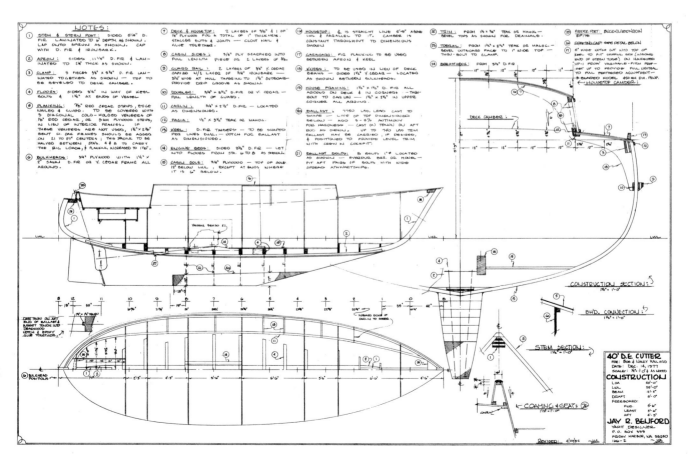

40' D.E. CUTTER
FOR: Bob & Nancy Willard
DATE: Dec. 14, 1977
SCALE: ¾" = 1'-0" (& as noted)

CONSTRUCTION

LOA — 40'-0"
LWL — 35'-0"
BEAM — 12'-6"
DRAFT — 5'-0"
FREEBOARD:
FWD. — 5'-6"
LEAST — 3'-6"
AFT — 4'-3"

JAY R. BENFORD
YACHT DESIGNER
P.O. BOX 399
FRIDAY HARBOR, WA. 98250
166-2

Chapter
21

Quiet Bird

41' Double-ended Cutter
Design Number 156
1977

What happens when a designer who specializes in cruising boats and lives on one of his own custom designs is commissioned to design a production boat that is to be both a cruising home and a fast passagemaker?

The parameters CMS Yachts gave us were to design a fast cruiser, based on our long experience in designing and living aboard practical cruising boats. She was to have a modern appearance outboard, and maximum crew comforts below decks. Separate staterooms were wanted forward and aft, with a spacious saloon amidships.

Quiet Bird, the CMS 41 is the result of that commission. She has a modern cutter rig to keep the sail sizes manageable for a small crew. She has a long fin keel and large skeg and rudder well aft to provide good tracking and control, and both are shaped to proven NACA foil sections. Her beam and powerful hull has good form stability, to help make her fast and weatherly.

The long trunk cabin is kept low in the bow for good visibility forward, yet still provides 6'10" headroom below. The anchor and winch reside in a recessed well at the bow, covered by a hatch when not in use. The cockpit seats are contoured for comfortable lounging. A molded-in fairing is provided for attaching a dodger, for shelter from the rain and sun. Stern dinghy davits are available.

The large chart table with comfortable seat is just to starboard of the companionway ladder, and has a large electronics locker alongside. There is a built-in dustpan below the grate at the base of the companionway ladder to facilitate housekeeping. To port is the enclosed master stateroom, with a large double berth with lockers below and a hanging locker. Aft of the ladder is the enclosed engineroom and shop, providing good engine access for servicing and maintenance, a workbench, and tool lockers. The very roomy lazerette has plenty of room for sail stowage in addition to being an "attic" for liveaboards.

The galley and head are amidships, where the motion will be easy, so the traffic coming off deck will not have to track water through the saloon. An optional gimballed range can be arranged outboard, and a gas bottle locker is available in the stern. The head faces aft, so it will be easy to use on either tack, and the compartment also has a shower. An optional layout has a separate shower stall.

The settees in the saloon are built with angled seats and backs to make lounging a pleasure, particularly with the fireplace at hand. Pilot berths are available as an option.

Ten opening ports, three skylight/hatches, and two dorade vents provide excellent light and ventilation below decks. Numerous lockers and storage compartments can be found throughout, with shelves outboard in the hanging lockers and bookshelves over the berths and settees.

Don Murphy, who owned *Quiet Bird,* number 2 of the CMS 41s, sailed her offshore, in a variety of conditions and experiences. When asked how he would rate her sailing qualities, he replied:

"Oh, fantastic. In my estimation, she was the most seakindly ocean cruising boat that I've ever been on. She was really a fantastic sailing boat. We got caught in about a force 10 off Cape Flattery, ran blindly into it with everything hanging out. We were in it for about twelve hours and never got one drop of water in the boat or in the cockpit. Another boat was behind us and radioed for help. I could barely see them through the mist and seas, but I could see the helicopter trying to assist them. I had to heave-to twice because I was the only one who wasn't sick in our crew of three.''

Later, *Quiet Bird* continued on to San Francisco: "We were off the Oregon coast, heading south. We had the main on and the 140% genoa. The winds were about 15 knots to start with. She was clipping on real nice. The winds picked up and picked up until they were running up to maybe 35 knots, with seas moderate. It was hard to estimate wind speed going downwind, but we had way too much sail up. *Quiet Bird* was going along at 14 knots. We checked it out by siting our distance, so I know it wasn't an erroneous log reading. It sounded like we were going through Niagara Falls, just sounded horrendous. But I knew Jay had designed her to be strong. . . .''

When queried about the CMS 41's tracking abiliy, Don was enthusiastic:

"She tracked very neatly. Fantastic. Good. That's all I can say. She was a great boat. I sold her (for health reasons) and have been kicking myself ever since for selling. She's probably one of the finest boats that I ever sailed.''

Don reported a meeting between *Quiet Bird* and a whale thusly:

"We were in the Sea of Cortez, coming from Porte Vallarte to Cabo San Lucas. We apparently hit the whale, which was below the surface, with our boat keel, and it was like we'd gone aground. The bow went down and the stern up. We'd been under power, and the propeller probably wounded him.

"The whale went out behind us about 75 yards, and turned around and attacked the boat. We could see him coming, just barely below the surface. Blood was sopping out around the head area, where he apparently got hit. He was building up a pretty good speed by the time he hit the boat. He hit about midships, quartering from the stern, and rocked us over about 20 degrees.

"Then he went back out again about the same distance and surfaced, and we got a real good look at him. He was probably about 35 feet long, and weighed as much as the boat. I think he was a sperm or grey whale. We thought he was going to attack again, but he went on his way. And we wasted no time getting going in the other direction.

"When we got to Cabo San Lucas, we had a diver go under the boat. There was no damage except for a little bottom paint that got scratched off.

"One thing that made that boat so tough was the sole grid arrangement that Jay designed into it. You know how most boats twist a bit, and maybe the doors don't fit so well after awhile in the boat. That never happened in this boat; never.''

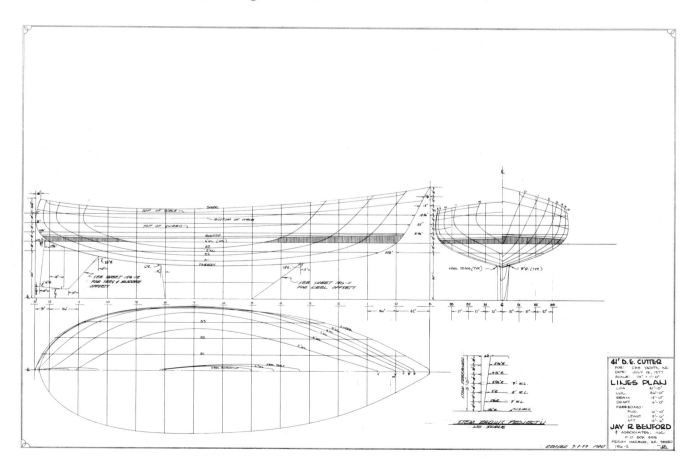

More on QUIET BIRD:

The plans for this 41' D.E. Cutter were drawn up in quite extensive detail, as the vessel was built in Taiwan. There we knew the boatbuilders were not experienced in the ways of the sea or the hows and whys of putting important details together for strength and durability in the marine environment. We therefore attempted to leave very little to the imagination. The results were pleasing to us, especially by the time the third boat came out and the reasoning behind our details was by then very evident. The structural integrity was maintained from the start; the fine detailing and smaller outfitting questions were ironed out after the first boat arrived, and before the third boat was finished.

The Clayton 41 plans were developed using the original cutter version plans as a base, with revisions drawn on the understanding that details not shown on the pilothouse version plans would be done as shown on the cutter version plans.

A number of our designs are done this way. We use the parent design for some of the basic detailing and draw up whatever changes are neccessary for the new version. This creates a new design at a more affordable price for the client, and we're all pleased with the good boat that results.

Howard Cain Photo

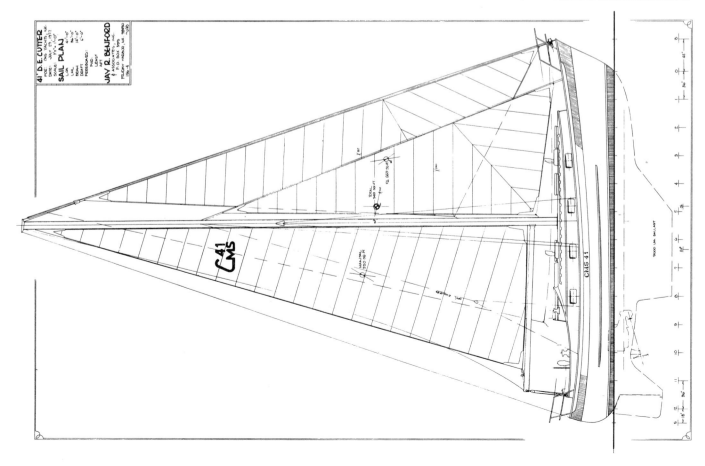

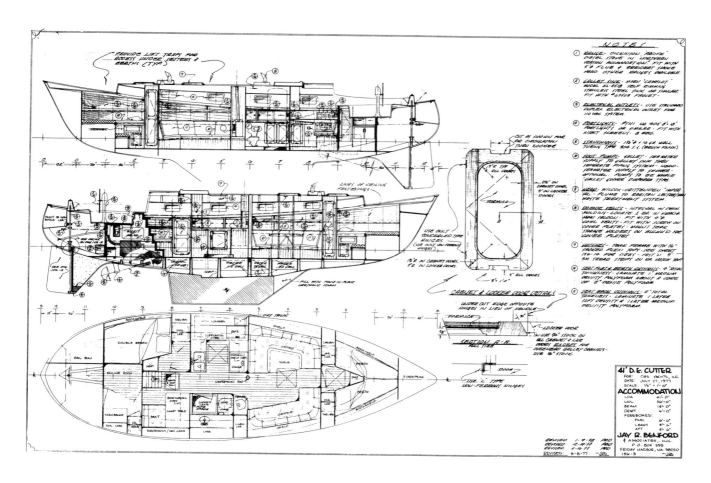

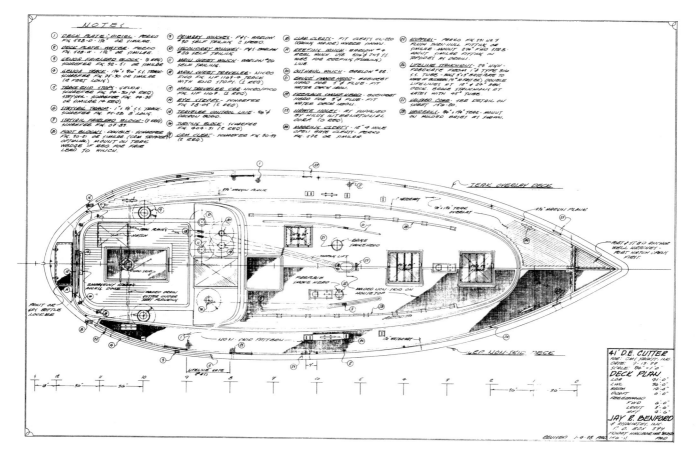

PARTICULARS:

Item	English	Metric
Length over all	41'-0"	12.50m
Length designed waterline	36'-0"	10.97m
Beam	14'-0"	4.27m
Draft	6'-0"	1.83m
Freeboard:		
Forward	6'-0"	1.83m
Least	3'-6"	1.07m
Aft	4'-6"	1.37m
Displacement, cruising trim*	26,000 lbs.	11,793 kg.
Ballast	8,300 lbs.	3,765 kg.
Ballast ratio	32%	
Displacement-length ratio	249	
Sail area	949 sq. ft.	88.16 sq. m
Sail area-displacement ratio	17.30	
Wetted surface	438 sq. ft.	40.69 sq. m
Sail area-wetted surface ratio . . .	2.17	
Entrance half-angle	22¼ degrees	
Prismatic coefficient	0.547	
Pounds per inch immersion	1,552	
GM	4.97'	1.51m
Water tankage	300 gals.	1135 liters
Fuel tankage	100 gals.	378 liters
Headroom	6'-10"	2.08m

*CAUTION: The displacement quoted here is for the boat in cruising trim. That is, with the fuel and water tanks filled, the crew on board, as well as the crews' gear and stores in the lockers. This should not be confused with the "shipping weight" often quoted as "displacement" by some manufacturers. This should be taken into account when comparing figures and ratios between this and other designs.

"In publishing the first edition of "Yacht Architecture" in 1895 I was able to state that the knowledge of the scientific principal on which yacht designing is based had been considerably extended since the publication of my large work entitled "Yacht Designing" in 1876. This can also be said of the period between 1885 and 1897, and no doubt the present generation of yachtsmen and those interested in yachts have a much more exact knowledge of the science of Naval Architecture than their predecessors had, owing to their having studied the numerous works published on the subject.

Yacht building can be better described by engravings than by writing, and the plates and woodcuts which are given will instruct the amateur in all the details of construction according to the practice of the best builders."

Dixon Kemp
Yacht Architecture, 1897

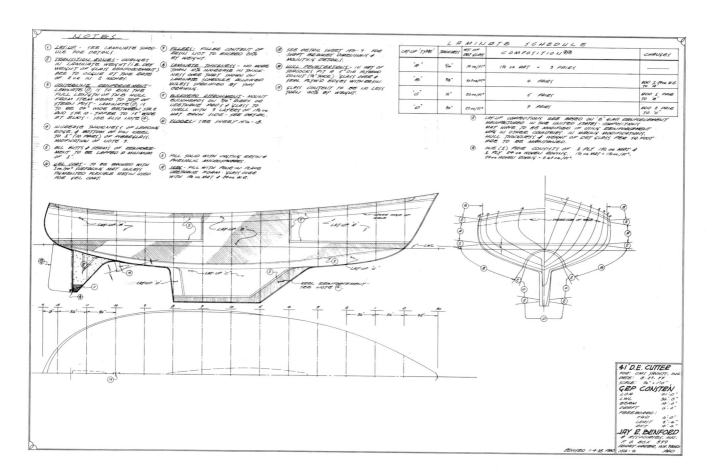

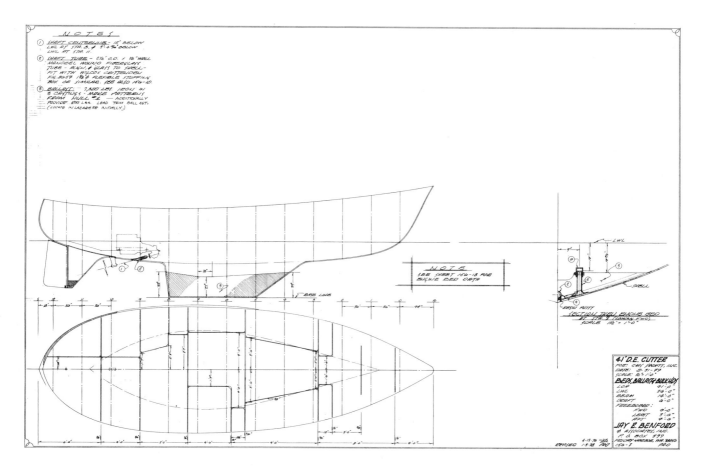

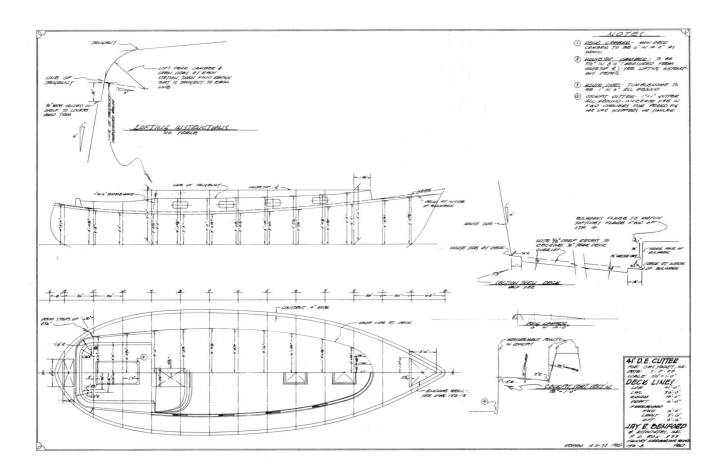

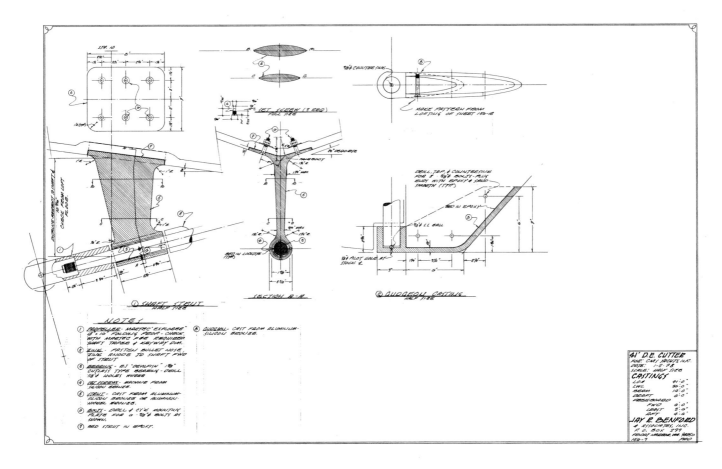

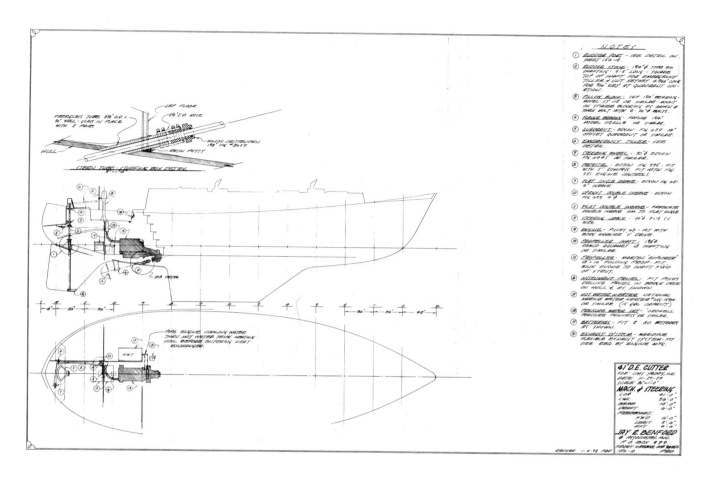

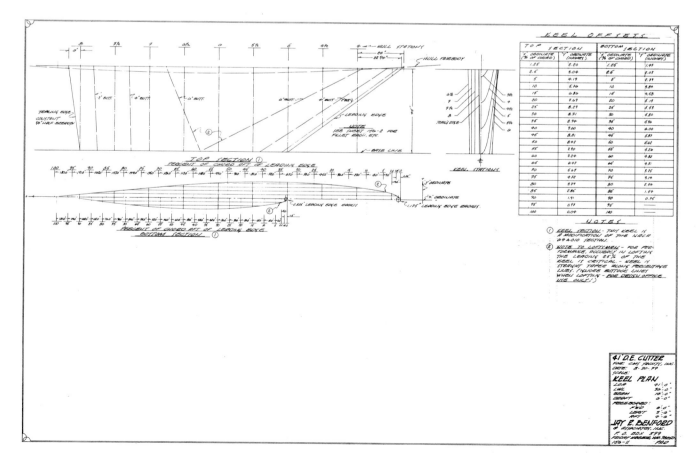

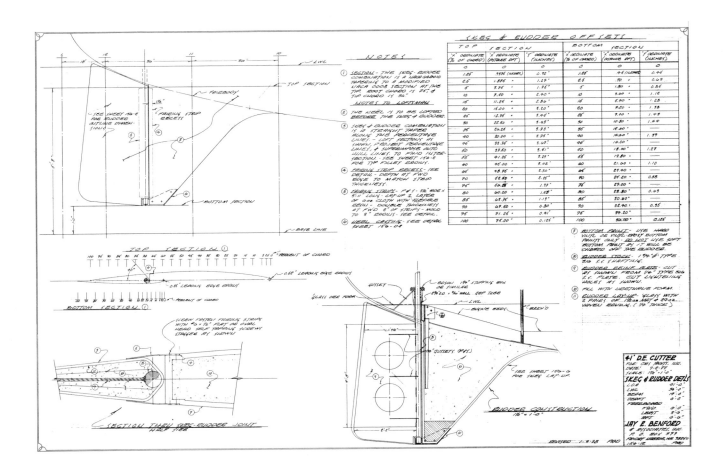

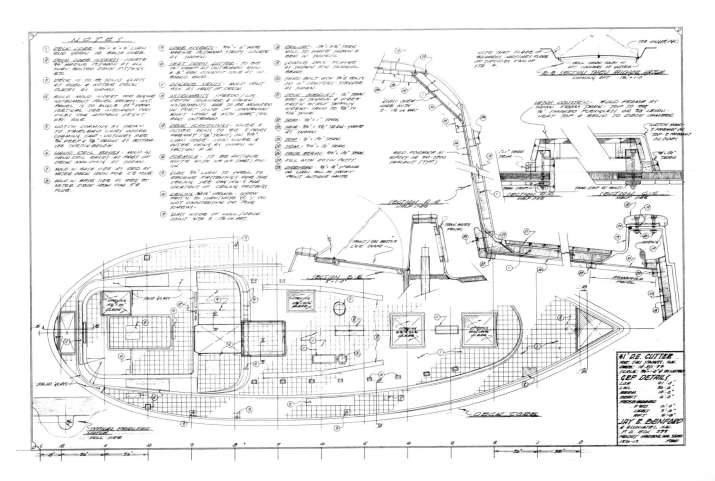

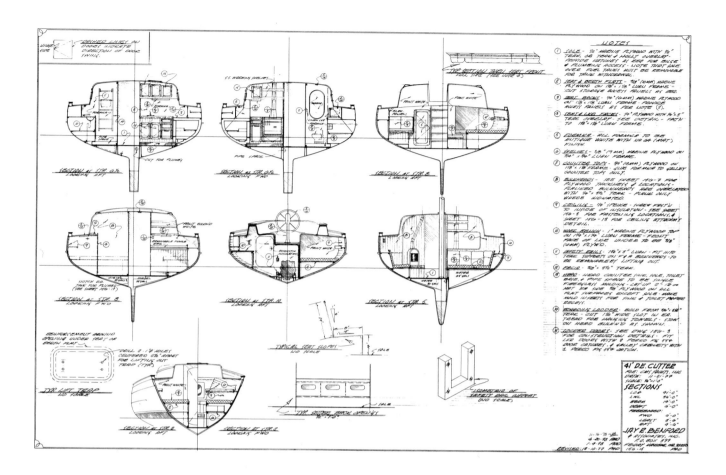

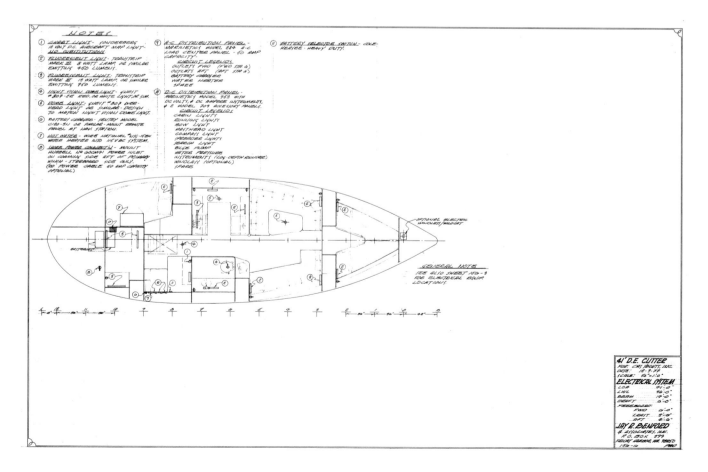

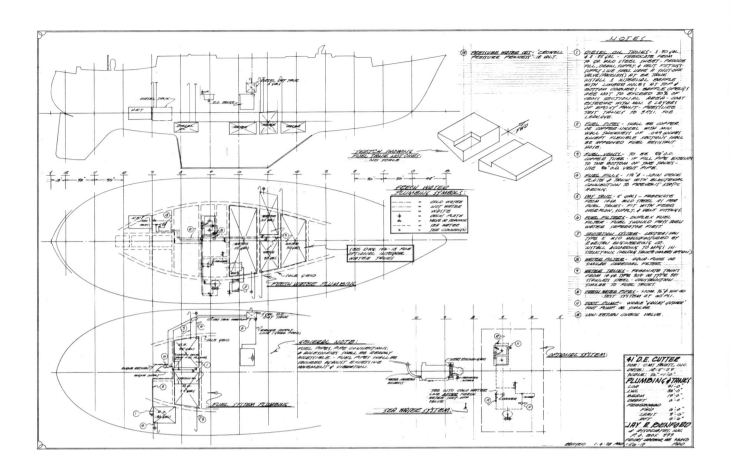

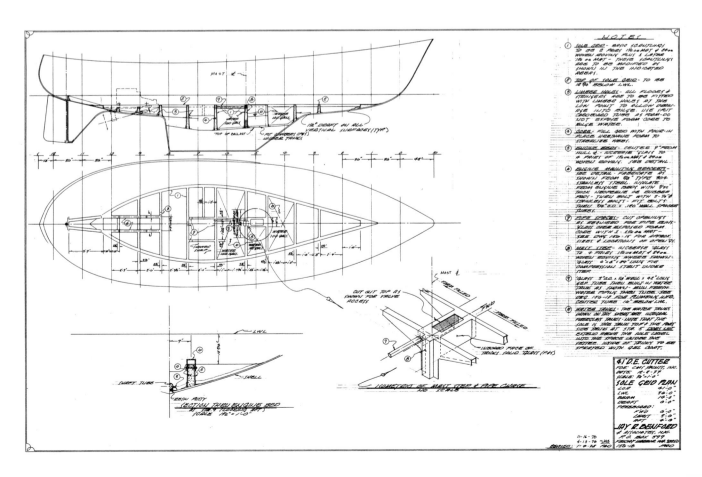

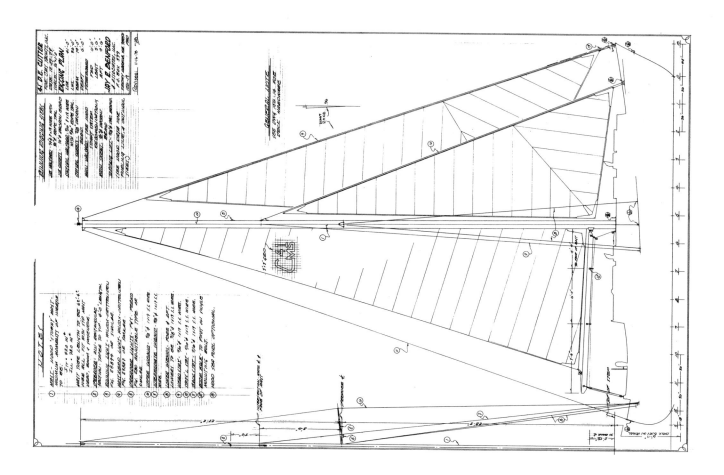

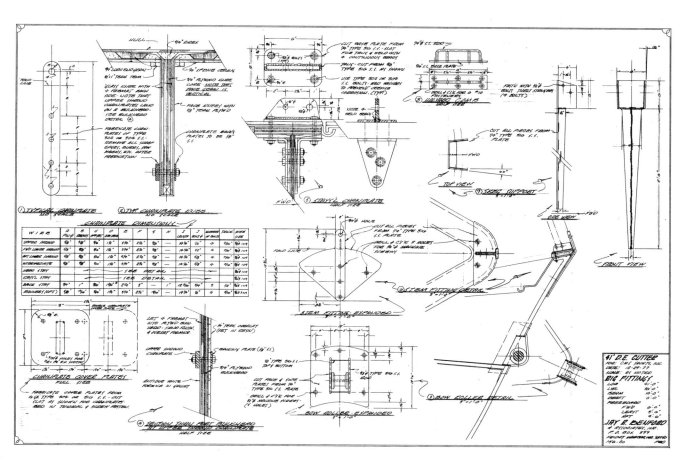

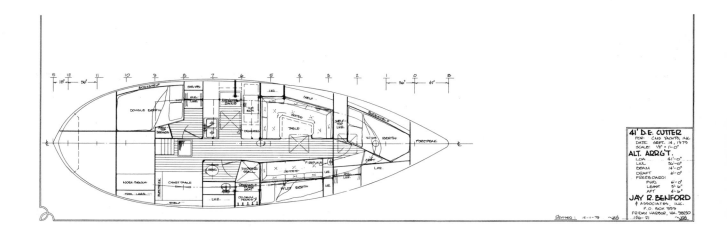

Pilothouse Version:

The pilothouse version of QUIET BIRD was developed in 1982 for Blue Sea of Taiwan, who now have the molds for the 41. They plan to build a new deck mold for this version. Clayton Enterprises of St. Louis will be marketing these pilothouse cutters. Their first boat, is being built to ABS classification, and is planned to be based in Newport Beach, California, for demonstrations.

This version has a very functional pilothouse, with sufficient elevation for the helmsman so he can see where he is going. To maintain the same area with the raised boom and foot of the mainsail, the foot was lengthened. Thus, the same mast, mast position, and fore triangle are used on both versions.

With the raised after deck and cockpit, there is a large aft stateroom with its own private head. Thus, each of two couples on board would have a private stateroom with a double berth and head. Additional guests could be put up in the pilothouse. The pilothouse seating did not have to be raised, as the windows are deep enough to see out from the seating positions. The helmsman is right next to the one-fold chart table, and there is a large sloping dashboard forward of the helm on which things can also be spread out.

The elevated cockpit provides excellent forward visibility over the pilothouse. Thus, the crew can be aware of what is going on at all times. All the running rigging leads to the cockpit, so there will be no need for a large crew spread all over the deck. The seatbacks are tall and well sloped to make this a comfortable place to spend many pleasurable cruising hours.

With the aft stateroom running right out into the stern, we had no place for a lazerette in this version. So, the forepeak was enlarged to make for a large bosun's locker between the chain locker and the forward stateroom. It is sealed off from the rest of the boat with a watertight bulkhead, so it can be used for stowage of the outboard motor and gas cans from the dinghy as well as painting supplies. There is also an access door into the chain locker to check on the chain stowage.

The only significant change from the layout shown on these drawings that ABS requested was the moving of the gas bottle locker from its side deck location. It is now going to be over part of the bosun's locker, with the access hatch to it to port of the bosun's locker hatch.

This version will be well appreciated in the northern climates, as well as by those in hotter climates who want to get some relief from being in the sun. She is well suited to living aboard for long periods of time, and would be a most comfortable way to travel. If fact, before I had the drawings completed, I made up a sketch of how the pilothouse could be rearranged to make it a combination drafting room and office, and revising the aft end like K'AN (the 40' pilothouse sloop shown elsewhere in this book) with a great cabin seating and dining area.

The variations can go on endlessly. This is one of the great things about yacht designing — the constant flow and exchange of ideas keeps up a high level of interest.

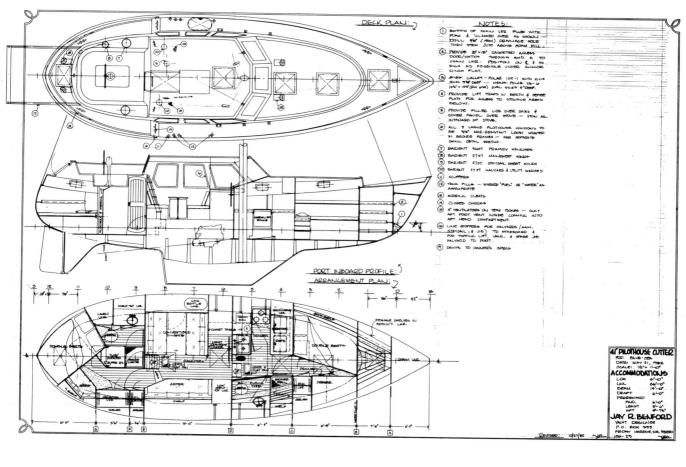

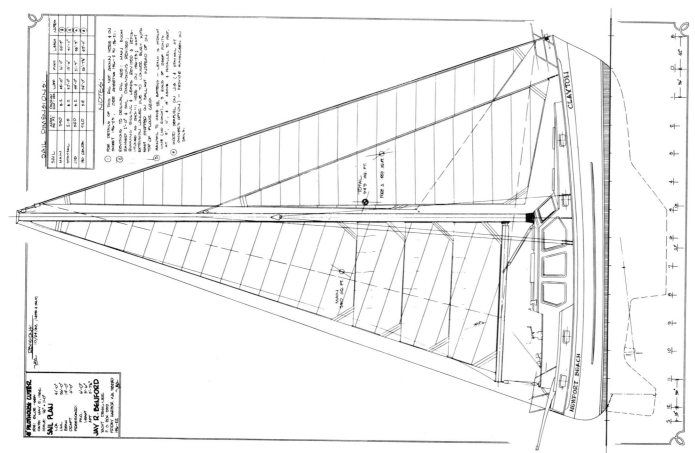

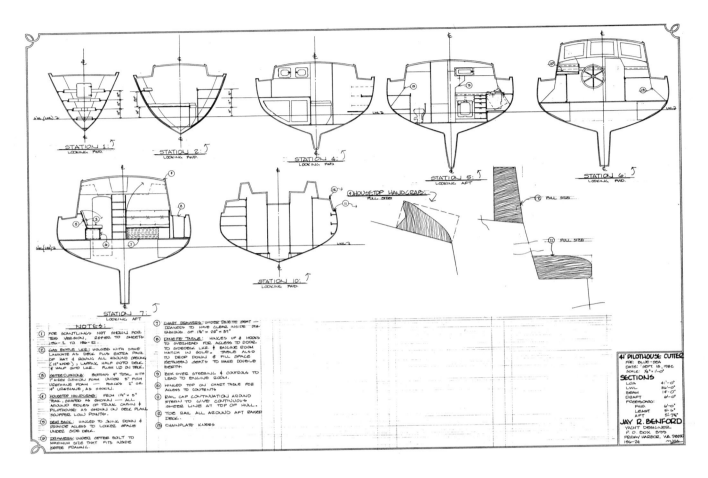

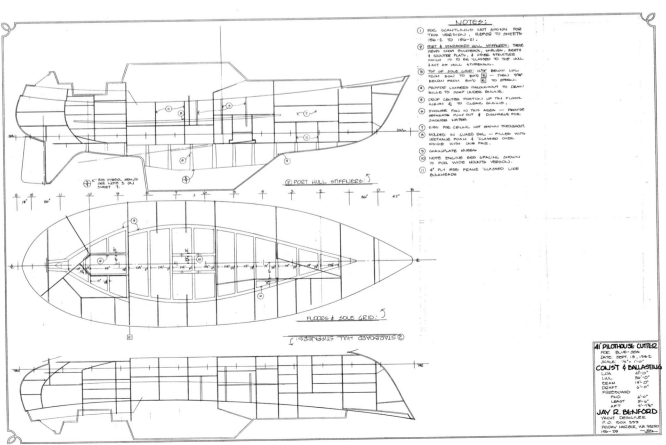

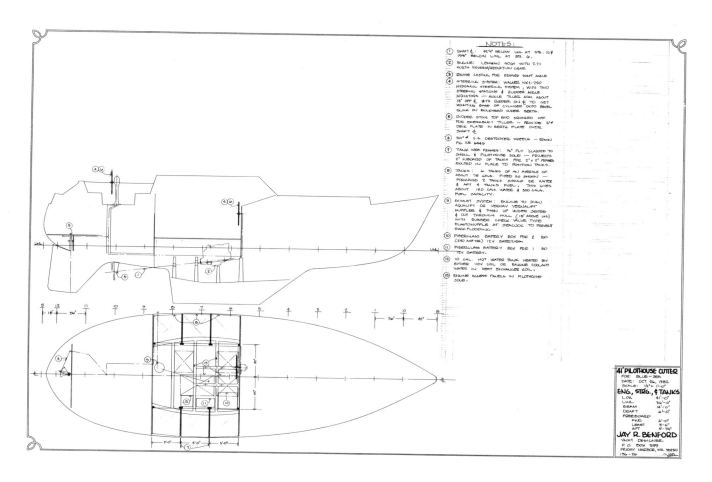

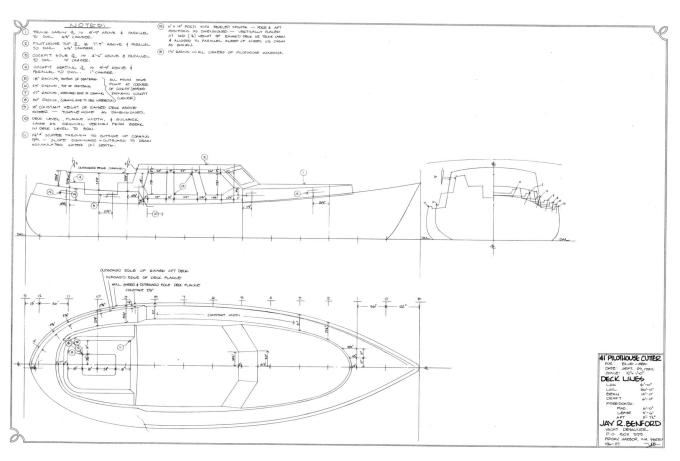

36-Foot Version

Before we even had the drawings for the 41 footer, QUIET BIRD, finished, we had a request from a client for a smaller version. This became the 36' double ended cutter shown in the following drawings.

While her outward style is much like the 41, her hull form is more related to the 39' PROMETHEUS and RANSOME, with a different keel.

Several features of her accommodations are worth mentioning. The forepeak bulkhead is sloped to increase the length of the berth and still keep the top of the bulkhead in position to take the load from the inner forestay. The sides of the trunk cabin are reinforced to take the inboard located shroud chainplates, making for a narrower sheeting angle. The engine is located amidships, in an insulated box, to keep its polar moment of interia low and provide easy access for servicing. The engine exhaust runs outboard under the sink counter with a side outlet.

This design was done for one-off 'glass construction, and would also be suitable for W.E.S.T. System, or cold-molded wood construction.

A couple of revisions to this design have been considered and would be practical. One would be a long, shallow keel, like *PROMETHEUS* or *CORCOVADO*, with about 4½' draft. This would add something in the range of one to two thousand pounds to the displacement, which she could carry well. The change over on keel and ballasting would end up with a boat with the same fine stability, and very little difference in sailing ability.

The other revision would be to alter the layout and deck houses to make a pilothouse cutter, like *CORCOVADO*, or a smaller version of the *CLAYTON 41*. This would be very practical, and the substantially lighter boat would be much less expensive to build and require a smaller engine with lower fuel consumption. Well worth considering . . . .

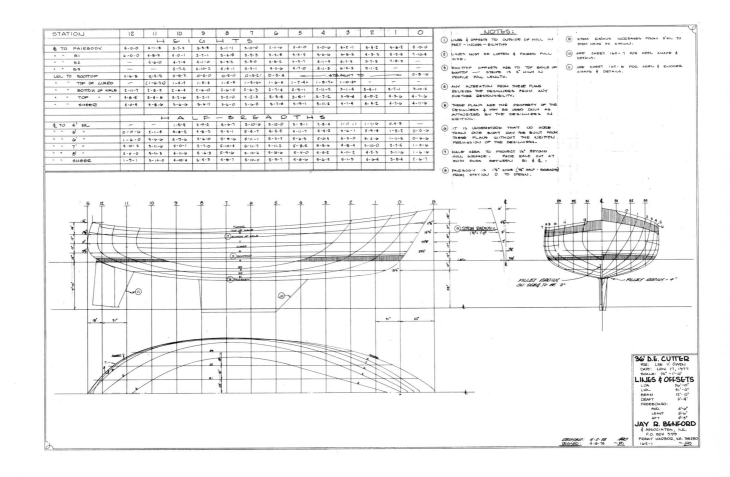

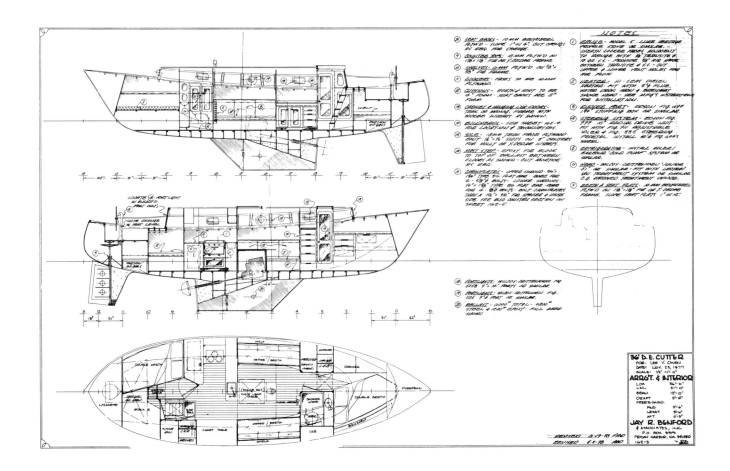

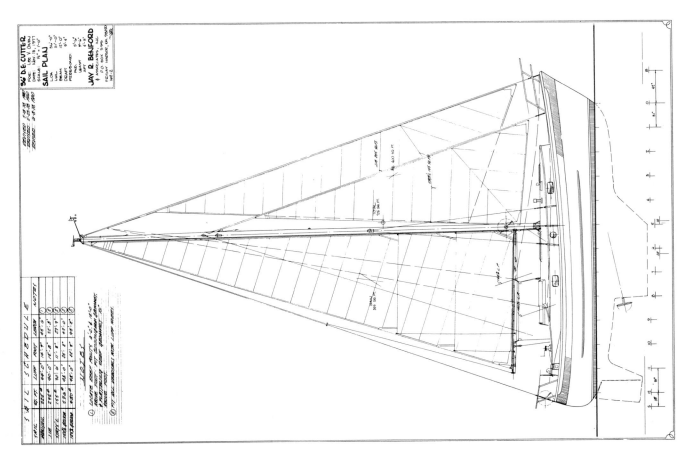

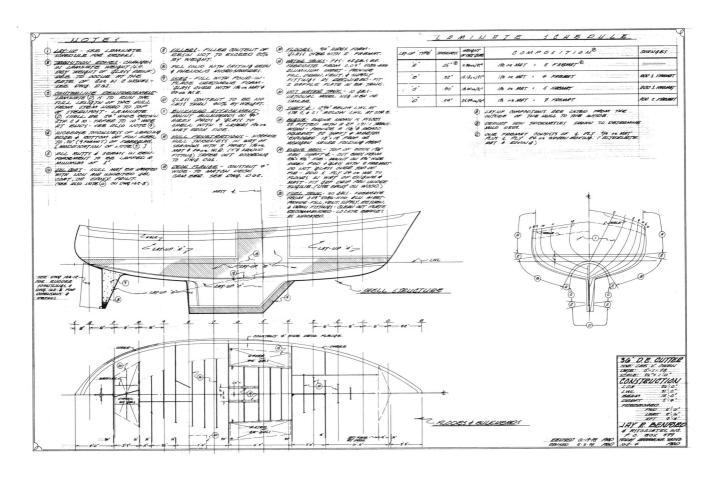

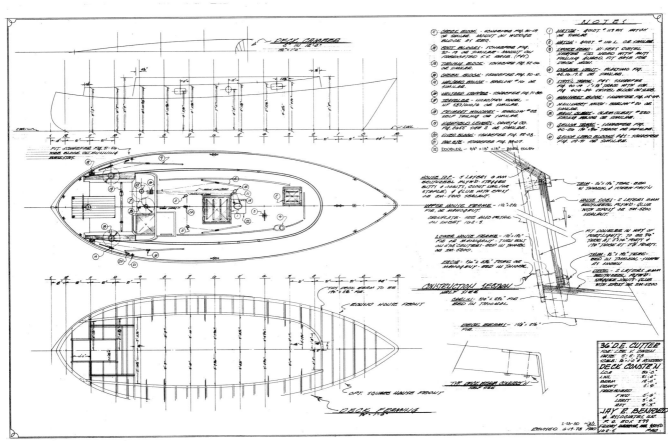

PARTICULARS:

Item	English	Metric
Length over all	36'-0"	10.97m
Length designed waterline	31'-0"	9.45m
Beam	12'-0"	3.66m
Draft	5'-4"	1.63m
Freeboard:		
Forward	5'-6"	1.68m
Least	3'-6"	1.07m
Aft	4'-3"	1.30m
Displacement, cruising trim*	17,000 lbs.	7,711 kg.
Ballast	6,000 lbs.	2,722 kg.
Ballast ratio	35%	
Displacement-length ratio	255	
Sail area	725 sq. ft.	67.35 sq. m
Sail area-displacement ratio	17.55	
Entrance half-angle	25 degrees	
Prismatic coefficient	0.556	
Water tankage	84 gals.	381 liters
Fuel tankage	60 gals.	227 liters
Headroom	6'-8"	2.03m

*CAUTION: The displacement quoted here is for the boat in cruising trim. That is, with the fuel and water tanks filled, the crew on board, as well as the crews' gear and stores in the lockers. This should not be confused with the "shipping weight" often quoted as "displacement" by some manufacturers. This should be taken into account when comparing figures and ratios between this and other designs.

To many, the creation of a yacht is a mysterious process, whereby the client's wallet and patience grow thinner. In fact, the construction of a new yacht often seems to be a severe test of a marriage. If the parties involved can make it through the whole process and are able to enjoy the fruits of their efforts together, they've passed the first test. The second test comes when they live aboard the boat. Can they get along in quarters much smaller than they have been used to ashore? Is it too much of a trial after the luxuries of modern society to live in close company with the elements (wind in the rigging, boat bouncing at her moorage, rain drumming down all night, inhabitants trying to get warm in winter or to stay cool in summer)?

Success in passing the second test usually means success as long-term boat owners.

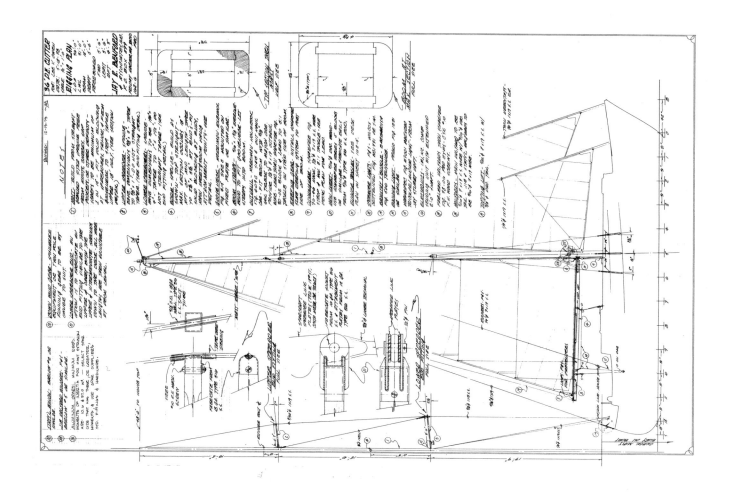

Chapter
22

Boundary Bay 44

For: Peter Nemeth and Jan Crowley
Design Number 184
1979

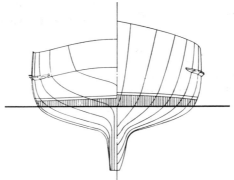

The commission for the Boundary Bay 44 presented an interesting challenge. I was to create a boat that was to have first-rate living accommodations for use in port and underway, as well as having an extremely simple rig: a cat ketch.

The hull form we designed has excellent form stability. Her firm bilges can be seen in the body plan. The sections also show the long foil shape of the keel. This is the same sort of shape I would use for a shorter fin keel, merely stretched out, and it gives good flow characteristics. I've used this shape with success on previous designs and found that it provides very good windward performance on a boat with shallow draft. The modest draft will be well appreciated in gunkholing.

The forefoot is cutaway to provide good response in maneuvering. Keel area is maintained aft to provide for good tracking and course keeping. The rudder area is ample and will provide for keeping her on course with small angles, thus minimizing the drag encountered by smaller rudders which have to be cranked over to much greater angles to steer the boats, with these large angles making the rudders act like brakes.

The stern shape is my favorite, giving a graceful and elegant appearance. It will also give a good account of itself in a seaway, lifting over the seas and

parting them like a double ender. There is plenty of deck space on the fantail stern's deck, and I've sloped the deep bulwarks aft to make a nice backrest for lounging on deck.

The midships cockpit is also shaped for comfort. The backrests are all high enough to give good support, and are well sloped to make for comfort. The seats are fitted with drains that direct any accumulation of rain or spray down to the cockpit scuppers, instead of leaving puddles to be sat in.

Down below, the accommodation plan provides comfort and privacy for two couples, with space for more on the settees and quarter berth. With the staterooms at each end of the boat, there is good separation, and the head and galley are accessible from either stateroom without disturbing the occupants of the other stateroom.

The head and galley, as well as the navigation area, are directly off the companionway. This easy access from the cockpit will mean that the settees and salon won't get soaked with seawater every time someone comes off deck for something from the galley or the head.

The Hundested prop system allows us to adjust the pitch of the prop to load the engine to full power at any rpm. It also allows us to feather the blades under

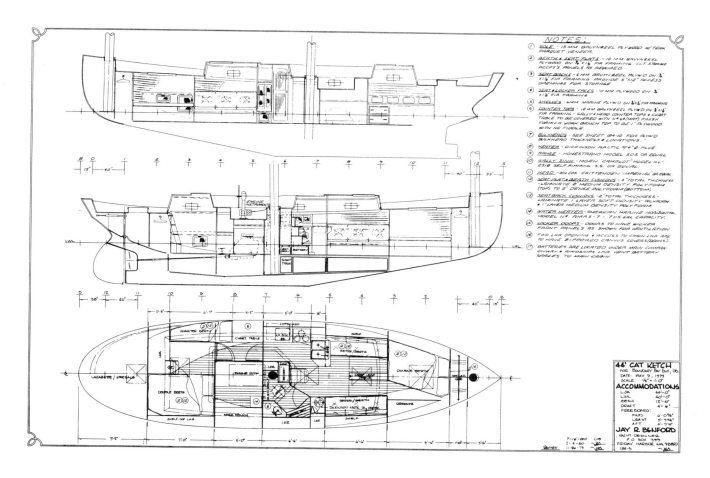

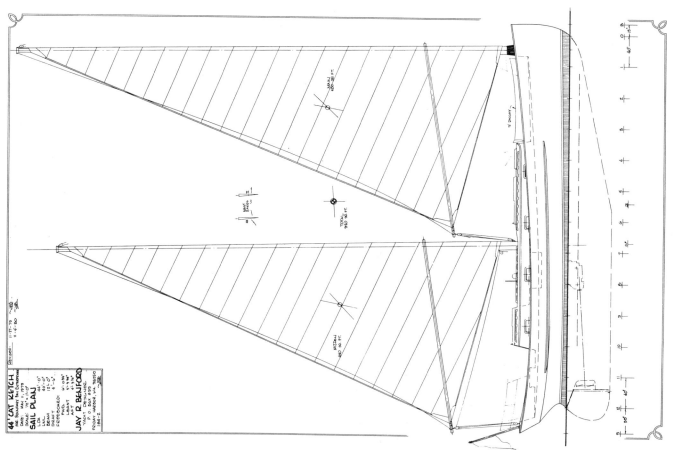

R.UDDER — KEEL

sail, to minimize drag. In sailing other designs of ours with this system, the results in speed are immediately noticeable on the log on cranking out the pitch. By cranking the pitch in the other direction, we can get down to a neutral position, and this is very useful for trolling. Also, in towing another vessel, reducing the pitch allows use of the full power of the engine to move both boats out of harm's way.

The results of this challenging design commission can be seen in the drawings for the boat. We're all delighted with the way she turned out.

Our clients' comments at the beginning of the project:

"Dear Jay,

Jan and I have decided to ask you to take on the project of designing our boat. The short visit we had with you in Friday Harbor in January convinced us that you are the right man for the job. We were impressed by the location and the atmosphere surrounding your offices and the wide range of designs that you have tackled."

Our clients' descriptive comments after the Boundary Bay 44 was designed:

"After several years of evaluation, we could not find a cruising boat that met our standards. Our demands were simple: we wanted a comfortable sailboat that would be capable of long range cruising. The boat had to sail well but could be easily handled by a couple, and of course we wanted a safe boat that we could trust when the going got rough. We also demanded that the whole thing should come in a pretty package.

Instead we found unsightly boats that sailed badly, but were safe; unsafe boats that were pretty, or ungainly gadget-filled machines that required a tireless crew of six for operation.

It was at this point that the concept of the Boundary Bay 44 was born. We commissioned well-known West Coast naval architect Jay R. Benford to design for Boundary Bay Boats, Ltd., a 44-foot cat-ketch that would be capable of offshore cruising with two to four adults and longshore chartering for six. The three prime requirements for the boat had to be sailing ability, simplicity and safety. This has resulted in the development of a very exciting craft to be introduced to the marine industry. An advancement of the state of the art of cruising yacht design — the Boundary Bay 44.

The hull of the Boundary Bay 44 is designed with swift passagemaking in mind. Construction is of Airex core fiberglass, resulting in higher impact strength, better sound and thermal insulation and greater hull stiffness. The full keel aft, a successful Benford design in the form of a long NACA foil section provides good tracking and windward ability as well as affording pro-

tection for the inboard rudder and propeller. The cutaway forefoot allows good maneuverability in tight spots. Her classic lines will draw admiration from any gathering of old salts. The pleasing design sweeps the eye from the commanding almost plumb bow along the lively sheer past the low-profile cabin to the beautiful and functional fantail stern. A far cry from the ungainly breadbox designs of many 'modern' cruising yachts."

TECHNICAL DATA:

Item	English	Metric
Length over all	44'-0"	13.41m
Length designed waterline	40'-0"	12.19m
Beam	12'-0"	3.66m
Draft	4'-6"	1.37m
Freeboard:		
Forward	6'-0¾"	1.85m
Least	3'-9¾"	1.16m
Aft	4'-9¼"	1.45m
Displacement, cruising trim*	22,850 lbs.	10,365 kg.
Displacement/length ratio	159.5	
Ballast	8,000 lbs.	3,629 kg.
Ballast ratio	35%	
Sail area	920 sq. ft.	85.47 sq. m
Sail area/displacement ratio	18.3	
Sail area-wetted surface ratio	2.2:1	
Water	160 gals.	568 liters
Fuel	75 gals.	284 liters
Headroom	6'-4½"	1.94m

*CAUTION: The displacement quoted here is for the boat in cruising trim. That is, with fuel and water in the tanks, the crew on board, as well as the crew's gear and stores in the lockers. This should not be confused with the "shipping weight" often quoted as "displacement" by some manufacturers. This should be taken into account when comparing figures and ratios between this and other designs.

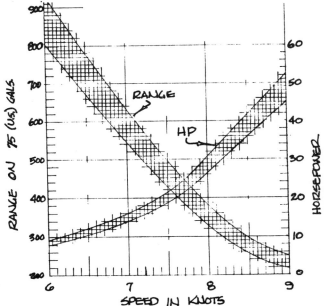

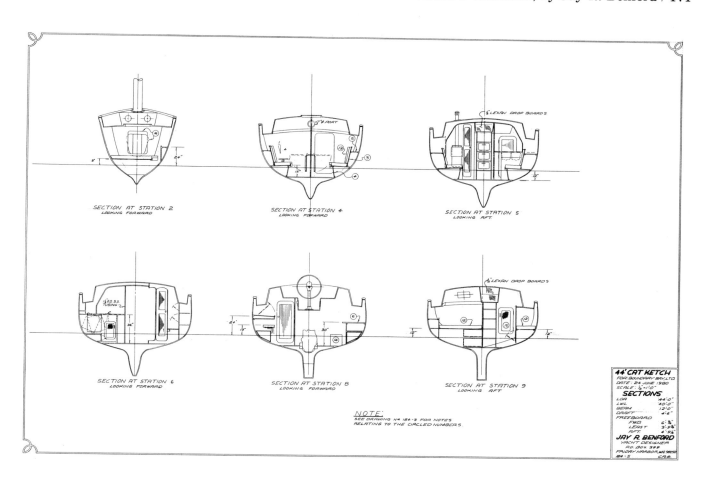

SECTION AT STATION 2
LOOKING FORWARD

SECTION AT STATION 4
LOOKING FORWARD

SECTION AT STATION 5
LOOKING AFT

SECTION AT STATION 6
LOOKING FORWARD

SECTION AT STATION 8
LOOKING FORWARD

SECTION AT STATION 9
LOOKING AFT

NOTE:
SEE DRAWING Nº 184-3 FOR NOTES
RELATING TO THE CIRCLED NUMBERS.

44' CAT KETCH
FOR BOUNDARY BAY LTD.
DATE: 24 JUNE 1980
SCALE: ⅜"=1'-0"

SECTIONS
LOA .... 44'-0"
LWL .... 40'-0"
BEAM .... 12'-0"
DRAFT .... 4'-6"
FREEBOARD
FWD. .... 6'-⅜"
LEAST ...... 3'-9¾"
AFT. .... 4'-3¼"

JAY R. BENFORD
YACHT DESIGNER
P.O. BOX 399
FRIDAY HARBOR, WA 98250
184-5   C.A.G.

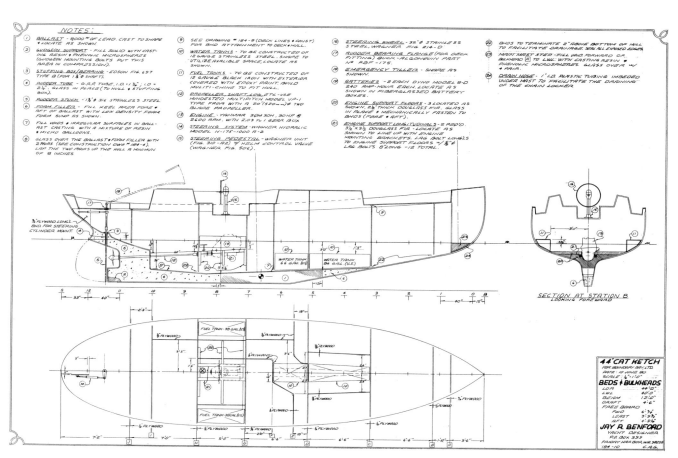

NOTES:

1) BALLAST - 8000 # OF LEAD. CAST TO SHAPE & LOCATE AS SHOWN.
2) GUDGEON SUPPORT - FILL SOLID WITH CASTING RESIN & PHENOLIC MICROSPHERES (GUDGEON MOUNTING BOLTS PUT THIS AREA IN COMPRESSION).
3) STUFFING BOX BEARING - EDSON FIG. 697 TYPE B (FOR 1⅜ Ø SHAFT).
4) RUDDER TUBE - G.R.P. TUBE, 1.D.=1¾", 1.D.= 2½", GLASS IN PLACE (TO HULL & STUFFING BOX).
5) RUDDER STOCK - 1⅜ Ø 316 STAINLESS STEEL.
6) FOAM FILLER - FILL KEEL AREA FORE & AFT OF BALLAST WITH LOW DENSITY FOAM. FORM SUMP AS SHOWN.
7) FILL VOIDS & IRREGULAR SURFACES IN BALLAST CASTING WITH A MIXTURE OF RESIN & MICRO BALLOONS.
8) GLASS OVER THE BALLAST & FOAM FILLER WITH 2 PAIRS (SEE CONSTRUCTION DWG #184-4). LAP THE TWO PAIRS UP THE HULL A MINIMUM OF 8 INCHES.

9) SEE DRAWING # 184-3 (DECK LINES & CONST.) FOR BHD ATTACHMENT TO DECK & HULL.
10) WATER TANKS - TO BE CONSTRUCTED OF 12 GAUGE STAINLESS STEEL. SHAPE TO UTILIZE AVAILABLE SPACE, LOCATE AS SHOWN.
11) FUEL TANKS - TO BE CONSTRUCTED OF 12 GAUGE BLACK IRON WITH EXTERIOR COVERED WITH EPOXY PAINT. BUILD MULTI-CHINE TO FIT HULL.
12) PROPELLER SHAFT, LOG, ETC.- USE HUNDESTED MULTIPITCH MODEL VP-1 TYPE FROM Q 20 (520mm) Ø TWO BLADE PROPELLER.
13) ENGINE - YANMAR 3QM 30H, 30HP @ 2600 RPM, WITH 2.03 TO 1 GEAR BOX.
14) STEERING SYSTEM - WAGNER HYDRAULIC MODEL N-175-1000 R-2.
15) STEERING PEDESTAL - WAGNER UNIT (FIG. 310-R2) W/ HELM CONTROL VALVE (WAGNER FIG. 506).

16) STEERING WHEEL - 32" Ø STAINLESS STEEL, WAGNER FIG 214-D.
17) RUDDER BEARING FLANGE (FOR DECK FITTING) BUCK-ALGONQUIN PART Nº ABF-175.
18) EMERGENCY TILLER - SHAPE AS SHOWN.
19) BATTERIES - 2 EACH DYNO MODEL 8-D 240 AMP-HOUR EACH. LOCATE AS SHOWN IN FIBERGLASSED BATTERY BOXES.
20) ENGINE SUPPORT FLOORS - 3 LOCATED AS SHOWN, 2½ THICK DOUGLASS FIR. GLASS IN PLACE & MECHANICALLY FASTEN TO BHDS (FORE & AFT).
21) ENGINE SUPPORT LONGITUDINALS - 2 REQ'D 3½ X 3½ DOUGLASS FIR - LOCATE AS SHOWN TO LINE UP WITH ENGINE MOUNTING BRACKETS. LAG BOLT LONG'LS TO ENGINE SUPPORT FLOORS W/ ⅜ Ø LAG BOLTS 8"LONG - 12 TOTAL.

22) BHDS TO TERMINATE 2" ABOVE BOTTOM OF HULL TO FACILITATE DRAINAGE. SEAL ALL EXPOSED EDGES.
23) MAIN MAST STEP - FILL VOID FORWARD OR BULKHEAD Ⓐ TO LWL WITH CASTING RESIN & PHENOLIC MICROSPHERES. GLASS OVER W/ 4 PAIR.
24) DRAIN HOSE - 1" I.D. PLASTIC TUBING IMBEDDED UNDER MAST TO FACILITATE THE DRAINING OF THE CHAIN LOCKER.

⅜ PLYWOOD LONG'L BHD FOR STEERING CYLINDER MOUNT.

WATER TANK 66 GAL (US)   WATER TANK 84 GAL (U.S.)

SECTION AT STATION 8
LOOKING FORWARD

FUEL TANK - 35 GALLONS

FUEL TANK - 35 GAL

44' CAT KETCH
FOR BOUNDARY BAY, LTD.
DATE: 10 JUNE 80
SCALE: ⅜"=1'-0"

BEDS & BULKHEADS
LOA .... 44'-0"
LWL .... 40'-0"
BEAM .... 12'-0"
DRAFT .... 4'-6"
FREE BOARD
FWD .... 6'-⅜"
LEAST ...... 3'-9¾"
AFT .... 4'-3¼"

JAY R. BENFORD
YACHT DESIGNER
P.O. BOX 399
FRIDAY HARBOR, WA 98250
184-10   C.A.G.

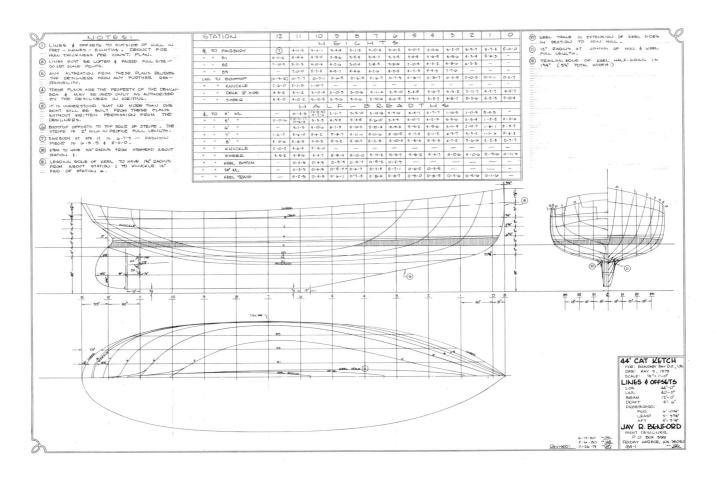

44' CAT KETCH
FOR: BOUNDARY BAY ENT., LTD.
DATE: MAY 3, 1979
SCALE: 1/2" = 1'-0"

LINES & OFFSETS

LOA	44'-0"
LWL	40'-0"
BEAM	12'-0"
DRAFT	4'-6"
FREEBOARD:	
FWD.	6'-0¾"
LEAST	5'-5¾"
AFT	4'-9¾"

JAY R. BENFORD
YACHT DESIGNER
P.O. BOX 399
FRIDAY HARBOR, WA. 98250
184-1

REVISED: 6-19-80
7-6-80
11-26-79

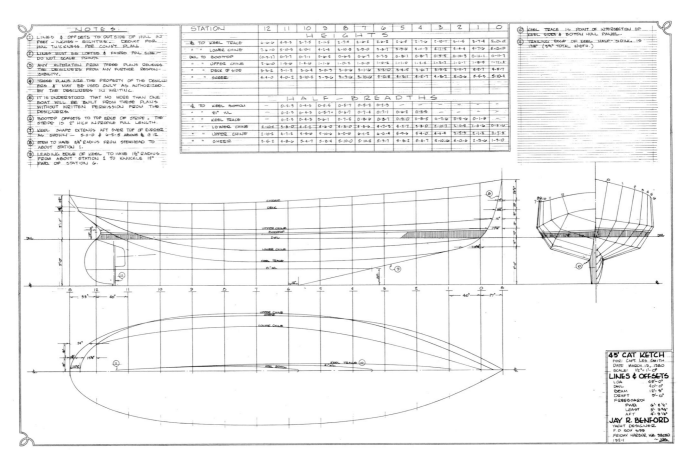

45' CAT KETCH
FOR: CAPT. LES SMITH
DATE: MARCH 13, 1980
SCALE: 1/2" = 1'-0"

LINES & OFFSETS

LOA	45'-0"
LWL	40'-0"
BEAM	12'-5"
DRAFT	5'-0"
FREEBOARD:	
FWD.	6'-1⅛"
LEAST	5'-3⅛"
AFT	4'-8⅛"

JAY R. BENFORD
YACHT DESIGNER
P.O. BOX 399
FRIDAY HARBOR, WA. 98250
192-1

45' Cat Ketch:

While we were completing the plans for the Boundary Bay 44, Captain Les Smith, a British Columbia Ferry captain, called us wanting plans for a steel boat with an unstayed rig. We told him of the work in process on the 44, and he liked the boat when he saw the plans. We agreed to do a steel version for him, and the plans shown here are the result. Since the structure for the steel boat weighs more than an equivalent fiberglass one, we had to increase the displacement. We took care of this in revising the lines for chine steel construction. The steel one has 6'' more draft, 30,420 pounds in cruising trim, carries 7,600 pounds of ballast, has a displacement-length ratio of 212, and a sail area-displacement ratio of 15.1 with the same 920 square foot rig. The interior was revised to provide a second head aft. This boat (or the 44) could carry a cutter rig like *ARGONAUTA*.

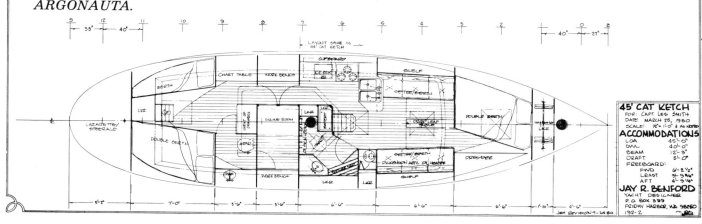

45' CAT KETCH
FOR: Capt Les Smith
DATE: MARCH 25, 1980
SCALE: ¼"= 1'-0" & As Noted

ACCOMMODATIONS

LOA	45'-0"
DWL	40'-0"
BEAM	12'-3"
DRAFT	5'-0"

FREEBOARD:
FWD	6'-2½"
LEAST	3'-9¾"
AFT	4'-9¼"

JAY R. BENFORD
YACHT DESIGNER
P.O. BOX 399
FRIDAY HARBOR, WA 98250
192-2

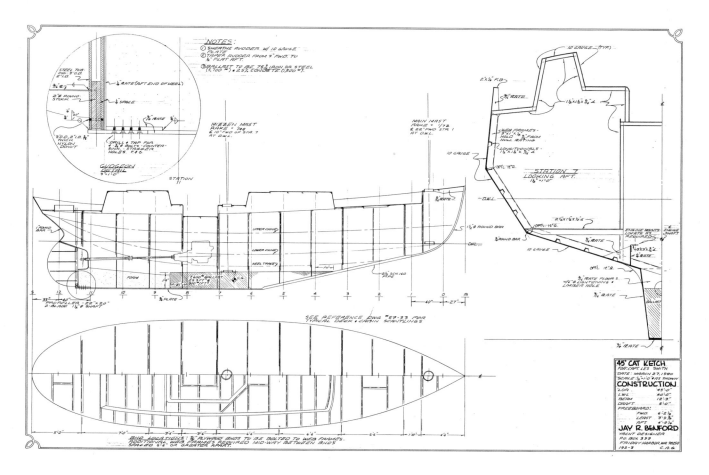

45' CAT KETCH
FOR: CAPT. LES SMITH
DATE: MARCH 27, 1980
SCALE: ½"= 1'-0" AS SHOWN

CONSTRUCTION

LOA	45'-0"
LWL	40'-0"
BEAM	12'-3"
DRAFT	5'-0"

FREEBOARD:
FWD	6'-2½"
LEAST	3'-9¾"
AFT	4'-9¼"

JAY R. BENFORD
YACHT DESIGNER
P.O. BOX 399
FRIDAY HARBOR, WA 98250
192-3

Chapter
23

Argonauta

45' Cutter
For: Marine Illustrator Stephen L. Davis
Design Number 195
1981

Argonauta is our design for the well known marine artist and illustrator, Stephen L. Davis. The Davis family plans to make her their home on completion. The boat is currently under construction at the Cecil M. Lange & Son boatyard in Port Townsend, Washington.

Argonauta's construction is cold-molded wood, using the W.E.S.T. System epoxies for glueing and sealing. She is planked with three skins of yellow cedar over fir longitudinal framing.

The hull form is an evolutionary development of a series we've been working on for a while. The fantail/eliptical counter stern is my personal favorite, and gives the boat a distinctive style and appearance all her own. Computer performance analysis, by George Hazen of Hazen & Stearn of Annapolis, indicates that she'll have fine sailing qualities, and her stability had the longest range of any that they had checked. They regarded her as virtually uncapsizable.

On deck, she has a contemporary cutter rig, laid out for easy handling by her small crew. She's got plenty of sail area to make her go in light and moderate conditions, and can be quickly shortened down in a blow.

The interior features private staterooms at each end of the boat. One is for the parents in the stern and one for their daughter in the bow. A variation possible is to have a double berth aft with a dresser opposite in place of the other berth, and the aft walk-in locker could become a second head.

There is a walk-through passageway from the aft cabin to the galley. Alongside this, there is a long galley counter, with an L-shape at the forward end housing the Dickinson oil range. The range is sited such that the hot side is free to radiate heat into the cabin, making for ease of warming the crew.

Opposite the galley is a large head compartment. There is a door in the head compartment leading into the engine room, for easy access to the engine and workbench. The passageway side of the engine enclosure will also be openable for easy servicing.

The saloon has opposing settee/berths, with a dropleaf table in between. This is open into the galley area, and will make for a roomy and pleasant social area.

The deckhouse/pilothouse will be Steve's work studio in harbor, and an operational pilothouse at sea. It will have a large workflat to starboard, over the passageway. To port, there will be a slightly lower settee and the inside control station. This settee will be raised so that the occupants will have a good view of their surroundings and the scenery going by.

Power is a Yanmar 3QM30 diesel driving a Hundested variable pitch prop. This prop can be adjusted from full neutral to full feather, for minimal drag under sail. We've used this system with success on several previous designs. With an exhaust pyrometer to measure the load on the engine, the pitch adjustment can be fine tuned to give maximum fuel economy.

Currently, she is planked up, with the interior roughed in, the deck on, and the house is being framed up and closed in.

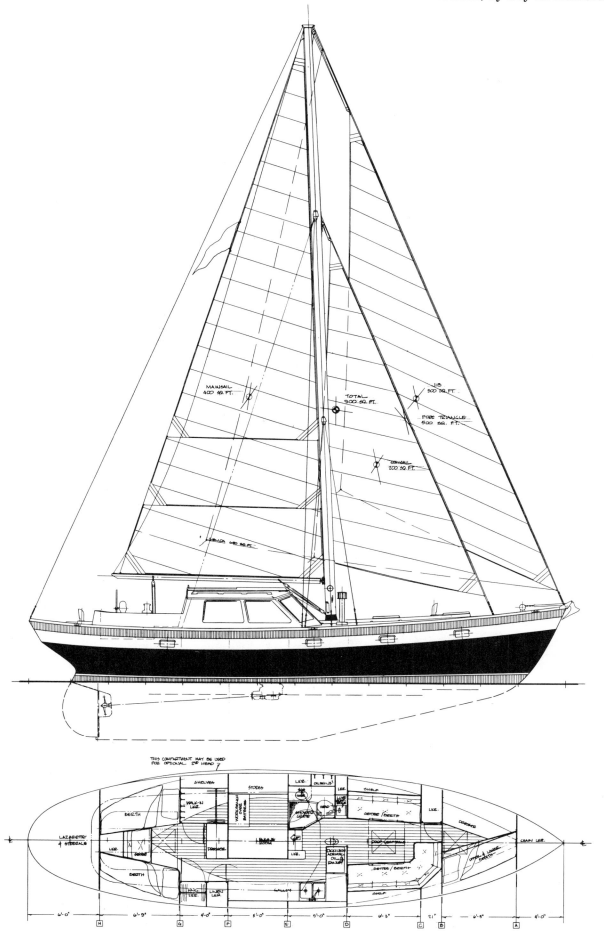

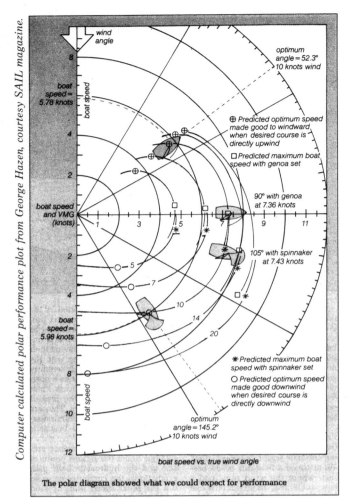

Computer calculated polar performance plot from George Hazen, courtesy SAIL magazine.

wind angle

optimum angle = 52.3° 10 knots wind

boat speed = 5.78 knots

boat speed

⊕ Predicted optimum speed made good to windward when desired course is directly upwind

□ Predicted maximum boat speed with genoa set

boat speed and VMG (knots)

90° with genoa at 7.36 knots

105° with spinnaker at 7.43 knots

boat speed = 5.98 knots

boat speed

✱ Predicted maximum boat speed with spinnaker set

○ Predicted optimum speed made good downwind when desired course is directly downwind

optimum angle = 145.2° 10 knots wind

boat speed vs. true wind angle

The polar diagram showed what we could expect for performance

PARTICULARS:

Item	English	Metric
Length over all	45'-0"	13.72m
Length designed waterline	37'-6"	11.43m
Beam	12'-3"	3.73m
Draft	5'-0"	1.52m
Freeboard:		
Forward	6'-6"	1.98m
Least	4'-6"	1.37m
Aft	5'-3"	1.60m
Displacement, cruising trim*	24,475 lbs.	11,102 kg.
Ballast (lead)	8,000 lbs.	3,629 kg.
Ballast ratio	33%	
Displacement-length ratio	207	
Sail area	900 sq. ft.	83.61 sq. m
Sail area-displacement ratio	17.08	
Wetted surface	427 sq. ft.	39.67 sq. m
Sail area-wetted surface ratio . . .	2.11	
Entrance half-angle	22½ degrees	
Prismatic coefficient	0.536	
Pounds per inch immersion	1,352	
GM	3.35'	1.02m

*NOTE: The displacement quoted here is for the boat in cruising trim. That is, with fuel and water in the tanks filled, the crew on board, as well as the crews' gear and stores in the lockers. This should not be confused with the "shipping weight" often quoted as "displacement" by some manufacturers. This should be taken into account when comparing figures and ratios between this and other designs.

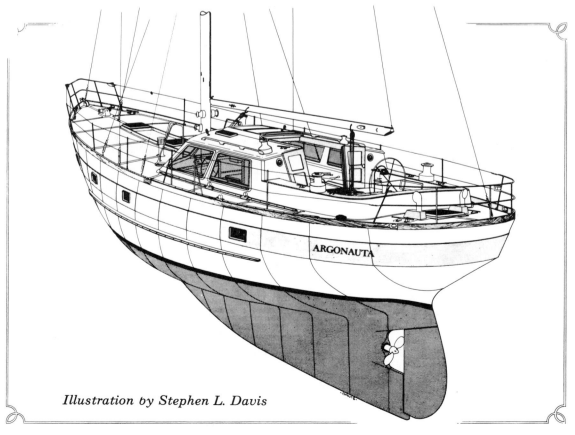

ARGONAUTA

Illustration by Stephen L. Davis

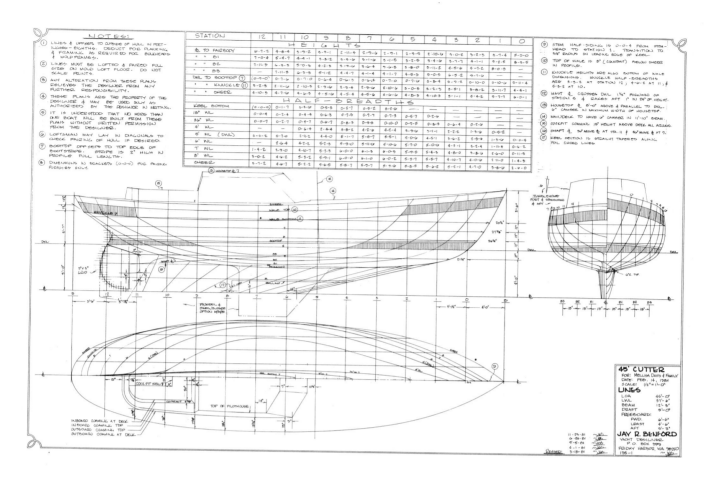

NOTES:

1. LINES & OFFSETS TO OUTSIDE OF HULL IN FEET-INCHES-EIGHTHS. DEDUCT FOR PLANKING & FRAMING AS REQUIRED FOR BULKHEADS & MOLD FRAMES.
2. LINES MUST BE LOFTED & FAIRED FULL SIZE ON MOLD LOFT FLOOR. DO NOT SCALE PRINTS.
3. ANY ALTERATION FROM THESE PLANS RELIEVES THE DESIGNER FROM ANY FURTHER RESPONSIBILITY.
4. THESE PLANS ARE THE PROPERTY OF THE DESIGNER & MAY BE USED ONLY AS AUTHORIZED BY THE DESIGNER IN WRITING.
5. IT IS UNDERSTOOD THAT NO MORE THAN ONE BOAT WILL BE BUILT FROM THESE PLANS WITHOUT WRITTEN PERMISSION FROM THE DESIGNER.
6. LOFTSMAN MAY LAY IN DIAGONALS TO CHECK FAIRING OF HULL IF DESIRED.
7. BOOTTOP OFFSETS TO TOP EDGE OF BOOTSTRIPE. STRIPE IS 2" HIGH IN PROFILE FULL LENGTH.
8. DIMENSIONS IN BRACKETS (0-0-0) FOR FAIRING PURPOSES ONLY.

STATION	12	11	10	9	8	7	6	5	4	3	2	1	0
HEIGHTS													
℄ TO FAIRBODY	6-7-2	4-8-4	3-9-2	3-3-1	2-11-4	2-9-6	2-9-1	2-9-5	2-10-6	3-0-2	3-2-3	3-7-4	5-0-0
" " B1	7-0-4	5-4-7	4-4-1	3-8-2	3-3-6	3-1-6	3-1-5	3-2-5	3-4-6	3-7-7	4-1-1	5-2-5	8-3-5
" " B2	7-11-3	6-3-3	5-0-3	4-2-3	3-9-6	3-6-4	3-6-3	3-8-0	3-11-2	4-5-6	5-7-2	8-0-3	—
" " B3	—	7-11-3	6-3-3	5-1-2	4-4-7	4-1-4	4-1-7	4-5-3	5-0-5	6-5-2	9-7-6	—	—
DWL TO BOOTTOP (7)	(0-9-0)	0-7-6	0-7-0	0-6-4	0-6-3	0-6-4	0-7-0	0-7-6	0-8-4	0-9-2	0-10-0	0-10-6	0-11-4
" " KNUCKLE (11)	3-2-3	2-11-6	2-10-3	2-9-6	2-9-4	2-9-6	2-10-6	3-0-3	3-2-3	3-5-1	3-8-2	3-11-7	4-4-1
" " SHEER	4-10-3	4-7-6	4-6-3	4-5-6	4-5-4	4-5-6	4-6-6	4-8-3	4-10-3	5-1-1	5-4-2	5-7-7	6-0-1
HALF-BREADTHS													
KEEL BOTTOM	(0-0-0)	0-1-7	0-3-6	0-5-3	0-5-7	0-5-2	0-2-6	—	—	—	—	—	—
18" WL	0-0-4	0-2-4	0-4-4	0-6-3	0-7-5	0-7-7	0-7-3	0-5-7	0-2-6	—	—	—	—
36" WL	0-0-7	0-2-7	0-4-7	0-6-7	0-8-3	0-9-3	0-10-0	0-9-5	0-8-5	0-6-4	0-2-6	—	—
4' WL	—	—	0-6-4	2-4-4	3-8-2	4-2-6	4-2-4	3-9-6	3-1-1	2-2-2	1-3-6	0-5-2	—
5' WL (DWL)	0-0-2	0-7-0	2-11-2	4-4-0	5-1-7	5-5-7	5-5-1	5-0-6	4-5-1	3-6-2	2-5-6	1-3-6	0-0-4
6' WL	—	2-6-4	4-2-2	5-2-3	5-9-0	5-11-6	5-10-6	5-7-0	5-0-6	4-3-1	3-2-4	1-11-4	0-6-2
7' WL	1-4-2	3-9-0	4-10-7	5-7-3	6-0-0	6-1-3	6-0-3	5-9-5	5-4-3	4-8-0	3-8-6	2-6-0	0-11-5
8' WL	3-0-2	4-6-2	5-3-2	5-9-1	6-0-0	6-1-0	6-0-2	5-9-7	5-5-7	4-10-7	4-0-6	2-11-0	1-4-3
SHEER	3-7-2	4-6-7	5-2-2	5-6-5	5-8-7	5-9-7	5-9-6	5-8-5	5-6-2	5-2-1	4-7-0	3-8-6	2-6-0

9. STEM HALF-SIDING IS 0-0-4 FROM STEMHEAD TO STATION 1. TRANSITION TO 3/4" RADIUS ON LEADING EDGE OF KEEL.
10. TOP OF WALE IS 8" (CONSTANT) BELOW SHEER IN PROFILE.
11. KNUCKLE HEIGHTS ARE ALSO BOTTOM OF WALE DIMENSIONS. KNUCKLE HALF-BREADTHS ARE 3-3-2 AT STATION 12; 4-6-2 AT 11; & 5-3-2 AT 10.
12. MAST ℄ CROSSES DWL 1½" FORWARD OF STATION 5 & RAKES AFT 1" IN 24" OF HEIGHT.
13. HOUSETOP ℄ 8'-0" ABOVE & PARALLEL TO DWL. 6" CAMBER IN MAXIMUM WIDTH OF HOUSETOP.
14. MAINDECK TO HAVE 6" CAMBER IN 11'-10" BEAM.
15. COCKPIT COAMING 15" HEIGHT ABOVE DECK ALL AROUND.
16. SHAFT ℄ 36" ABOVE ℄ AT STA. 11 & 46" ABOVE ℄ AT 7.
17. KEEL SECTION IS STRAIGHT TAPERED ALONG FOIL CHORD LINES

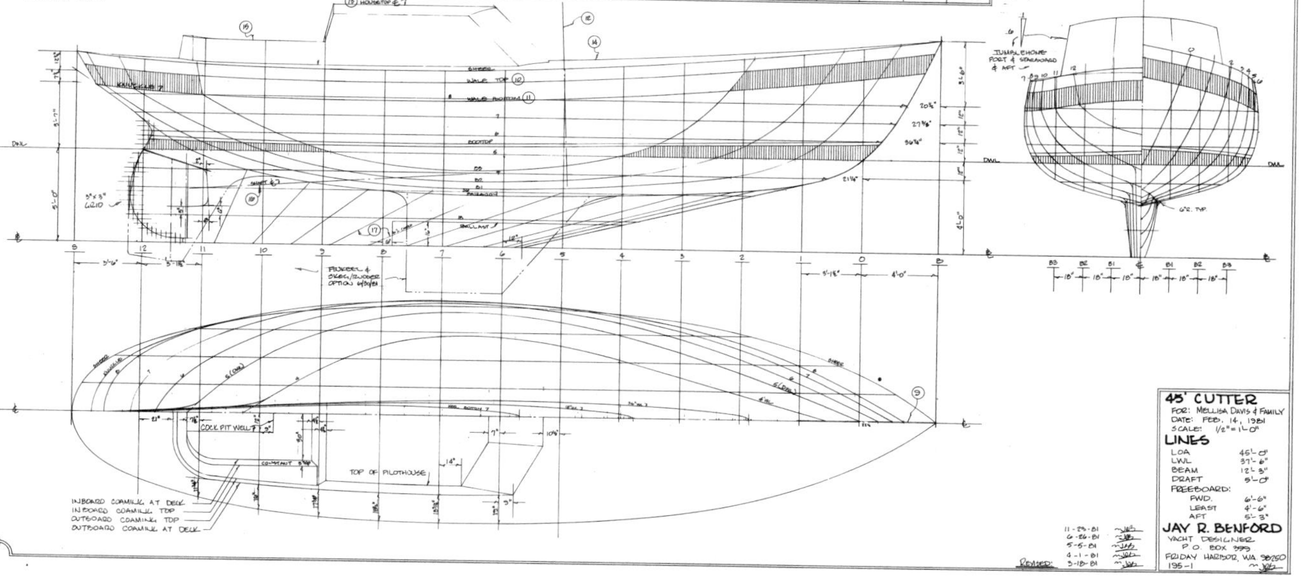

45' CUTTER
FOR: MELLISA DAVIS & FAMILY
DATE: FEB. 14, 1981
SCALE: 1/2" = 1'-0"
LINES
LOA 45'-0"
LWL 37'-6"
BEAM 12'-3"
DRAFT 5'-0"
FREEBOARD:
FWD. 6'-6"
LEAST 4'-6"
AFT 5'-3"
JAY R. BENFORD
YACHT DESIGNER
P.O. BOX 399
FRIDAY HARBOR, WA 98250
195-1
REVISED: 3-18-81 4-1-81 5-5-81 6-26-81 11-23-81
INBOARD COAMING AT DECK
INBOARD COAMING TOP
OUTBOARD COAMING TOP
OUTBOARD COAMING AT DECK
TOP OF PILOTHOUSE
COCKPIT WELL

NOTES:

1. PLANKING: 3 DIAGONAL LAYERS 5/16" YELLOW CEDAR.
2. LONGITUDINAL STRINGERS: 1 & 2 – 7/8" × 1½", 3 & 4 – 1" × 1½", 5 & 6 – 1⅛" × 1½", 7 & 8 – 1¼" × 1½", 9 & 10 – 1⅜" × 1½", 11/12 & 13 – 1½" × 1½" – ALL D. FIR.
3. CLAMP: 4 PIECES 3/4" × 3½" — INBOARD 1½" × 1½" CORNER CUT OFF AS SHOWN.
4. APRON: 3 PIECES 3/4" × 11"
5. LONGITUDINAL DECK FRAME: 1½" × 3½" TAPERED TO 1⅛" AT TOP — LIMBER AS REQ'D. AT HATCHES. D. FIR.
6. LONG'L. DECK FRAME: 1½" × 3½" D. FIR.
7. TOE RAIL: FROM 1½" × 3½" - TAPER TO 1" AT TOP
8. DECK: 3 LAYERS 10MM (3/8") PLY — 1⅛" TOTAL.
9. FLOORS: FROM 5/16" × 4" Y. CEDAR — 5 PLIES ACROSS ℄ TAPERING TO 2 PLIES OUTBOARD AS SHOWN.
10. BULKHEADS: 12MM BRUYNZEEL (OR 1/2" FIR MARINE) PLYWOOD — NO VOIDS IN CORE OR FACE PLIES.
11. BULKHEAD FRAMING: 1½" × 3½" ALL AROUND EDGES OF BH'DS. AT CONNECTION TO SHELL. NOTCH FOR STRINGERS ((2))
12. BALLAST: 8,000 LBS. LEAD (WITH 2 TO 5% ANTIMONY) - SEE "LINES" FOR SHAPE.
13. BALLAST BOLTS: 9 BOLTS 7/8" ⌀ MONEL OR EVERDUR BRONZE — SINGLE BOLT ON ℄ FWD. & 4 PAIRS OF BOLTS AFT — SPREAD PAIRS AS FAR OFF ℄ AS POSSIBLE.
14. DEADWOOD: D. FIR OR Y. CEDAR
15. WORM SHOE: IRONBARK OR GUM
16. ENGINE BEDS: FROM 3½" × 7" D. FIR.
17. WALE: 5/16" Y. CEDAR
18. KNUCKLE FRAME: 3 PIECES 3/4" × 3½" — BEVEL TOP AS SHOWN FOR DRAINAGE — RUN FULL SECTION FROM STERN AROUND TO STA. 10 & TAPER DOWN TO 3/4" × 3½ AT 9.
19. MOLD FRAMES: ("M") LOCATED AS NOTED, IN ADDITION TO BULKHEADS, IN INITIAL SETUP. REMOVE AFTER PLANKING IS COMPLETED.
20. STEERING SYSTEM: 16" QUADRANTS & 6" SHEAVES FOR CABLES — PROVIDE LIGNUM VITAE OR MICARTA BEARINGS ((B)) AS SHOWN
21. RUDDER: STOCK 1¾" ⌀ EVERDUR OR MONEL — WELD ON 3 3/8" × 4" × 8" PIECES — SANDWICH INSIDE SHAPED PLYWOOD BLADE — EPOXY SATURATE & SEAL & SHEATH SAME AS KEEL — PROVIDE COUPLING JUST ABOVE STUFFING BOX.
22. ENGINE: YANMAR 3QM30 2:1 RED.
23. PROP SYSTEM: HUNDESTED VP-1 FROA STERN TUBE 1.5m, TOTAL SHAFT 2.4m LONG. REVOLVE CONTROL UNIT TO KEEP BELOW SOLE.
24. SHAFT ℄: 25" BELOW DWL AT [H] & 15⅛" BELOW DWL AT [F]. NOTE NOTCH ON ℄ STRUCTURE REQUIRED FOR MOUNTING OF PROP SYSTEM.

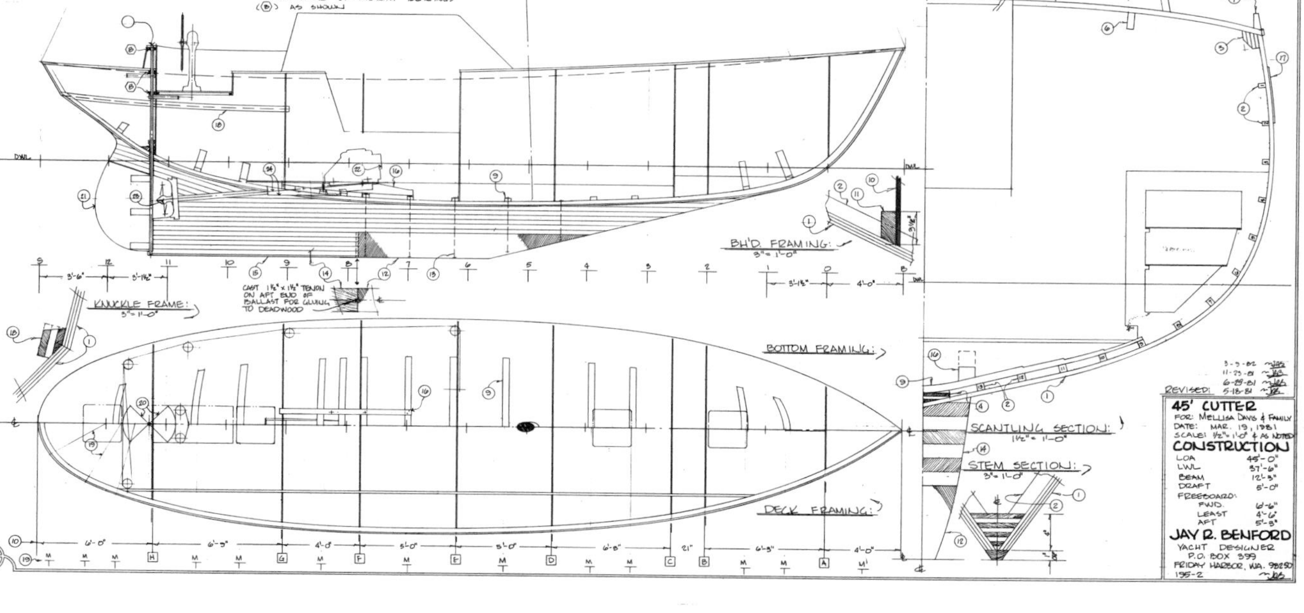

BH'D FRAMING: 3" = 1'-0"
KNUCKLE FRAME: 3" = 1'-0"
BOTTOM FRAMING
DECK FRAMING
SCANTLING SECTION: 1½" = 1'-0"
STEM SECTION: 3" = 1'-0"
45' CUTTER
FOR: MELLISA DAVIS & FAMILY
DATE: MAR. 19, 1981
SCALE: 1/2" = 1'-0" & AS NOTED
CONSTRUCTION
LOA 45'-0"
LWL 37'-6"
BEAM 12'-3"
DRAFT 5'-0"
FREEBOARD:
FWD. 6'-6"
LEAST 4'-6"
AFT 5'-3"
JAY R. BENFORD
YACHT DESIGNER
P.O. BOX 399
FRIDAY HARBOR, WA. 98250
195-2
REVISED: 5-18-81 6-29-81 11-23-81 3-9-82

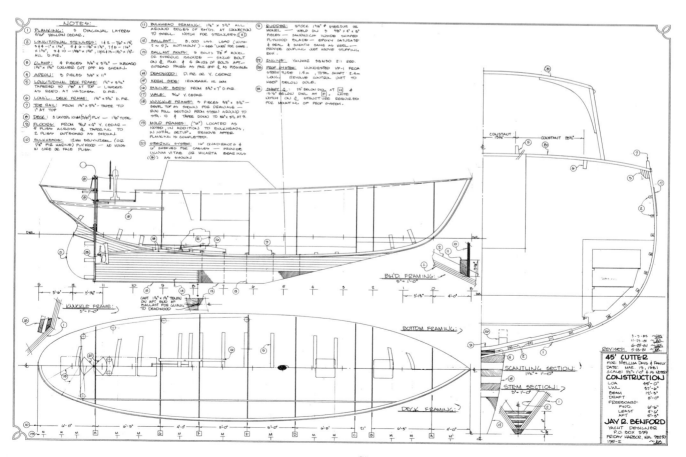

Chapter
24

Inscrutable

45' Lug Schooner
For: Marg and Dale McNeil
Design Number 144
1977

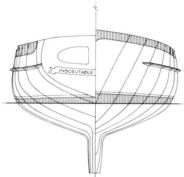

Cruising people on long ocean voyages often seem to have lots of time to fantasize about their ideal "next boat". Only a few of them follow through and actually undertake to make the dream a reality.

Marg and Dale McNeil are members of that very select group. After spending six years cruising their Spencer 35, *Bag O Winds,* around the South Pacific, they sold her and returned to British Columbia to pursue their dream.

When they came to see us to discuss their new boat in the summer of 1976, they had a set of nicely detailed preliminary drawings outlining their concept in great detail. We had met them earlier while they were outfitting for their long cruise, and I remembered that Dale had been a draftsman for Boeing then. The clarity of their sketches and ideas reflected this skill and the amount of time they'd spent evolving them.

We spent the following fall and winter working on the evolution of the final detail drawings. We had an extensive and enjoyable interchange of ideas with the McNeils. The final drawings give some idea of the special features that are incorporated in this vessel.

General Concept:

The general concept is for a vessel to be a home

afloat. It is suitable for both coastal cruising and ocean crossings. The McNeils' operating philosophy is that ocean passages are viewed as something to be made as easy to accomplish as possible in order to get to the more pleasant coastal cruising areas.

In following these principles to their natural conclusion, the layout they conceived is admirably suited to this style of cruising. The middle portion of the boat is given over to those functions that are used on passages, as this area has the least motion. This central core has two passage berths, the head, the navigation area and the galley. Forward and aft are the areas that are used while living aboard in quiet waters.

Hull Form Considerations:

The McNeils requested a keel long enough to properly support the boat for hauling and beaching. Such a beaching operation would also use shear legs for additional transverse support, so the keel would have to provide the main fore and aft support. The bottom of the keel is about a foot wide, thus providing good bearing for spreading the load on the bottom.

The keel is an elongated NACA foil section, as is the rudder. There is plenty of area for lateral resistance and the foil shape will provide for good windward per-

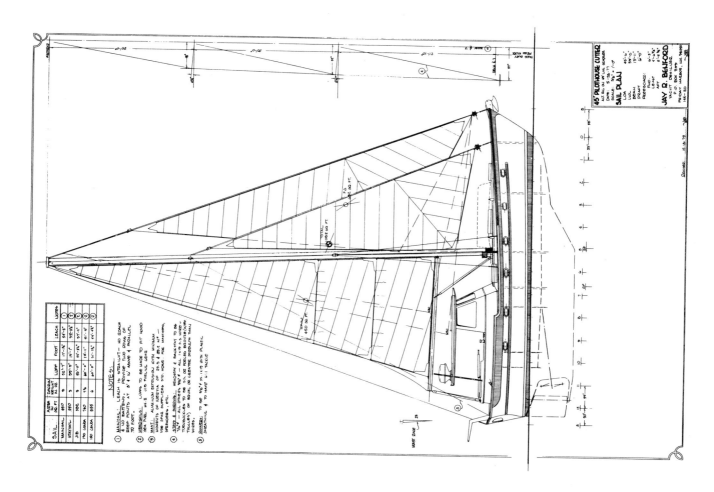

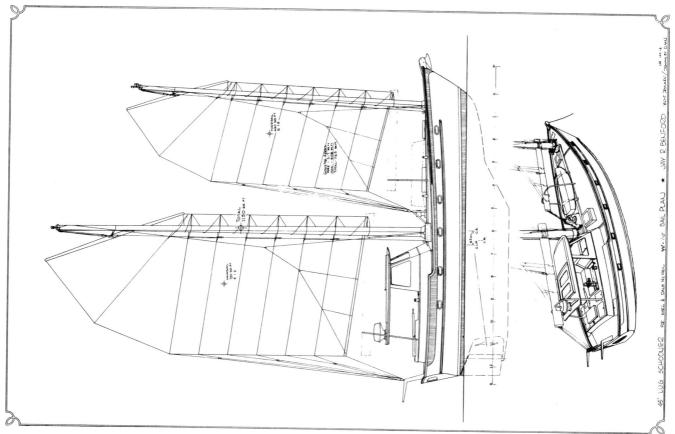

formance. The length and position of the keel were also intended to give good directional stability under sail, as well as to try to minimize any tendency to sail around at anchor.

The hull form has good definition of the keel and hull as separate entities, with a small radius at the connection. This type of hull keeps the center of buoyancy higher than is found on the traditional wineglass sectioned boats. The higher CB location increased the initial stability, giving the good form stability wanted.

Rudder and Steering:

The rudder is partially balanced, to ease the loads on the tiller. There is a heavy bronze casting supporting the bottom of the rudder, and providing protection for the propeller. The drag linkage connecting to the tiller in the cockpit keeps the steering from interrupting the master berth. The tiller will be hooked up with a tiller auto-pilot inside the deck box it passes through. This will be accessible to the helmsman via the hatch shown on the cockpit layout drawing.

Construction:

Hull construction is Airex cored fiberglass. The 'glass skins are substantial, befitting a conservative cruising boat. The core is omitted at the hull to deck joint and in all of the keel area. These are the high stress areas and have extra 'glass reinforcement.

With an unstayed rig, such as this lug schooner rig, the stresses on the structure are different than on a conventional stayed rig. This is because of the way in which the stresses from the driving force of the rig are transmitted into the hull. In a stayed rig, there is a lot of longitudinal bending stress when the stays are tuned to keep the rig tight. With a stayed rig, the loads are taken at the mast step and at the deck, where the side loading of the rig tries to twist the hull.

To counteract these rigging loads, we have worked out a special method of applying Airex. Instead of letting the two skins on either side of the Airex work independently, we join them together in predetermined areas. The areas in which the skins are joined have been carefully worked out to give the required rigidity to the hull. This means some careful work is required of the builder in doing the special reinforcing. But the results in strength and longevity will be well worthwhile.

The construction of the deck is similar to the hull, except that end-grain balsa is used for the core. There are solid wood and plywood inserts in the higher stress areas to increase the local load carrying ability. Additionally, some C-Flex is used for diagonally strapping the deck to take the twisting loads.

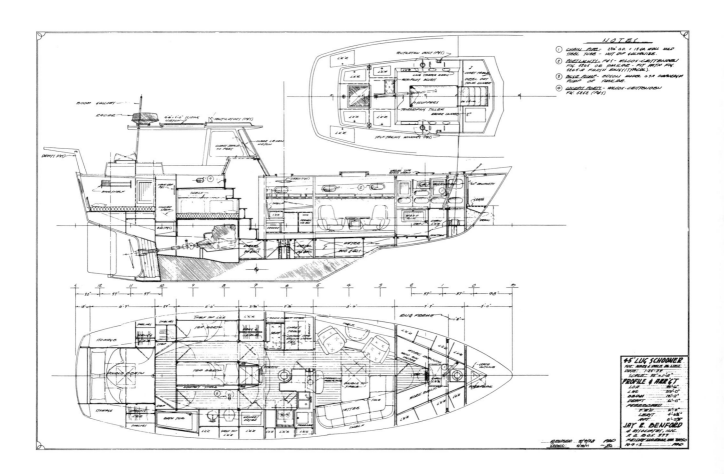

Machinery:

The main engine is planned to be a Ford 4-220 60hp diesel. This will connect to the Hundested variable pitch prop to give infinite variation on the prop pitch, from neutral to fully feathered for minimized drag under sail. The reverse and reduction gear on the engine will provide proper shaft speed for efficient powering and permit use of conventional controls on the engine for maneuvering. This engine should give a top speed of about 8⅓ knots under power.

An alternative, being considered, is to use the Sabb 30hp diesel with variable pitch prop. This will provide one less knot of top speed under power, and not have quite as much effectiveness powering against adverse condition, but the additional economies of this installation make it attractive.

Lug Schooner Rig:

The lug schooner rig represents the McNeils' choice for an easily handled large boat. Their experience sailing another lug rigged boat proved to them that they could set this one up to be entirely handled from the cockpit. This includes hoisting, reefing, and lowering both foresail and mainsail.

The McNeils are developing the rigging details based on the Hasler-McLeod principles. Hasler-McLeod

are perhaps best known as the developers of the rig on *Jester*, the OSTAR racer.

For light airs, they may add light jibs, set flying in front of each mast. These two ghosters will add 725 square feet to the total sail area set.

Optional Cutter Rig:

This is an optional rig created for those who liked the basic concept of the boat, but felt more at home with a more conventional rig. It has less weight aloft as well as a lower center of effort, so should be even more stable than the lug rigged version. The construction is more than adequately strong to take the loads of this rig, and only minor changes will be required to the accommodation plan because of the new mast position.

Deck Plan:

The deck layout includes clear top hatches over the workshop, the galley, the chart table, and the owners' berth aft. There is room on deck to carry a good sized dinghy, and good visibility over it for the helmsman.

There are two athwartships toerails on deck. The forward one is to prevent aft flow of dirty water from the anchor gear. The aft toerail just in front of the pilothouse, has a scupper at each outboard corner, to

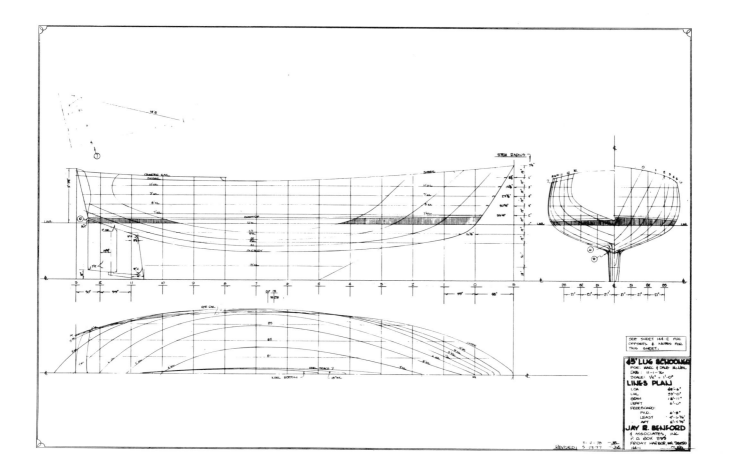

direct the water collected at these low points of the deck. In normal service, this will simply drain overboard. When the tanks are getting low, and the decks have been reasonably cleaned by the rain, a valve can be turned to direct the flow from the scuppers into the water tanks.

Pilothouse:

The original concept for the pilot house was for it to be more truly a hard dodger, providing protection from the elements. The cockpit was to be scuppered in the normal manner.

We have followed this philosophy in the design, and the pilothouse structure can be viewed as expendable without exposing the rest of the boat to being flooded.

Interior:

Most of the features of the interior are apparent on the drawings. However, two points are worth additional comment. One: the bulkheads in way of the masts are double walled, with stiffeners holding them apart. These provide very good support for keeping the boat in shape while absorbing the rig loads. Two: the cabin sole has a slight slope throughout, with a low point at the base of the companionway ladder. Thus

any water getting below will drain to this point and facilitate interior cleaning.

Project Status:

Building at Powell River, B.C., the McNeils have the construction well along. Their progress has been interrupted periodically when they have taken jobs professionally building other boats. The photos I've seen indicate the work is being done to a high standard.

Photo courtesy of Dale and Margaret McNeil

PARTICULARS:

Item	English	Metric
Length over all	45'-6"	13.87m
Length designed waterline	39'-0"	11.89m
Beam	13'-11"	4.24m
Draft	6'-0"	1.83m
Freeboard:		
Forward	6'-3"	1.91m
Least	4'-6 3/8"	1.38m
Aft	5'-5¾"	1.67m
Displacement, cruising trim*	35,200 lbs.	15,966 kg.
Ballast	10,500 lbs.	4,763 kg.
Ballast ratio	30%	
Displacement-length ratio	265	
Sail area:		
Lug Schooner	1150 sq. ft.	106.84 sq. m
Cutter	1082 sq. ft.	100.52 sq. m
Sail area-displacement ratio:		
Lug Schooner	17.13	
Cutter	16.12	
Wetted surface	505 sq. ft.	46.9 sq. m
Sail area-wetted surface ratio:		
Lug Schooner	2.28	
Cutter	2.14	
Entrance half-angle	22½ degrees	
Prismatic coefficient	0.54	
Pounds per inch immersion	1,771	
GM	4.4'	1.34m

Integral bilge tanks:

Water		300 gals.	1136 liters
Fuel		205 gals.	776 liters
Headroom		6'-6"	1.98m

*CAUTION: The displacement quoted here is for the boat in cruising trim. That is, with the fuel and water tanks filled, the crew on board, as well as the crews' gear and stores in the lockers. This should not be confused with the "shipping weight" often quoted as "displacement" by some manufacturers. This should be taken into account when comparing figures and ratios between this and other designs.

Photo courtesy of Dale and Margaret McNeil

INSCRUTA-BLE's building mold, ready for the Airex foam to be applied. Her easily driven hull form can be seen in this photo and the one on the preceding page. She easily could be redesigned for cold-molding.

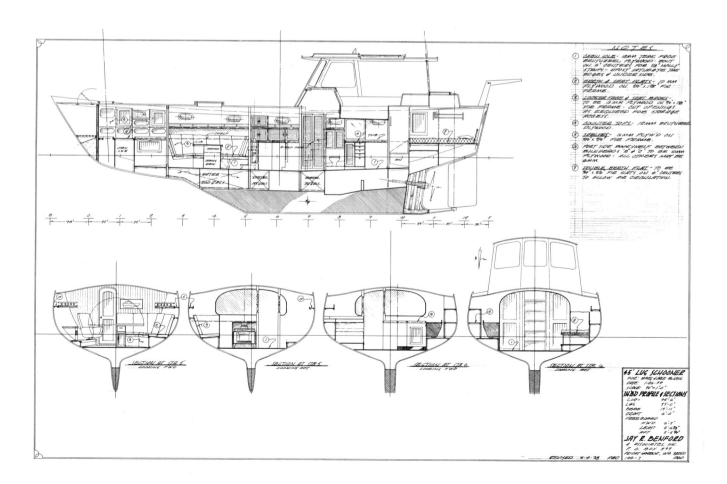

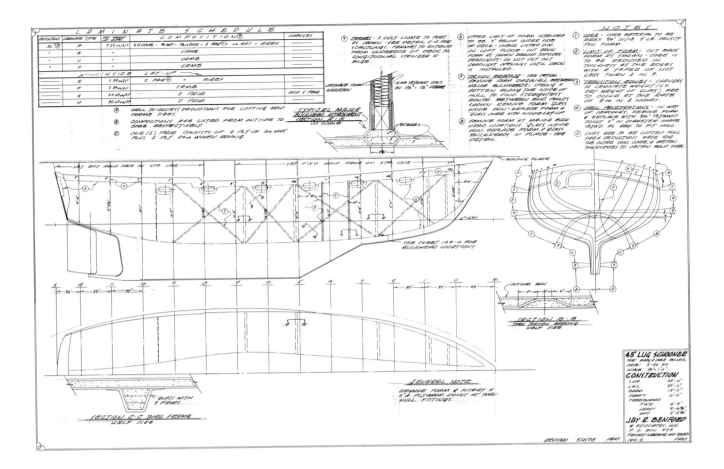

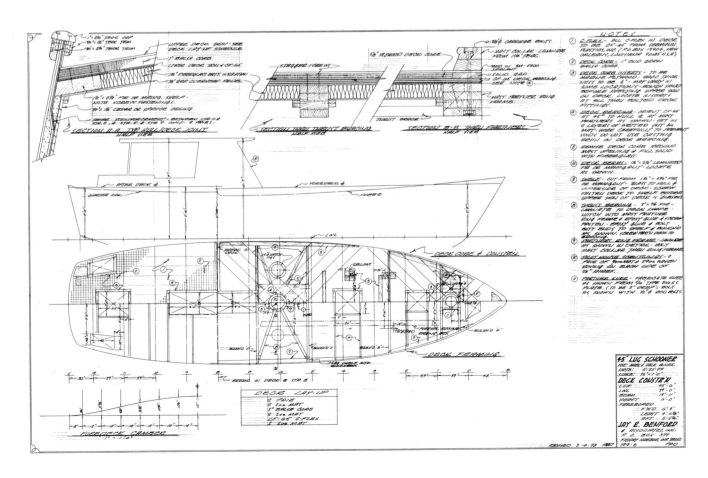

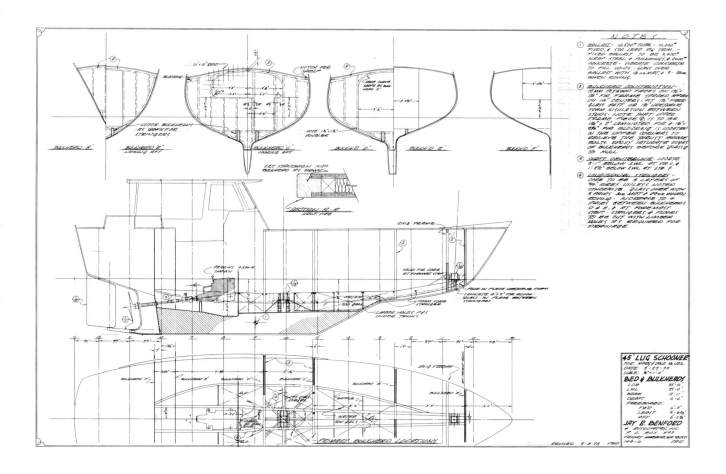

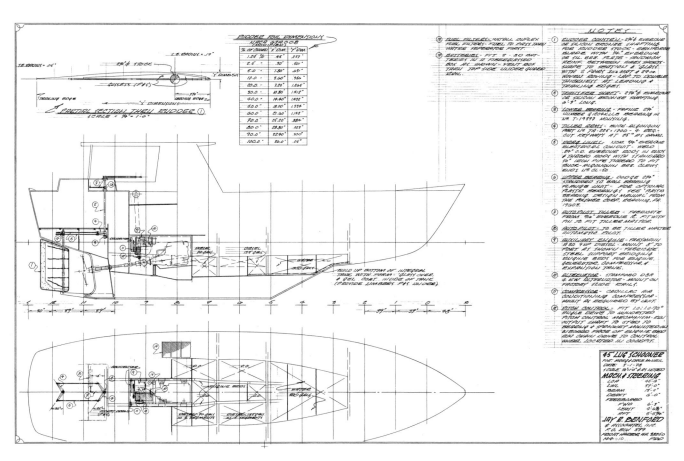

Chapter
25

Orphan Annie

45½' Cutter or Ketch
Design Number 190
1979

Every few years we are faced with the frustration of finishing a nice design and then finding the owner/client has a change of plans which preclude building the boat. Liking each of these designs, we are then faced with trying to find a new home for the orphan.

This 45½-footer is one of those orphans. She is of good breeding and would make a good home for some loving sailors. She was originally designed for production in Airex cored fiberglass, and could be done as a one-off in Airex or cold-molded wood construction.

The two rigs share the same mainmast and fore triangle. The ketch has a shorter main boom and smaller mainsail. The mizzen mast permits flying a mizzen staysail for extra light air drive and provides a good platform for the radar scanner. The fore staysail stay attaches to the chain locker bulkhead, insuring that the load from the sail will not distort the foredeck. The shrouds are inboard, attached to heavy knees, permitting a narrow sheeting angle for the headsails and easy fore and aft access.

The deck has bulwarks that increase in height towards the bow. There are several hatches with clear tops to let in light and air.

The cockpit, unlike most boats with inside steering, is elevated enough to permit the helmsman good visibility over the deckhouse. This cockpit also features seatbacks high enough to give good back support, and they are sloped to provide a comfortable lounging position. This elevated cockpit also provides very beneficial headroom below.

The layout of the aft cabin takes advantage of the headroom afforded by the cockpit. The bridgedeck provides the headroom for the passageway into the aft head. The cockpit seats provide the headroom in the aft cabin's passageway and in the head compartment.

The aft head is spacious enough to feature a washer and dryer. The tub/shower is one step down under the footwell in the cockpit, so there is headroom there as well.

The interior layout features comfort and privacy for two couples, with room for a few more to come along. With inside steering in the deckhouse, she can be comfortable cruising in almost any weather. The deckhouse also has a large galley and dinette and chart table.

The forward and aft staterooms both have double berths, and both adjoin private heads. The aft stateroom has light and air from the ports in the topsides and transom, and from the angled skylight/hatch aft of the cockpit.

The steering system is a Wagner hydraulic system, with two steering stations. The main engine is to be either a Perkins 4-236 or Ford 4D220 diesel with conventional reverse and reduction gear. This is to be hooked to a Hundested variable pitch prop. The 90 degrees of blade rotation on the prop will be used to give both full neutral and full feathered positions. Adjustment in between will be done with the exhaust pyrometer and vacuum gauge on the engine. This gives flexibility to achieve superior fuel economy when powering and to minimize drag under sail. We have used this setup on a number of others of our design with great success.

The hull and keel form is an evolutionary development of previous successful designs of ours. There is quite distinct definition between the body of the hull and the keel. The keel is an elongated NACA foil section, which we have found to provide excellent results. The boat has high form stability and a relatively low-center of gravity, creating a very stiff boat. She has a fine entry and a bow shaped to keep the spray off the decks. The "numbers" in the accompanying particulars table will help give an idea of how well she will perform.

All in all, this is an excellent cruising boat. We hope we will find some sailors who would like to adopt her and give her a good life.

PARTICULARS:

Item	English	Metric
Length over all	45'-6"	13.87m
Length designed waterline	37'-6"	11.43m
Beam	14'-0"	4.27m
Draft, cruising trim*	5'-6"	1.68m
Displacement, cruising trim*	33,500 lbs.	15,195 kg.
Displacement-length ratio	284	
Ballast	10,000 lbs.	4,536 kg.
Ballast ratio	30%	
Prismatic coefficient	0.54	

Pounds per inch immersion	1730	
Entrance half-angle	20 degrees	
Wetted surface	504 sq. ft.	46.82 sq. m
Sail area — cutter	1032 sq. ft.	95.88 sq. m
ketch	1050 sq. ft.	97.55 sq. m

Sail area/wetted surface ratio:

cutter	2.05	
ketch	2.08	
Water	280 gals.	1060 liters
Fuel	300 gals.	1135 liters
Headroom: deckhouse	6'-7"	2.01m
aft cabin	6'-7"	2.01m
forward cabin	6'-5"-6'-7"	1.96-2.01m
Bridge clearance	59'-8"	18.19m
GM (est.)	4.7'	1.43m

*CAUTION: The displacement quoted here is for the boat in cruising trim. That is, with fuel and water in the tanks, the crew on board, as well as the crew's gear and stores in the lockers. This should not be confused with the "shipping weight" often quoted as "displacement" by some manufacturers. This should be taken into account when comparing figures and ratios between this and other designs.

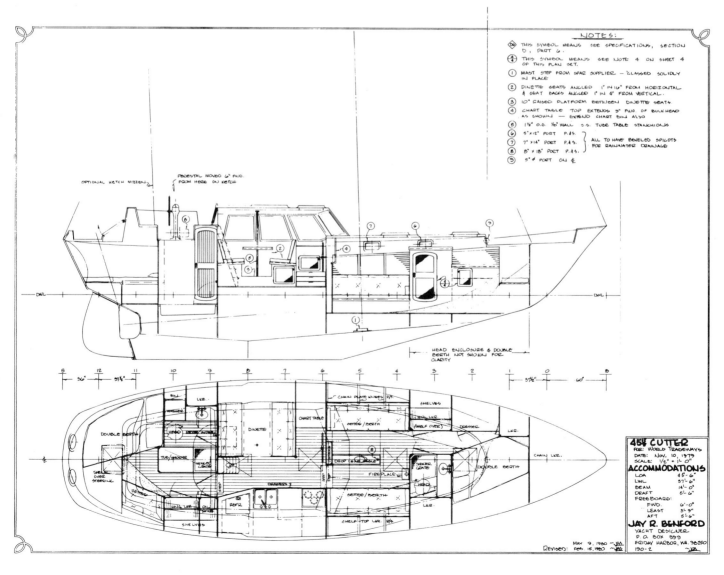

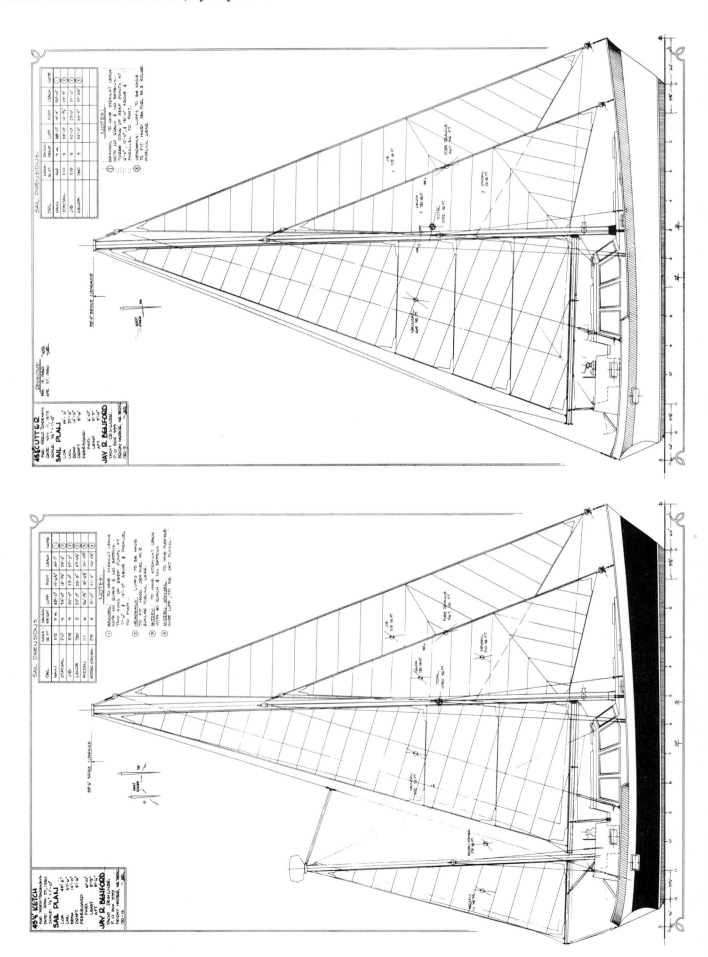

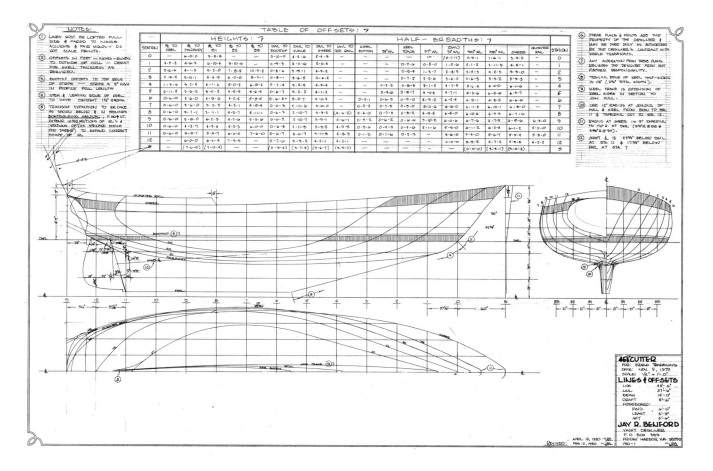

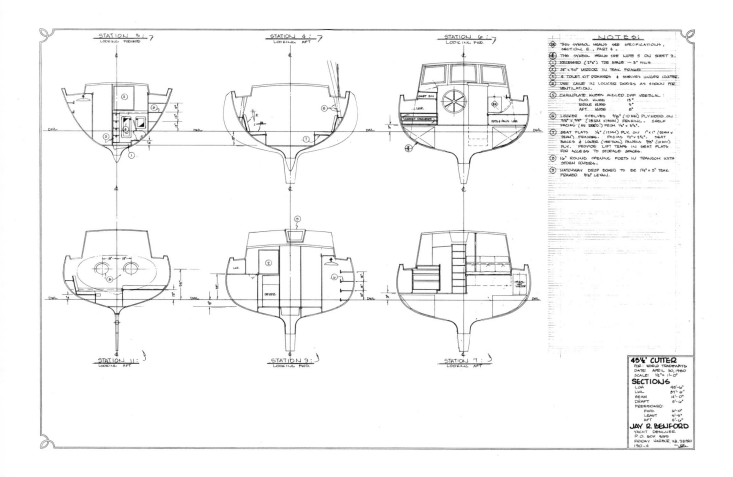

Chapter
26
Harambee

60′ Ketch
For: Herman and Gail Husen
Design Number 53
1969

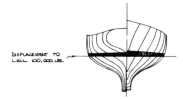

DISPLACEMENT TO
L.W.L. 100,000 LBS.

Designing a yacht always involves a combination of many things beyond setting pencil to paper. One of the important aspects not often considered by outside viewers is the designer's need to analyze the particular philosophy of the people who are intending to use the yacht. Creating a custom design in particular, this one facet can become quite intriguing. We very much enjoyed learning of the living/working philosophy of Herman and Gail Husen, and having the chance to help them see their own particular way of life become epitomized in the transition from dream to reality.

As the designer works with his clients, there is much exchange of ideas as the initial concepts form themselves on paper. Our work doesn't ever end there, especially with custom design, for as the drawings come to life in the shop, and interior spaces come into sharper perspective under the reality of construction, the clients are then best able to reach their final refinement of how a particular space will be most comfortable and suited to their needs. Although the design is very closely defined with the last of the preliminary drawings and on into the finalized detailed construction drawings, there's always "fine tuning" as the new ideas are tried and fitted into the grand puzzle.

One of the most gratifying aspects of custom designing is the chance to see new ideas take shape, and also the joy in seeing a custom-built boat come to life with a good deal of tender loving care. To a designer, this is infinitely more satisfying than seeing a chorus line of look-alikes pop out of a mold without any special, personal attention to detail. It takes time to build a good boat, and the result is a long term investment which imbues in its crew the desire to maintain their yacht on a level that is very much different from the fleeting once-over that characterizes both the construction and the presold "effortlessness of maintenance" of her molded sisters.

The 60′ ketch, *Harambee,* is a fine example of how much gratification can be derived from custom designing. Her skipper and first mate, Herman and Gail Husen, came to us after carrying paying guests aboard their 40′ schooner, *Sindbad* for four years in the San Juan Islands, Canadian Gulf Islands, and up the coast to Alaska. Having lived aboard *Sindbad* and worked her for this length of time, they had quite well defined ideas of what they desired of their next boat. She was to be a larger vessel, one which would give the crew separate (and private) quarters from their charter guests. The vessel was to continue to be their home, with all the privacy that a home should provide, but she was to be laid out, both in the way of below and above decks (interior arrangement to rigging) so as to be a successful charter yacht.

With experience in boat construction and repair — all the way from dinghies to larger tugboats/liveaboards — the Husens planned to build their new vessel themselves. The new design was to include a comfortable galley, with freezer, refrigerator, diesel stove, dishwasher and good counter space, and was to be located so that the cook would be included in the social gatherings, without, at the same time, leaving potato peelings in the charter guests' laps. The galley and this social area were to be naturally well lit, so that all who were working and/or socializing would be able to view the scenery at the same time. The master stateroom was to have its own head with bath/shower and also to be separated from the rest of the working/socializing part of the vessel. There was to be a separate laundry facility with washer and dryer unit built in. There was also to be room for Gail's player piano, and an area for a warm fireplace which would help to take the chill off the sometimes-cold Pacific Northwest airs. There were to be three private staterooms to accommodate two per stateroom: one stateroom to have a double berth, with the rest being singles. The maximum charter party which the Husens were planning to have at one time was to be a party of six, as groups larger than this can lose their sense of togetherness during the kind of personal charter work which the Husens were accustomed to providing. Additionally, Coast Guard regulations and requirements increased manyfold if the party grew larger than six. Stores carrying ability was desired to be considerable for any long passagemaking which could be in the offing.

The rig was to be a ketch, with a goodly amount of sail area to push her along handsomely in the light airs which are common to summer sailing in the Pacific Northwest. However, if possible, some way was to be

Jay R. Benford, Photo

designed that the large sail area could be broken down into individual sails of such size that each could be readily and quickly single-handed, should sail need to be taken in during a sudden change in conditions. Ideally, a person of light build — such as Gail Husen — should be able to handle the sails by herself, if need or desire be. Additionally, safety in positioning the various rigging parts was to be given careful consideration for the novice sailors who may come aboard during a charter excursion.

Power requirements were specified to be sufficient for motor cruising during calm airs, should the charter party and/or crew desire to be able to reach a specific point within a predetermined time span. The vessel should be easily maneuvered for responsiveness in light air conditions, turning ability to windward, and prompt reaction at dockside.

Aesthetics were an important consideration. Having had their appetites whetted by the charm of the traditional boat in *Sindbad*, the new vessel was to have a similar grace of sheer and overall lines. The Husens wished to be able to look back at *Harambee* with pride as she lay at anchor, and to enjoy seeing photos of their vessel as they sailed through equally beautiful surroundings.

How to satisfy all these requirements in one design was a challenge, the solution to which evolved itself over many meetings with the Husens, and during the course of construction, and even ongoing operation

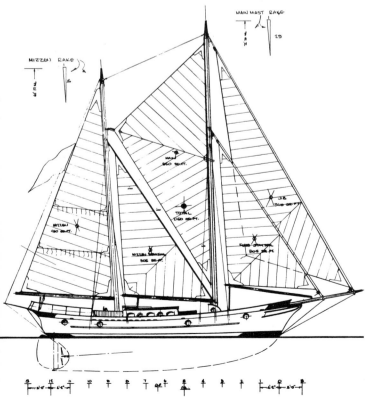

of, the vessel. The accompanying illustrations show the result of over six years of careful planning, back-breaking construction, and continuous interchange of ideas, questions and comments.

The master stateroom was designed aft in the layout, separated from the social area midships and guest staterooms forward. It is well lit by transom windows and portlights, and is spacious, consisting of a large double berth fully aft thwartships, with a small settee at the forward foot of the berth for comfortable reading and/or socializing. Over the settee is a large skylight which adds further to the cheery lightness of this area.

To starboard is a lovely desk with lockers over and under, while a large hanging locker is situated to port. Immediately forward of the master stateroom is a utility area to starboard (with washer, dryer, sink, good counter space and storage drawers) and commodious head (with bath, shower, sink and lockers) to port, and engine room between.

One of the finest areas during the daytime aboard *Harambee* is the dining/galley area midships. The galley counter to starboard was expanded by designing in a protrusion inboard from the galley counter, making room for a double sink. The dishwasher and re-

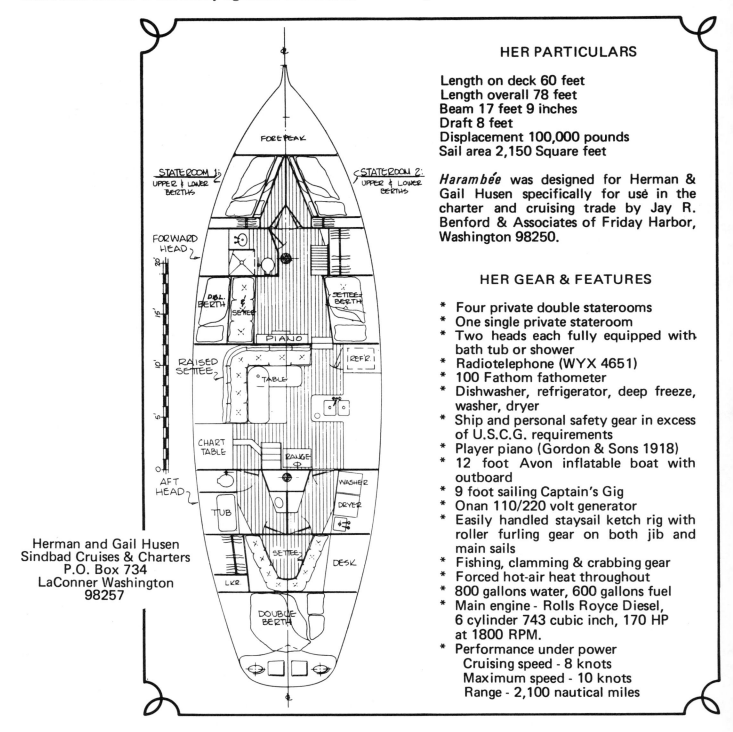

HER PARTICULARS

Length on deck 60 feet
Length overall 78 feet
Beam 17 feet 9 inches
Draft 8 feet
Displacement 100,000 pounds
Sail area 2,150 Square feet

Harambée was designed for Herman & Gail Husen specifically for use in the charter and cruising trade by Jay R. Benford & Associates of Friday Harbor, Washington 98250.

HER GEAR & FEATURES

* Four private double staterooms
* One single private stateroom
* Two heads each fully equipped with bath tub or shower
* Radiotelephone (WYX 4651)
* 100 Fathom fathometer
* Dishwasher, refrigerator, deep freeze, washer, dryer
* Ship and personal safety gear in excess of U.S.C.G. requirements
* Player piano (Gordon & Sons 1918)
* 12 foot Avon inflatable boat with outboard
* 9 foot sailing Captain's Gig
* Onan 110/220 volt generator
* Easily handled staysail ketch rig with roller furling gear on both jib and main sails
* Fishing, clamming & crabbing gear
* Forced hot-air heat throughout
* 800 gallons water, 600 gallons fuel
* Main engine - Rolls Royce Diesel, 6 cylinder 743 cubic inch, 170 HP at 1800 RPM.
* Performance under power
  Cruising speed - 8 knots
  Maximum speed - 10 knots
  Range - 2,100 nautical miles

Herman and Gail Husen
Sindbad Cruises & Charters
P.O. Box 734
LaConner Washington
98257

frigerator are forward of the protrusion. The diesel stove is midships, against the aft bulkhead of the galley. The raised settee is situated high enough to allow the crew and guests a good view out the many, large ports, some of which open for ventilation during hotter weather. The dining table is a wonderfully unique idea, thought out by Don Blevins, a friend of the Husens. It consists of two, swinging leaves mounted on a stanchion, and which can close, scissor-like, one leaf over the other, both leaves swinging either together or separately to allow easy access or egress from the settees. This arrangement also makes it most simple to get at the freezer, which is built into the raised box area upon the perimeter of which the settee itself sits. As the settee was built raised in this manner, there was discovered to be enough room for an additional crew member in a crew's bunk outboard of the freezer and below the level of the settee — an area completely naturally closed off from general sight at all times. Aft of this stowage/bunk area to port is the chart table, which is immediately handy to the main companionway out to the midships/aft cockpit.

The center of the socializing — especially on cooler evenings — was to end up forward of midships, with a delightfully warm area, cheered overhead by a large skylight, and below decks by a bulkhead fireplace opposite the player piano. This saloon could be divided later in the evening by means of a curtain, into two private staterooms, one of which is home to a double berth, near the foot of which is the fireplace. Forward of this social/stateroom area is a head/shower to port, companionway rising up to a scuttle, and large hanging locker outboard to starboard. The foc'sle contains Staterooms 1 and 2, each with upper and lower berths, leaving the forepeak to be a chain and general stowage locker. It is also home to the 3 KW generator set.

The deck layout is grand for both working and socializing. Ample sidedecks make passage fore and aft efficient and safe, with 9 to 16 inch bulwarks along the length, and of course waist-high lifelines guide the way, in addition. Booms are located a goodly height above unwary guests. Evening barbecues can readily be prepared and shared on the aft deck, with still plenty of room forward on deck for other activities. A comfortable enclosure around the cockpit area extends itself inward to provide seats for guests to "advise" the skipper of the course to take. Visibility from the cockpit area is good over the cabin, scuttle, and bow.

The ketch rig grew on the boards to be a wishbone configuration on the main, so as to maximize sail area between the masts, yet divide the mainsail into two, easily-handled sails. Forestaysail at 305 square feet and jib at 510 square feet are both on roller furling, again readily handled by a shorthanded crew at any time. Later, the 550 square feet main trysail was also modified for roller furling — one of several successful design evolutions as the vessel came into shape. The wishbone is presently not being used, in favor of a single boom, as we all consider this part of the rig to be still under development, as so far, the single boom is working out satisfactorily. The mizzen at 480 square feet and the mizzen staysail at 305 square feet are also handy from the viewpoint of the singlehandler.

Harambee's hull shape grew from a typical displacement hull shape, to allow plenty of room for stores and people working and living aboard. Still, her hull lines allow her to ghost along nicely in light airs, which surprises her owners, to be responsive at the helm, yet to hold her course well. During most of the summer sailing weather in the San Juans, she heels gently to about ten or fifteen degrees, leaving dishes in place on the counters below decks, while in very heavy going, she'll heel only about 20 degrees. With her 100,000 pound displacement, she is as stable and comfortable as one could be in heavy weather, with no pounding, and a very gentle motion in the seas she has encountered in the years of service to date. She enjoys light boat sailing qualities, with heavy boat comfort.

Her engine is a Rolls Royce, 6-cylinder, 743 cubic inch gem which moves her along easily, and extremely smoothly under power alone. She has 170 shaft horsepower at 1800 rpm, and with her 36" x 21", 2-bladed propeller through a 2:1 gear, she'll readily push 8-2/3 knots at 1250 rpm or 10(+) knots at 1750 rpm (hull speed).

Harambee sails responsively and smartly. Her crew are happy in their work, and have taken their numerous charter parties on some exhiliarating sails and cruises amongst the myriad of the San Juan Islands. At time of writing, they are just bringing their eighth charter season aboard *Harambee* to a close. As both Gail and Herman are attractive, extremely personable, and highly competent individuals, they make each of their charter parties feel very much a part of the boat: — living up to the meaning behind *Harambee's* name — "Let us all pull together." *Harambee* has certainly pulled together nicely, and she has been able to book these seasons of charter work largely by word of mouth advertising. A fine yacht, put together and run by a fine crew, *Harambee* is a grand example of how much satisfaction can be brought to the yacht designer who has the good fortune to work with productive clients. Such clients have a well defined concept of what they desire; based on prior experience, they are able to execute the construction details most handsomely. They are receptive to new thoughts, yet can offer sound and imaginative ideas in turn back to the designer.

Chapter
27
Antonia
131' Luxury Yacht

131' (40 Meter) Ketch
For: Armando Vasone Filho
Design Number 191
1980

What man has not dreamed of owning a large yacht with every luxury? A few men act to make their dreams come true. Our commission to design the 40 meter (131') ketch ANTONIA is the result of one man's action in pursuing his dream.

In the spring of 1980 I was approached about the possibility of designing a large sailing yacht. Two other designers had already presented preliminary design ideas. As the client's ideas evolved on what sort of boat he wanted, each of the boats was quite different.

A native of Brazil, Armondo Vasone Filho wanted to take advantage of the abundant and reasonably priced wood available there by building locally in wood. Initially, he had planned to build in the traditional method used in the commercial fishing vessels there; carvel planking on sawn frames.

Then, on reading and studying John Guzzwell's book, **Modern Wooden Yacht Construction,** Mr. Vasone decided that cold-molded construction would be the best method. He also decided to hire John Guzzwell as a consultant on the construction, as well as for advice on the project in general, based on John's extensive offshore sailing experience.

John Guzzwell was then just commencing construction of a second vessel to my 37 foot pilothouse cutter

design. I was given an opportunity to make a proposal to the client, who was receptive to my ideas. Since John and I lived on neighboring islands, it would be easy for us to work together on the project. We had already established a good working relationship over the past three years, during the building of the first of the 37 foot cutters. We also realized that the design and building of a sailing yacht of this size was a rare thing, and felt it was an adventure not to be missed.

Mr. Vasone's previous considerations had been towards building a type of vessel that was traditional both in design and construction. By the time of his discussions with me, he had decided to build using cold-molded construction instead of carvel planking. We were in agreement that the cold-molded construction would produce a boat with better longevity and make it a better investment.

My previous work with cold-molding had shown me that it is possible to build a lighter structure than was possible with carvel construction. A lighter boat would require less horsepower and sail area to drive it, and thus could be operated with a smaller crew. With reduced sail area, we should also reduce the wetted surface to maintain good light air performance. This led me to a model with much less wetted surface and more contemporary shape. I felt this would take best advantage of the lightness and strength of the cold-molded construction.

In our discussions on the best appearance for the boat, both Mr. Vasone and I agreed that an eliptical counter stern would present the best appearance, blending in well with the slender proportions of the hull. Given a free hand, on a displacement vessel, this would be my personal choice for stern shape.

The design work on ANTONIA followed our standard procedure. We analyzed the requirements of the owner, quantifying them into estimated weights for the equipment and structure of the vessel. Then a weight estimate for the whole vessel was done, so we could make a preliminary determination of the ballast requirement. Working over the weight estimates of the center of gravity and metacentric height, we arrived at the right amount of ballast to give the desired level of stability.

With these calculations in hand, we could start the actual development of the lines, by selecting a prismatic coefficient suited to the service of the boat and matching the midsection area to the waterline length and displacement required. This is a very quick design calculation, and assures the designer that he will not have to draw several sets of lines to come up with one of the correct displacement.

The final scantlings for the structure took advantage of the Honduras mahogany we were using. This mahogany, swietenia macrophylla, is native to Brazil, and is being used for almost all the structure. The structure is being put together with rescorcinal and epoxy glues, as well as mechanical fasteners, and is epoxy sealed inside and sheathed with Dynel set in epoxy resin outside.

Scantlings specified for ANTONIA'S construction are 45mm (1.77'') planking, consisting of 4 diagonal layers and a final longitudinal layer. The longitudinal framing is 80mm x 80mm (3.15'' x 3.15'') on about 400mm (16'') centers amidships.

Mr. Vasone requested that we design ANTONIA with twin screw propulsion, for ease of maneuvering. The main engines chosen were Caterpillar model 3306, turbocharged and aftercooled, with Twin-Disc MG509 2:1 reduction gears. To minimize drag under sail, the propellers are to be feathering variable-pitch units. We have used this system on quite a number of our designs to success. The most recent example is the 37' Pilot-house Cutter, CORCOVADO, built by John Guzzwell. CORCOVADO's owner says that he feels that the propeller system is the key to realizing the design's full potential both under sail and power.

The propeller system used, the Hundested VP-5, comes with about 90 degrees of available blade rota-

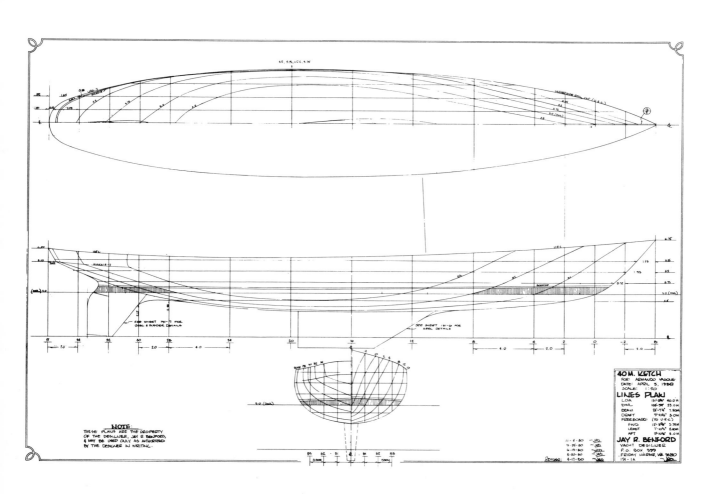

tion. This is intended to be used in place of a reverse gear. However, we are using a reduction gear to provide a more efficient propeller speed with a larger diameter propeller. This reduction gear also comes with a reverse gear, and lets us use the 90 degrees of blade rotation so that we can go from full neutral through trolling speed to cruising speed up to a fully feathered position. With proper engine instrumentation, we can gauge engine loading to produce some very economical cruising under power.

Mr. Vasone also desired the ability to power 3,000 miles at about 10 knots. The weight of fuel required for this led us to cut back a bit on the water tankage, to keep the overall weight of the vessel reasonably light. In normal operation, the generators will be running much of the time. We decided to fit a watermaker to take advantage of their waste heat. This will supplement the water capacity and allow full usage of the bathtubs as well as the washing machine and dishwasher.

The accommodations are laid out with the owner's party aft, the guests amidships, and the crew forward. The drawings show the layout pretty well, and all those aboard should be quite comfortable.

The deck layout has room for three small craft, in addition to the three deck lounges — at the stern, and

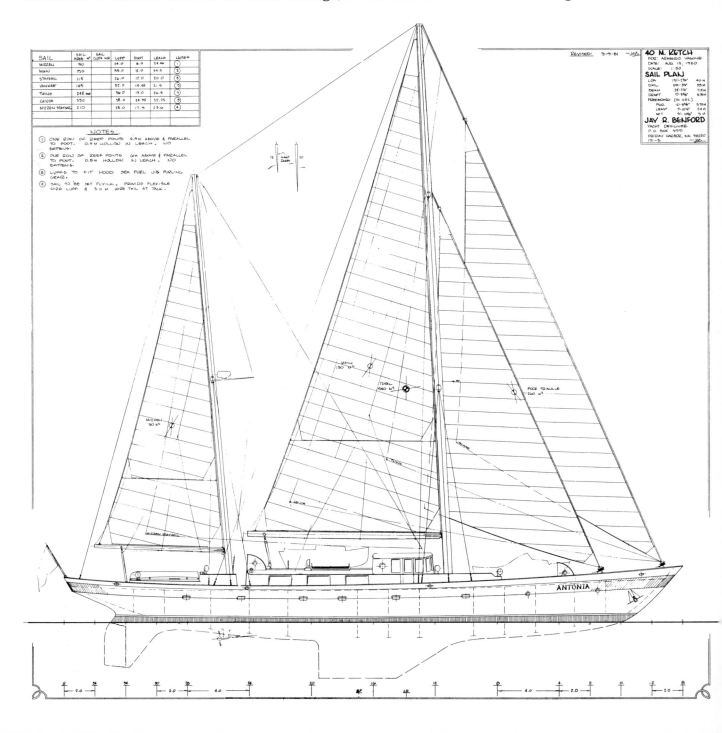

by each mast. The forward position of the pilothouse will contribute to the safe operation of the boat, giving better visability from the helm.

A yacht of this size is capable of carrying her crew to all parts of the world in style and comfort. We have been pleased to take part in her creation and will look forward to sailing her in the near future.

Particulars

Item	English	Metric
Length over all	131.23'	40.0m
Length datum waterline: Hull ...	98.43'	30.0m
Total ..	108.27'	33.0m
Beam, maximum	24.61'	7.5m
Beam, datum waterline	20.94'	6.38m
Draft	12.30'	3.75m
Displacement: Hull	205,000 lbs.	92,986kg.
Total	228,750 lbs.	103,759kg.
Longitudinal center of Buoyancy (Distance aft of station O):		
Hull..................	54.68'	16.67m
Total.................	55.17'	16.82m
Wetted surface: Hull	1537 sq. ft.	142.81 sq. m
Total	2147 sq. ft.	199.47 sq. m
Prismatic coefficient: Hull	0.542	
Total	0.467	
Displacement-length ratio:* Hull	95.97	
Total	80.46	

Midsection coefficient: Hull	0.719	
Waterplane coefficient: Hull	0.660	
Total	0.596	
Metacenters (above datum waterline)		
Transverse	8.15 ft.	2.49m
Longitudinal	189.57 ft.	57.78m
Vertical center of buoyancy (below datum waterline) ...	1.87 ft.	0.57m
Sail area	5812.5 sq. ft.	540 sq. m
Sail area-displacement ratio** ..	24.86	
Sail area-wetted surface ratio...	2.71	
Pounds per inch immersion	7253	
Entrance half angle	12 degrees	

*Displacement in long tons divided by one-hundredth of the waterline cubed.

**Sail area in square feet divided by the displacement in cubic feet raised to the two-thirds power.

CAUTION: The displacement quoted here is for the boat in cruising trim. That is, with the fuel and water tanks filled, the crew on board, as well as the crews' gear and stores in the lockers. This should not be confused with the "shipping weight" often quoted as "displacement" by some manufacturers. This should be taken into account when comparing figures and ratios between this and other designs.

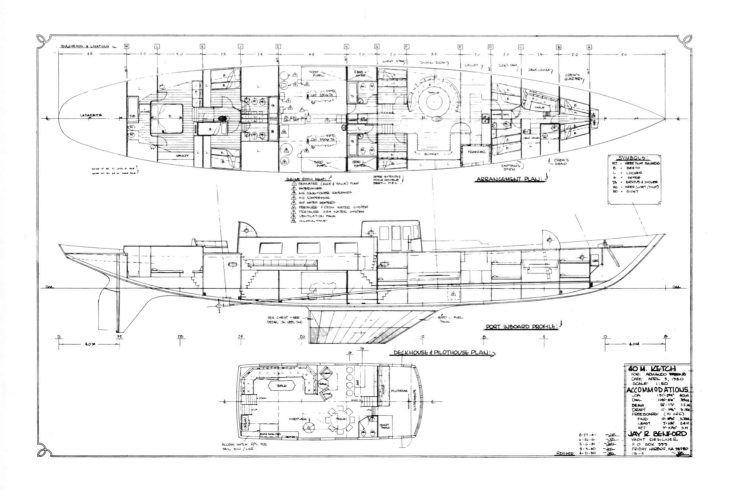

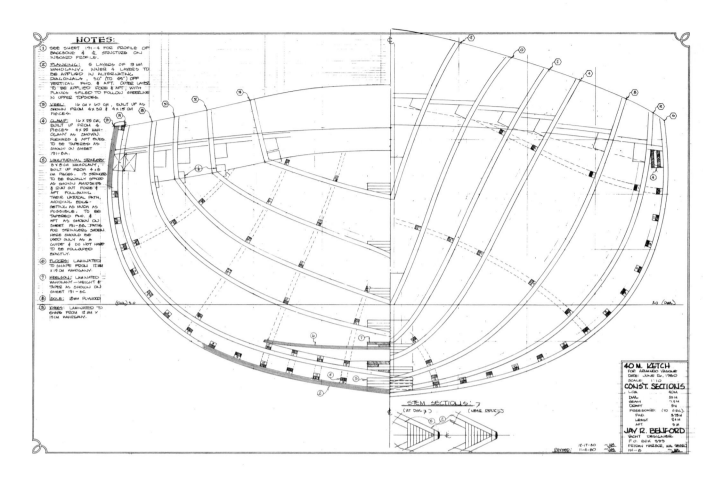

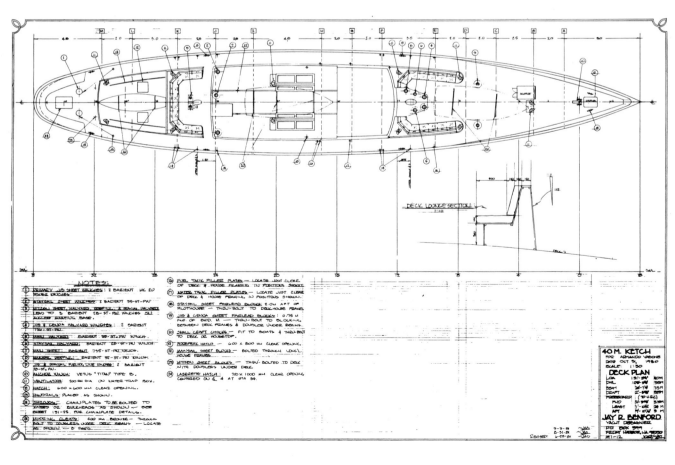

Framing completed, above. Below, last layer of planking going on, sheathing completed, and rolling over the completed hull.

Above and below; ANTONIA's bow showing the longitudinal framing being completed and the first diagonal skins of planking being glued in place. More information on this method of construction is in John Guzzwell's **Modern Wooden Yacht Construction** and **The Gougeon Brothers on Boat Construction.**

ANTONIA photos courtesy Armando Vasone Filho

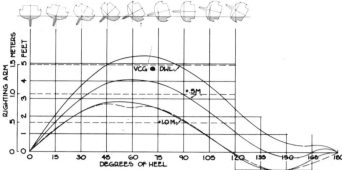

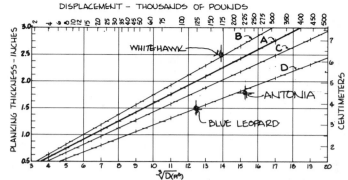

A part of the computer design analysis we did on *ANTONIA* included a stability study. The righting arm curves are shown above. Four conditions are plotted; with the vertical center of gravity (VCG) at the designed waterline (DWL), with the VCG 0.5 meters above the DWL, with the VCG 1.0 meters above the DWL, and the dashed line showing the effect of having her floating 0.25 meters deeper (about 10 inches) with the corresponding greater displacement and the VCG at 1.0 meters above the DWL.

The small section drawings above the curves give some idea of what is happening to the boat as she heels. At about seventy degrees her keel and rudder will have lifted out and all steering control will have to wait until she rights herself. At about sixty degrees, the deckhouses start to immerse, adding to the rise in the center of buoyancy and helping to extend the range of her stability.

One of the Society of Naval Architects and Marine Engineers (SNAME) papers written on yacht stability after the vessel losses in the Fastnet race a couple of years ago made suggestions on the relation between positive and negative stability. The positive part of the stability is the part above zero righting arm, or base line, and the negative part is the portion below the base line. Their suggestion was that the positive/negative ratio be 6/1 or greater. *ANTONIA* meets this suggestion at the +1.0 meter condition, and we have calculated that her VCG should be below this level, giving her a greater margin of safety.

In beginning the structural design for *ANTONIA,* we had to do quite a bit of research to decide on the best approach to determine her scantlings. The above planking thickness graph is part of the result of this research.

Line A represents normal carvel planking thickness, as called for in Nevins' Rule. Line B is 10% greater thickness, and is about the norm for cold-molded boats built with no framing other than bulkheads. Bruce King's lovely *WHITEHAWK* is a good example of this type of structure. Line C is 10% less thickness than A and is a guide to conservative scantlings used on Longitudinally framed cold-molded boats. Line D is 25% less than A and is a guide to boats with a combination of transverse and longitudinal framing and cold-molded shells. The Giles design for the high performance motorsailer *BLUE LEOPARD* is a successful design with this sort of structure.

ANTONIA is slightly below line D in planking thickness. In choosing this final thickness, we took advantage of the greater strength of the Honduras Mahogany over the commonly used softwoods. Craig Goring who worked with me on this design, doing engineering, rigging, structure, and systems design, researched information that showed we could vary the thickness downward as the strength of the material went up. Thus, even though the specified thickness is slightly lower than line D, we felt it was a conservative scantling. The section modulus calculations backed this up.

Another part of the computer design analysis we did was a floodable length calculation. The curve below shows the results of that computation. As designed, she has one compartment floodability throughout and in some cases has two compartment floodability. If the subdivision of the boat by her watertight bulkheads was slightly rearranged, it would be possible to have two compartment floodability throughout.

ANTONIA's speed and range curves, at right, are the results of our calculations of her endurance on the 10,000 litres of fuel tankage and assuming a displacement close to her designed conditions. The benefits of slowing down for longer range are obvious.

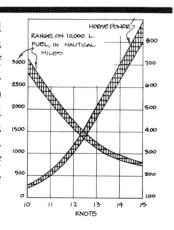

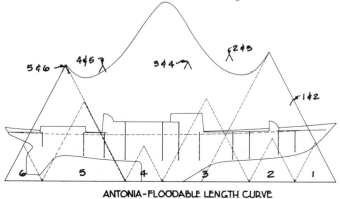

ANTONIA-FLOODABLE LENGTH CURVE